*Criminal Genius
in African American and US Literature,
1793–1845*

Criminal Genius
in African American and US Literature, 1793–1845

ERIN FORBES

Johns Hopkins University Press
Baltimore

© 2024 Johns Hopkins University Press
All rights reserved. Published 2024
Printed in the United States of America on acid-free paper
2 4 6 8 9 7 5 3 1

Johns Hopkins University Press
2715 North Charles Street
Baltimore, Maryland 21218
www.press.jhu.edu

Cataloging-in-Publication data for this book is available.

A catalog record for this book is available from the British Library.

ISBN 978-1-4214-4375-1 (hardcover)
ISBN 978-1-4214-4376-8 (paperback)
ISBN 978-1-4214-4377-5 (ebook)

*Special discounts are available for bulk purchases of this book.
For more information, please contact Special Sales at specialsales@jh.edu.*

CONTENTS

Acknowledgments   vii

Introduction. "Nourished in Vice"   1

1 Zombies of Civic Virtue   27

2 The Convict's Corpus   54

3 Outlaw Humanism   95

4 The Southampton Insurgency   131

5 Fugitive Aesthetics   165

Conclusion. New Forms of Crime   188

Notes   197
Index   229

ACKNOWLEDGMENTS

There have been times when I thought this book would never find its way to publication. I am delighted that it has and grateful to be able to thank, in print, those who have helped along the way, some of them quite a long time ago now and others much more recently.

Before I ever thought I would write a book of literary criticism, before I ever knew that such beasts existed, I was fortunate to learn from wonderful English and history teachers at Plainville High School. Elaine Brasile and Chuck Radda fed my curiosity and taught me to how to write, while the late Holly Bergen motivated me and the late Walter Caswell believed in me. At Reed College, Lisa Steinman and Robert Knapp continually blew my mind by showing me how literature can create whole worlds. Betsy Duquette made me want to be like her when I grew up and proved to be a valuable mentor for many years afterward. For offering fantastic models of scholarly engagement, intellectual generosity, and lively pedagogy during my PhD years at Princeton, I thank my advisors Eduardo Cadava, Bill Gleason, and Jennifer Greeson, along with Daphne Brooks, Kathleen Davis, Diana Fuss, Meredith Martin, Starry Schor, Cornel West, and Michael Wood.

For inspiring me, mentoring me, and keeping me grounded as a new assistant professor at the University of Wyoming, and for their careful reading of my work, including many drafts of these chapters, I am deeply indebted to Frieda Knobloch, Teena Gabrielson, and Quincy Newell. My landing at the University of Bristol in the United Kingdom has been a happy one, due in no small part to Tom Davies, Ben Dillet, Helen Fulton, Billie Gavurin, Josie Gill, Casey Hale, Siân Harris, Ed Holberton, Cathy Hume, Danny Karlin, Rowena Kennedy-Epstein, Madhu Krishnan, Sam Matthews, Elaine McGirr, Saima Nasar, Dot Price, Tara Puri, Lizzie Robles, David Russell, Kirk Sides, Karen Skinazi, Mimi Thebo, and Emily Tiplady.

I have received invaluable feedback on the manuscript both directly and following talks, panels, and the like from, I fear, more people than I will remember to name here. My gratitude to all of you, including Daniel Abdalla, Ulli Adelt, Nicole Aljoe, Angela Ards, Susan Aronstein, Branka Arsić, J. K. Barrett, Bridget Bennett, Juliana Braun, Tara Bynum, Russ Castronovo, Sandy Clark, Lara Cohen, Michael Cohen, Emily Coit, Thomas Contstantinesco, Hannah Crawforth, John Dorst, Paul Erickson, John Ernest, Ben Fagan, Renée Fox, John Funchion, Lindsey Grubbs, Jeanne Holland, Briallen Hopper, Michelle Jarman, Tal Kastner, Lauren LaFauci, Stacey Margolis, Neill Matheson, Katie McGettigan, Samuel Moriarty, Fred Moten, Hannah Lauren Murray, Sarah Boddy Norris, Jordan Norviel, Susan Oliver, Danielle Pafunda, Tracy Patton, Matthew Pethers, Kerry Pimblott, Jason Potts, Lloyd Pratt, Lindsay Reckson, Ric Reverend, Cécile Roudeau, Kelly Ross, Caskey Russell, Stephen Shapiro, Gus Stadler, Jordan Stein, Simon Stern, Ed Sugden, Tzu Chien Tho, Keri Walsh, Marcus Watson, Jonathan White, Gretchen Woertendyke, Arielle Zibrak, Christina Zwarg, and the much-missed Bob Torry.

For crucial feedback and support during the final stages, I thank J. Michelle Coghlan and Hilary Emmett. I also thank the members of the DFG research network Voices and Agencies: America and the Atlantic, 1600–1865, including Ilka Brasch and Elena Furlanetto, along with Alanna Bossel, Gesine Brede, Lukas Etter, Abigail Fagan, Philip James Grider, Marcel Hartwig, Caroline Koegler, Nicola Paladin, Cameron Seglias, and Katerina Steffan.

My work has been supported by the University of Bristol and the University of Wyoming, along with the American Antiquarian Society through a Kate B. and Hall J. Peterson Fellowship and the Huntington Library through a Mellon Fellowship, and by Princeton University's English Department, Center for the Study of Religion, Program in American Studies, and Center for African American Studies. I extend a warm thank-you to the British Association of Nineteenth-Century Americanists, as well as the organizers and audiences at the UCLA Americanist Research Colloquium, the University of Nottingham's Department of American Studies, the American Antiquarian Society, the Huntington Library, Royal Holloway, University of London's Centre for Victorian Studies, and the University of Oxford's Rothermere American Institute.

I am grateful to copyeditor Carrie Watterson and the folks at Johns Hopkins University Press, including Catherine Goldstead, Matt McAdam, Adriahna Conway, Kristina Lykke, and Hilary Jacqmin, as well as the anonymous readers whose advice greatly improved the book.

For love, support, and good company, I thank my family, Jon and Barbara

Baskin; Diana, Ian, Brenda, Jack, and Spencer Forbes; Jennifer Heins; and Judy Rosenbaum.

Jason Baskin has read every word from start to finish. He is my rock: clever, kind, dependable, funny, and strong. I dedicate this book to him and to our daughters, Lena and Talia, who light up my world. Every day with you three is a lucky one.

*Criminal Genius
in African American and US Literature,
1793–1845*

INTRODUCTION

"Nourished in Vice"

As he exited his cell to meet the executioner in 1859, John Brown left a note that read, "I John Brown am now quite certain that the crimes of this guilty land will never be purged away but with Blood."[1] His dying words joined an increasingly voluble chorus that condemned the harms perpetrated under US enslavement as criminal. In its first decades of existence, the United States garnered an international spotlight for its violent regime of enslavement, such that, by 1820, despite the efforts of early US poets, playwrights, and painters to establish a national literature, the English wit Sydney Smith proclaimed, "The Americans are a brave, industrious, and acute people; but they have hitherto given no indications of genius. . . . In the four quarters of the globe, who reads an American book? Or goes to an American play? or looks at an American picture or statue? . . . Finally, under which of the old tyrannical governments of Europe is every sixth man a slave, whom his fellow-creatures may buy and sell and torture?"[2]

Smith dubbed the United States "the native home of the needy villain," an iniquitous nation-state in which creative genius was not possible.[3] His writings caused an uproar in the US press, which leapt to defend American cultural production while sidelining any indictment of enslavement. Smith's English patrons also balked at his critique. Their diminished support makes sense. Although this negative brand of American exceptionalism has proved to have real staying power, slavery was not the United States' unique "original sin." Smith's own merchant father sought West Indian and colonial North American fortunes (but was nearly bankrupted during the Revolutionary War). Moreover, as Smith's British benefactors well knew, institutional New World enslavement was a crucial source of their own wealth.[4]

Black Bostonian activist and lecturer Maria W. Stewart took a longer, more globalized view of racial hostility than did either Brown or Smith. Her 1833 "Address to the African Masonic Hall" underscored the explicit transnationality of enslavement's atrocities: "The unfriendly whites first drove the native American from his much loved home. Then they stole our fathers from their peaceful and quiet dwellings, and brought them hither . . . obliged our brethren to labor . . . nourished them in vice and raised them in degradation."[5] Where Brown pronounces the United States "guilty" and Smith describes it as a cultureless criminal state, Stewart argues that enslavement's harms reach much further. A transnational governmental crime ("they stole our fathers") also, in turn, produced Black criminality (the sons of said fathers were then "raised in degradation"). Enslavement's degradations were begun and perpetuated by "unfriendly whites" throughout the Atlantic world. This "unfriendliness" encompassed criminal expropriation of Indigenous people's lands and racial slavery's establishment. Thus, in Stewart's view, a previously "peaceful and quiet people" metamorphosed into a criminal underclass that abandoned respectability: Africa's violently displaced millions, "nourished . . . in vice." The production of Black criminality, as Stewart clearly perceived, was endemic to an international system of settler colonialism and racialized enslavement.

Taken together, these excerpts from Brown, Smith, and Stewart highlight the disparate ways that enslavement comes to entail criminality. Per Brown, an enslaving polity becomes criminal in a figurative sense. Smith shows that the enslaving state becomes criminal in a moral sense, and Stewart underlines how, in a legal sense, a settler colonial system of enslavement also ultimately produces criminals out of the populations it oppresses and exploits. At the same time, to understand how the United States constructed a racialized criminality, it is also important to note that links between enslavement and crime predate settler colonialism in the Americas. European, African, and Middle and Near Eastern polities had for centuries held that criminal status justified enslavement. Thus, contrary to overly simplified historiographies, early modern Europeans understood most African peoples they encountered as sovereign subjects, not brutish hordes to be enslaved or plundered at will. Working to dislodge the persistent but inaccurate "savage-to-slave" historical narrative, Herman L. Bennett argues that Europeans initially accepted that Africans had "the right to exist unmolested until such time that they violated natural law."[6] From the sixteenth through nineteenth centuries, Europeans consistently excused the atrocities of colonialism and settler colonialism as "fitting punishments for infidels who had sinned against natural law," as Bryan Wagner reminds us.[7] This idea that criminal acts render sovereign subjects fit for enslavement, rooted in Roman, Arabian, and African jurisprudence, was reinvigorated in eighteenth- and nineteenth-century Euro-American penal reforms (recall that British engineer William Cubitt invented the treadmill "to reform offenders by teaching them habits of industry").[8] This notion was also on sharp display in the wake of the Civil War and indeed remains with us in the present day.

In 1865, the US Constitution's Thirteenth Amendment abolished all forms of slavery except "as punishment for a crime whereof the party shall have been duly convicted." Michelle Alexander and Ava DuVernay have brought this connection between criminality and enslavement sharply to public attention with the book *The New Jim Crow* (2010) and the documentary film *13th* (2016), which show how the Thirteenth Amendment has formed the conditions of possibility for enslavement's afterlives in twentieth- and twenty-first-century US regimes of racialized criminality and mass incarceration. For nearly a century before the Civil War, American jurists had avoided any explicit mention of enslavement in the Constitution: it was the Thirteenth Amendment, as H. Bruce Franklin notes, that "actually wrote slavery *into* the Constitution of the United States, but only for those people legally defined as criminals."[9] Cognizant of this fact, most scholarship exploring racialized criminalization begins from this post–Civil War moment. When legal enslavement collapsed, scholars argue, racialized oppression did not disappear. Instead, it masked itself, with slavery continuing "by another name" via penal institutions, carceral practices, and of course extrajudicial executions, that is, lynchings.[10] "The convicted criminal," as Angela Naimou underscores, is "the successor to the legal slave."[11] The legal legacies of enslavement haunt later forms of juridical personhood. Yet racialized criminality is not simply a hauntological or aftereffect of enslavement; the links between racialization and criminalization shaped New World slavery itself.

The pages that follow offer a longer view of this now well-documented post–Civil War shift, from controlling populations racialized as Black with slave patrols and chattel slavery, to deploying police power and the penal system. As Wagner has discussed, during the period of legal enslavement, "the power to police was considered not as a state prerogative but as a racial privilege of all whites over all blacks, slave or free."[12] Yet a malleable, racialized criminality predated, and helped to shape, the system of legal enslavement that developed in the United States, as much as it also paved the way for racial slavery's afterlives in Jim Crow and mass incarceration. In other words, racialized criminality is not solely a product of the post-Reconstruction era but stalked Black Americans across the Atlantic, from colonial to US labor camps, to debt bondage and the penitentiary, and to violent policing, systematized mass incarceration, and judicial surveillance regimes. The human suffering resulting from criminality's racialization has been, and continues to be, unfathomable. Yet taking a longer view shows us something surprising: that, particularly before the passage of the Thirteenth Amendment, the processes of racialized criminalization also generated creative, fugitive possibilities that radically undermined white supremacist regimes and the respectability frameworks they imposed.

At the center of these moments of possibility lies a dynamic formation that I am calling "criminal genius." A full treatment of how enslavement shaped and was shaped by regimes of police power is beyond the scope of this book, yet across these pages I show that careful attention to *racialized criminality* in the first half of the long nineteenth century reveals key connections to conceptions of *creative genius*. Their merger relied on a distributed agency, shared across multiple human and nonhuman entities, that unsettled efforts to consolidate white supremacy. Attention to criminal genius in its various iterations in African American and US literature before the Thirteenth Amendment therefore offers a new perspective on current discussions of enslavement's carceral afterlives. The criminal genius this book explores is by no means the stock caricature canonized in late Victorian and early twentieth-century literature and popular culture; it is rather a racialized and aestheticized mobilization of distributed agencies that resisted individualist legal and political frameworks. *Pace* Sydney Smith, art and atrocity were by no means mutually exclusive in the early United States. Not only were race and criminality crucially linked before the Thirteenth Amendment, but these links were frequently marked by radical, transformational worldviews. At the intersections of Blackness, criminalization, and aesthetics, an ambiguously racialized criminal genius, "nourished in vice," to borrow Stewart's phrase, strained against the bounds of respectability and law to enact more equitable modes of belonging, imagine more just worlds, and create more connective modes of being human.

The United States' violent historical canvas of Indigenous dispossession and forced African migration and labor did, of course, significantly mark its cultural production. Yet numerous US and African American literary examples topple Smith's premise that criminality and creativity are mutually exclusive. From Ahab to the invisible man to Hannibal Lecter to Omar Little, US cultural production charts a constellation of criminal geniuses who are lawless, ruthless, brilliant, methodical, and creative. Before the Civil War, American writers captured the criminal genius, this "most cherished villain," through a variety of memorable characters who not only bridge genius's classical, Romantic, and modern conceptions but also trouble the lines between fiction and reality.[13] They include Charles Brockden Brown's Ormond, Nathaniel Hawthorne's Hester Prynne,

Harriet Beecher Stowe's Dred, Herman Melville's Babo, William Wells Brown's Clotel, and Rebecca Harding Davis's Hugh Wolfe. Yet my study of criminal genius does not focus on characters in literary fiction like these. Instead, it examines the "storyworlds" around which early US conceptions of law, art, Blackness, personhood, agency, and ultimately the category of the human all constellate. In this sense, criminal genius is a key sociogenic category across the long nineteenth century, and the period's deeply complex literary "villains" illustrate how unruly the multiple convergences of crime and art were and how central racialization was in shaping US criminal genius before the passage of the Thirteenth Amendment. Looking at this longer prehistory helps shift our current understanding not only of the figure of criminal genius itself but also of the now-familiar conjuncture of race and criminality, offering a wider angle of vision than current critical and law-and-literature frameworks.

Genius, as a concept, always contains elements that are inherently transgressive and frequently criminal. Yet, of course, in the Western humanistic tradition, understandings of what constitutes genius have evolved from tutelary spirit in the premodern period to supreme artistry developing from the early modern period through the Enlightenment, culminating in the Romantic period's valorization of originality. Today, the idea of genius is less robustly linked with creativity. Since the mid- to late nineteenth century, it has primarily denoted logical intelligence. Each of these phases of genius informs the others, and, importantly for my study, each also links to contemporaneous understandings of criminality. The relative lack of scholarship in this area is thus surprising. As criminologist James C. Oleson notes, "preclassical explanations for crime frequently relied upon the devil, demons, witches, and evil spirits," yet "little has been written on the relationship between crime and the classical conception of genius (genius as an attendant spirit)."[14] Likewise, although the belief that "creative people are more willing to violate conventions, norms, or rules" remains widely shared (and, per Enlightenment and Romantic thinkers, considered a prerequisite for genius), nevertheless, "the relationship between creative genius and crime has been little studied."[15] The idea that uncommon intelligence and outsized personal magnetism are a boon to criminal activity has captured our collective imaginations across fiction and film since the nineteenth century. This view also underpins the "great man" historiography that has concentrated around figures like (perhaps most famously) Napoleon and also inspired real-life crimes like Nathan Leopold and Richard Loeb's 1924 murder of fourteen-year-old Bobby Franks in an attempt to execute the "perfect crime."

Criminal genius thus necessarily lies somewhere between the spheres of reality and imagination. Leopold and Loeb's case exemplifies the fact that literary figures imbued with criminal genius inspire real-world instances. Loeb was obsessed with crime novels, and the pair wanted to experience the thrill of the perfect murder; their case in turn inspired numerous novels, plays, and films. At every turn the formation of the criminal genius evades the very social-scientific approaches that were initially created to restrain it. Oleson laments the fact that "in the absence of relevant scholarship, fictional representations are among the only ways we can know the criminal genius."[16] Indeed, the relative lack of contemporary scholarship on the topic owes much to the formation's unruly mergers of fantasy and fact. It was only with the rise of criminology in the late nineteenth century that crime and genius were first linked and pathologized (via quantifications such as IQ, as well as skull and brain measurements). Yet it was precisely criminal genius's *fictionality*—its rootedness in the aesthetic realms of connectivity and imagination, its potential for world breaking and world making—that were its most salient features.

Criminal genius does not neatly align with the exceptional individual in the period under consideration here, in contrast to later iterations. Instead, the instances I explore in these chapters highlight why crime itself was a favorite subject for imaginative writing: it bridges human beings with the world as well as with one another. Even when both perpetrator and victim are individuals, crime designates a fundamentally collective concept: coming from the Latin *crimen* (misdeed) and *cernere* (to discern), the word links *action* to *actor*, and to the third-party assessment of both. That is, the act of judging something to be a crime is part of what constitutes it as such. Crime links directly to Enlightenment conceptions of the aesthetic as a universally shared, objective judgment on beauty, as with the Kantian *sensus communis*. From a legalistic point of view, crime likewise involves collectivities because an act is "criminal" insofar as its harm implicates society: in the world of jurisprudence, criminal matters involve shared public harm, a violation of social standards even in cases where there is only one "criminal" and one "victim." By contrast, matters arising among individual private parties are designated as "civil." Moreover, as we saw in the excerpts from Brown and Smith above, the category of "crime" can of course also be used in a moral sense, where once again it shapes normative, collective conceptions of personhood and society. In such instances, the word is used to condemn certain behaviors or practices, as when abolitionists described enslavement as a "crime" despite its patent legality. Indeed, they used the term "crime" precisely to indict and overturn enslavement's legality.

The acts of judgment that are inherent in understanding, and struggling over, what counts as crime also inform who counts as "criminal." Determining who is and is not criminal is fundamental to establishing both individual personhood and sociality. These concerns are, of course, also—and not coincidentally—fundamental to the reading and writing of literary fiction across the eighteenth and nineteenth centuries. Indeed, as Lisa Cacho has shown, criminalization is a racialized sociogenic process that, however counterintuitively, does not arise from the act of lawbreaking itself. Rather, criminality and related forms of "differential inclusion" within the US legal system arise "as *effects* of the law." These effects form the legal system's very foundation.[17] Cacho thus carefully distinguishes between a process of misrecognition, "being stereotyped as criminal" and "being criminalized."[18] She provides a powerful example of criminality being "*unrecognizable* without a black body" with a pair of Associated Press photos taken in the wake of Hurricane Katrina. One caption describes a Black man "looting a grocery store" alongside another describing "resourceful" white people "finding bread and soda from a local grocery store." In the pages that follow, I bring Cacho's argument directly into a literary studies frame. Criminalization is not misrecognition or misapprehension, not an epistemological *mistake* that can be corrected by uncovering additional knowledge or supplying further information: it is, rather, a constructed *process* inextricable from racialized "ideological and material processes" that, taken together, "turn some people into criminals by making it all but impossible for them to be law-abiding."[19] As I will argue in the chapters that follow, literary production is crucial in both shaping and subverting these processes. The "criminal" is, emphatically, not a static category. Although Cacho's work focuses on twenty-first-century criminalization, the media's role in "creating or fabricating criminals," of course, has a longer history.

Attending to this earlier history of criminalization, each of my chapters looks at how a series of adjacent racialized figurations—the zombie, the convict, the outlaw, the insurgent, and the fugitive—stretches the boundedness of the voluntarist legal subject, who exercises individual will to choose between lawful and criminal activity, in early African American and US literature. Looking at how criminalization is produced not by acts of lawbreaking per se but rather through sociogenic processes, including the literary, the ensuing chapters provide part of that backstory. I begin with the vilification of Philadelphia's Black community during and after the 1793 yellow fever epidemic as depicted in pamphlets like Mathew Carey's *A short account of the malignant fever*, which portrayed virtuous actors as will-less malefactors akin to the Haitian zombie. I then turn to the bodies of print surrounding two late eighteenth-century convicts to reveal a distributed agency that unsettled attempts to consolidate white supremacy in the era before Jim Crow and the rise of explicitly racialized incarceration. I continue by examining David Walker's rejection of white ontologies of being for Black people, operating outside the bounds of law; the shaping and reshaping of the insurgent Nat Turner's figuration as a divinely inspired or "mad" genius in the 1830s periodical press; and finally the fugitive landscapes and literal maroons that haunt the highly aestheticized nineteenth-century literary productions of Edgar Allan Poe. At the end of *Black Skin, White Masks*, Frantz Fanon writes that "the real *leap* consists in introducing invention into existence."[20] The varied iterations of criminal genius I examine respond to Fanon's "leap," his invitation to imagine a past, present, and future untethered from static capitalist ontologies of the human.

Today, as action against violent policing, carceral policies, and mass criminalization sweeps the globe, the delimitation of who counts as criminal and the role of racialization in early constructions of the criminal other are clearer than ever and their history that much more important to interrogate. In the late eighteenth-century United States, violent, sensationalized accounts of crime flooded popular periodicals. In her essential study of early American crime writing, Karen Halttunen argues that this rise of monstrous representations of the criminal arose directly from a desire "to comprehend radical human evil within the larger intellectual context of Enlightenment liberalism, which did not recognize radical human evil." For Halttunen, the criminal emerged as moral monster rather than an "everyday sinner" because of "explanatory breakdowns" within an Enlightenment context. Thus, she argues, "gothic conventions of the fundamental mystery of murder—its intrinsic unknowability—and its fundamental horror" arose when reason fell short.[21] Yet Halttunen's account of criminal depictions in early America moving from ordinary sinner to inhuman "moral alien," significantly, does not attend to crucial contexts of race and enslavement.[22]

It is impossible to adequately understand this shift as simply an impasse in the period's philosophizing. Material factors also shaped this evolution in understandings of criminality, and the period's racialized constructions of human taxonomy were paramount. In seventeenth-century crime literature, an individual convicted of a crime as heinous as child murder could be described as "savage," "damned," and even animalistic without losing claim to humanity. But by the late eighteenth century, criminal monstrosity functioned far differently: to be criminal was to be unrecognizable as human in the epistemological sense or, in Cacho's terms, "ineligible for personhood."[23]

This excision from the realm of the recognizably human, over the course of the long nineteenth century, became increasingly bound up with racialization.

The desire to justify racial slavery and white supremacy during this period likewise catalyzed a shift in understandings of the criminal as categorically inhuman. Sylvia Wynter and Giorgio Agamben have both variously argued that humanity as a concept had, by the late eighteenth century, shed its theocentric underpinnings. It became a more exclusionary category. From a theological perspective, humanity had been assumed: an inherent quality, present from birth. The theological question that preoccupied readers of early American crime periodicals such as Cotton Mather's execution sermons was not whether a living malefactor was sufficiently human but rather whether they would be worthy of salvation after death. Wynter marks the Enlightenment as the era that solidified a "redescription of the human outside the terms of the . . . 'sinful by nature' conception" to produce what has become "the struggle of our new millennium . . . between the ongoing imperative of securing the well-being of our present ethnoclass (i.e., Western bourgeois) conception of the human, Man, which overrepresents itself as if it were the human itself, and that of securing the well-being, and therefore the full cognitive and behavioral autonomy of the human species itself/ourselves."[24] Wynter labels this white, masculinist, propertied, Euro/American self-conceptualization "Man" with a capital *M*, to designate the ways Man "overrepresents" his (definitively *his*) being as "the being of being human itself."[25] The classification of *Homo sapiens* in Linnaeus's defining eighteenth-century work *Systema Naturae* is key to the redescription Wynter describes.

For Linnaeus, the human is a taxonomic anomaly insofar as it is identified and classed according to a potential ability rather than any objective physical quality or characteristic. Agamben notes "the irony with which [Linnaeus] does not record—as he does with the other species—any specific identifying characteristic next to the generic name *Homo*, only the old philosophical adage: *nosce te ipsum* [know yourself]."[26] What is important about *Homo sapiens*' taxonomic anomaly is that it "assigns not a given, but rather an imperative as a specific difference. . . . *Man is the animal that must recognize itself as human to be human.*"[27] Humans are not born such but rather must become "human" by making use of a particular set of abilities and practices. Linnaeus's *Homo sapiens*, human because he utilizes his ability to recognize or know himself as human, necessarily engages in processes of representation. To be human one must undertake a performance: by representing oneself (to oneself, to others) as human, one becomes human. If humanity is thus a representational process, it is also an aesthetic, classificatory project that systematically advantaged some "types" of humans: white, propertied, psychologically and physiologically normative men. When late nineteenth-century criminologists like Havelock Ellis and Cesare Lombroso sought to lock the criminal into classificatory schemes as proximate to the animal as to the human, they built on this foundation. Their work extended earlier "American school" ethnological projects such as Samuel George Morton's *Crania Americana* (1839), which attempted to provide scientific evidence to support a burgeoning Euro-American race science.

Of course, conceptions of humanity as fundamentally performative were not unique to the eighteenth century: they are embedded in etymology of the word "person," which is, in a linguistic and colloquial if not always a legal sense, closely aligned with "human being." From Old French *persone*, via the Latin *persona*, "actor's mask, character in a play," later "human being," the conception of a "person" implies that an act or performance *precedes* designation as a human. John Locke, often identified as the first theorist of individual identity, famously delimits "person" as a "forensic" descriptor. He writes, "Wherever a man finds what he calls himself, there, I think, another may say is the same person. It is a forensic term, appropriating actions and their merit; and so belongs only to intelligent agents, capable of a law, and happiness, and misery."[28] The definitive marker of what it means to be a human person, on this view, is the ability to be apprehended by law and a liability, at least potentially, for crime. This leaves a broad scope for exclusion, but it also leaves multiple routes back into humanity's fold. To establish oneself as a person, for many otherwise excluded individuals, one must first become a criminal, proving oneself "capable of law" in the breaking of it.

Criminal genius's formation in the first half of the long nineteenth century reveals that the slippage inherent in Lockean forensic personhood also makes possible radical redefinitions of the human. Crucially, this happens in tandem with the cultural shift in understanding the criminal as a racialized moral monster. From the late eighteenth century to the present day, the material sites and discourses used to construct criminality have remained unruly, with science, medicine, law, politics, print culture, and the literary imagination all playing key roles. On the one hand, settler-colonial imperatives have criminalized Black and Indigenous lifeways and thereby enacted racialized dispossession and exploitation across multiple, often overlapping sites (the slave ship, the labor camp, the reservation, the factory, the boarding school, the ghetto, the penitentiary). In this way, the "criminal" emerged as a racialized cultural production in the Americas, in order to, as Dylan Rodriguez explains, shore up "a primary *discursive position* against which a Euro-American and Western civilizational imperative consistently defines itself as an orchestration of vindicated, state-legitimated, ritual (national, racial, heteropatriarchal) violence."[29] At the same time, across US history, cultural and legal definitions of crime have stood in sharp tension, beginning with the nation's early decades, when many called legal enslavement criminal, even as enslaved people themselves were, for the most part, recognized as legal persons only insofar as they could be held criminally liable.[30] In the friction resulting across such convergences, Blackness and criminality shaped an aesthetic discourse of genius that turns out to be far more dynamic than familiar Romantic genealogies would suggest.

As we have begun to see, genius in the period considered here was strongly associated with criminality, and in the decades leading up to the Civil War, the category of genius increasingly took on a generally unacknowledged, indeed outlawed, racialized agency. Percy Bysshe Shelley, answering accusations of genius's criminality, famously declared poets "the unacknowledged legislators of the world" in 1821. He argued that "the imputations [against poets] of real or fictitious crime" must ultimately become mere "dust in the balance."[31] To many of his contemporaries, however, associations of genius and crime were more to be embraced than defended against. Indeed, we find Romantic literary production overflowing with representations of outlaw figures. They include exoticized, exciting "banditti" at various borderlands where, as J. Hector St. John de Crèvecoeur also emphasized at the end of his 1782 *Letters from an American Farmer*, races blend and merge. Crèvecoeur focuses on the American West, but Italy and Scotland are likewise frequent settings. Such tales center a criminal genius who troubles Enlightenment rationality, whiteness, and "civilization." Though they often display a certain heroism, the agency of borderland outlaw figures is marked by collective fugitivity rather than individual respectability. Typifying this, Farmer John seeks refuge for his family in a "wigwham [sic]" among Native Americans in "the wilderness," where he plans, as "a sojourner, as a fellow hunter and labourer" to escape the ravages of war.[32] I explore this Romantic preoccupation with liminal landscapes in chapter 5, where the terraqueous spaces of Southern swamplands likewise become key sites for Romantic genius not despite but because of the fact that they were well known to be home to maroons. These self-emancipated people formed communities that both overtly and covertly undermined the regime of enslavement and white supremacy. Outlaws, bandits, prisoners, fugitives, and maroons are all differently positioned with respect to legal frameworks and material histories, yet each of these transgressive figures links criminality and genius. They do so via an unacknowledged racialized agency, which was not confined to a particular phenotype but emerged through dynamic, sociogenic processes that generated liberatory possibilities from within a larger climate of anti-Blackness.

As outlined above, it has become a commonplace that genius, from the twentieth century to the present day, has most often been associated with white, elite, masculine hyper-individualism or superintelligence. In the late eighteenth and early nineteenth centuries, when the category of genius centered instead on artistry and originality, it contained clear, if implicit, connections to racialized Blackness and feminized rhetorics of generativity. Typifying the view of Romantic genius, Scottish rhetorician Hugh Blair proclaimed in 1783 that "genius always imports something inventive or creative."[33] And Ralph Waldo Emerson, with characteristic concision, in 1837 declared, "Genius creates."[34] The term's associations with excessive intelligence do not explicitly emerge until later in the nineteenth century, and when they do, they appear in eugenicist works such as Francis Galton's *Hereditary Genius* (1869). Mining this vein, Nathaniel D. Mitron Hirsch would theorize a hyper-white category of genius, above the classification of *Homo sapiens*: "Genius is another psychobiological species, different as much from man, in his mental and temperamental processes, as man differs from the ape."[35] Yet categorizations relating to genius do not simply reify gendered and racialized taxonomies of the human. They also profoundly unsettle them. In the earlier period under scrutiny here, genius, in designating expansiveness and creativity, often revealed alternatives to familiar liberal, normatively white and masculine conceptions of human personhood.

A disappointingly static historiography of white male genius remains one legacy of eugenicist conceptions of genius as hyper-intelligence. This mistaken perspective has consistently situated genius in exclusively white, masculinist, European frameworks. According to this view, eighteenth-century philosophers like Alexander Baumgarten and Immanuel Kant produced an idealized discourse of genius, alongside its attendant philosophical concept, the aesthetic, which English writers such as David Hume, Edmund Burke, and, later, Thomas De Quincey developed. And, the story goes, each of these elite white male figures did all this somehow in isolation from the political economies of enslavement and colonialism in which they were enfolded. Of course, Charles Mills, Robert Bernasconi, and others have offered important corrective analyses of how histories of imperialism and enslavement shaped these white European thinkers, and indeed how their philosophizing in turn shaped the development of colonialism and slavery. Yet creative genius's normative whiteness remained largely uninterrogated until Simon Gikandi's magisterial *Slavery and the Culture of Taste* (2011) offered a long-overdue, if partial, analysis. Gikandi demonstrates that Anglophone standards of beauty and refinement in fact developed in relation to brutal histories of enslavement: "Slavery and taste came to be intimately connected even when they were structurally construed to be radical opposites."[36] Elucidating long-denied intimacies of art and bondage, Gikandi argues that "both the institution of slavery and the culture of taste were fundamental in the shaping of modern identity . . . [and] they did so not apart but as nonidentical twins."[37] Yet oppressed peoples ultimately harness the culture of taste to stake their claim to liberal humanity. The chapters that follow both extend and depart from the foundation Gikandi provides.

Rather than establishing how Black artists use culture to claim liberal humanity, I look instead to counter-formations of a universal human being grounded in the material and spiritual experiences of the oppressed. Most of the figures I study here are gendered male. Reparative and recovery histories have emphasized their masculinity, seeking to return them to the domain of the human by underscoring their resistance and bold individuality. Such projects, however, reify racialized colonial gender orders that "grant civilized status only to those men and women who inhabit the domain of the human" through gender hierarchies, the absence of which "defines the nonhuman, racialized, naturalized non-Europeans, who are sexed but genderless."[38] By contrast, I emphasize the collective and material aspects of criminal genius, though without denying its voluntaristic elements. In identifying a formation of criminal genius grounded solidly on the experiences of those excluded from evolving, abstract Enlightenment formations of the human and the citizen as agentic subjects, I contribute to a diverse and growing body of scholarship seeking to delineate alternate universalisms by centering histories of racialization and enslavement.[39]

In the early United States, a racialized theory and praxis of criminal genius that strains against colonial gender hierarchies develops among Black and white writers and actors. Exemplifying both, William Wells Brown, a self-described "American fugitive," defines genius as impossible aspiration, beset by adversities:

> There is a great diversity of opinion with regard to genius, many mistaking talent for genius. Talent is strength and subtilty of mind; genius is mental inspiration and delicacy of feeling. Talent possesses vigor and acuteness of penetration, but is surpassed by the vivid intellectual conceptions of genius. The former is skillful and bold, the latter aspiring and gentle. But talent excels in practical sagacity; and hence those striking contrasts so often witnessed in the world—the triumph of talent through its adroit and active energies, and the adversities of genius in the midst of its boundless but unattainable aspirations.[40]

Throughout his compendium of biographical sketches, *The Black Man, His Antecedents, His Genius, and His Achievements* (1863), Brown distinguishes genius from talent: where the latter is strong, bold, active, acute, and practical, genius is delicate, gentle, boundless, vivid, and unattainable. Where talent achieves triumph, genius meets with adversity. Brown expands on this definition as approaching divinity: "To possess genius, the offspring of which ennobles the sentiments, enlarges the affections, kindles the imagination, and gives to us a view of the past, the present, and the future, is one of the highest gifts that the Creator bestows upon man."[41]

Brown emphasizes genius's "softer" qualities of kindness, creativity, and expansiveness, yet he also often attaches the category to masculine "great names," just as we see in his Victorian contemporaries Carlyle and Emerson. For Brown, such figures include Benjamin Banneker, Toussaint Louverture, and Frederick Douglass, with their astonishing achievements in science, politics, and rhetoric, respectively. Yet this is only one aspect of genius in Brown's view. Although his title (*The Black Man*) suggests otherwise, Brown's geniuses are not exclusively male; he includes chapters on figures like Phillis Wheatley and Charlotte L. Forten. Moreover, intriguingly, for Brown, genius is sometimes nameless: his sketch "A Man without a Name" tells of a fugitive from enslavement sentenced to a brutal flogging for protecting his sister from a white man's sexual assault. The nameless man stood, without legal rights of his own, condemned by law for what he termed "the crime of having within me the heart of a man."[42] At first glance, this display of chivalry aligns with a hypermasculinity. In Brown's fuller vignette, however, the entire genius of the man without a name, his claim to inclusion in the illustrious company Brown has assembled, is precisely his "gentle" aspiration to kindness. Kindness is a quality that becomes criminal for the enslaved. Brown sets out to record these instances of Black genius to give "the community" and the world at large "sketches . . . vindicating the Negro's character."[43] He emphasizes that the conditions of possibility for genius under enslavement's adversities were manifold.

For Brown, Black experience typifies the conditions of possibility for genius and for redefinitions of the human. One key foundation for this perspective was established, however inadvertently, by white English poet and critic Edward Young in 1759. Young's important early formulation of creative genius emphasizes genius's inherently unnatural qualities. He opines that it necessarily "rejects all human means" to produce that which is entirely new or original.[44] He frames genius in apposition to conscience, an inner guide operating beyond the restraint of laws or rules: "With regard to the moral world, conscience, with regard to the intellectual, genius, is that god within. Genius can set us right in composition, without the rules of the learned; as conscience sets us right in life, without the laws of the land."⁴⁵ Alongside its extra-human and unlegislated aspects, genius, for Young, contains an element of the unexpected. Where attainment in the arts might be presumed to fall to the well resourced, genius is precisely available to those from whom it might be least expected: "What . . . mean we by genius, but the power of accomplishing great things without the means generally reputed necessary to that end."⁴⁶ This is quite a different perspective from today's view, traceable directly, and troublingly, to eugenics, which holds genius as the exclusive, heritable domain of the elite.

Thomas De Quincey, another white Englishman widely read on both sides of the Atlantic, also laid Brown's groundwork. De Quincey is important to any discussion of nineteenth-century genius and criminality, as he introduced the word "aesthetic" into the English language from German in his satirical "Murder Considered as One of the Fine Arts" (1827). In a later essay in *Tait's Edinburgh Magazine* (1834), he differentiates talent and genius along lines very similar to Brown's: "Talent and genius . . . are not merely different, they are in polar opposition to each other. Talent is intellectual power of every kind, which acts and manifests itself . . . through the will and the active forces. Genius . . . is that much rarer species of intellectual power which is derived from the genial nature—from the spirit of suffering and enjoying—from the spirit of pleasure and pain. . . . It is a function of the passive nature."⁴⁷

As in Brown's later formulation, De Quincey links talent with an individual will to power. Genius, both rarer and more humane, "is derived from the genial nature." De Quincy, again like Brown, implicitly codes talent as white and masculine, the domain of the "will and active forces" characterizing the conqueror class. Such racialization of whiteness as active, voluntarist, and powerful hews to what had come to be called "Saxon" qualities in the literature of the period. Thomas Jefferson, who, famously, wanted to feature warriors Hengist and Horsa on the new Great Seal of the United States, traces the American legal system to a "Saxon" inheritance of individual liberty. In similar terms Emerson deifies Saxons as "all masculine, all brutish strength" with "an excess of virility."⁴⁸ Implicitly rather than overtly, De Quincey's example highlights the transnational and multi-directional reach of racial enslavement for developing Gikandi's "cultures of taste." Where talent aligns with these characteristics of masculine whiteness, De Quincey intimates that genius, by contrast, was Black and feminine.

For Young, Brown, and De Quincey, then, genius is softer, more concerned with pleasure, and generative yet aligned with passivity. These traits are more feminine than masculine, and, drawing again on the example of Jefferson, we can also see that they were all traits frequently associated with degendered Blackness in the period. Jefferson writes that Black people's "existence appears to participate more of sensation than reflection" than that of white people.[49] Similarly, Kant claims that people of African origin lack a "drive to activity."[50] Such associations provided insidious justification for enslavement or "proof" of Black deficiency. But in certain fleeting and probably unintended iterations, like De Quincey's, and like Brown's more self-aware later delineation, conceptions of genius that have roots in rank race science and remain problematically racialized, at the same time, point toward more expansive understandings of a humanity unbound by liberal agency. Taking a cue from Hortense J. Spillers, "it is our task to make a place for this different social subject," racialized and out of sync with colonial gender hierarchies, not to "join the ranks of gendered femaleness" (or maleness) but rather to "gain the *insurgent* ground."[51]

It is important to emphasize that the criminal genius that is the subject of this book has little in common with those figures Ibram X. Kendi terms "extraordinary negroes" hailed as exceptional by white patrons and audiences to diminish their threat. The political work of exceptionality has long been recognized as eroding collective interest, as Arthur Schomburg explains: "By virtue of their being regarded as something 'exceptional,' even by friends and well-wishers, Negroes of attainment and genius have been unfairly disassociated from the group, and group credit lost accordingly."[52] Equally, such "extraordinary" figures are easily enfolded into the kinds of eugenicist narratives that come to whitewash criminal genius in the late nineteenth century. They include child prodigy and poet Phillis Wheatley, whom Black British writer Ignatius Sancho famously dubbed the "Genius in Bondage," or the mathematician Benjamin Banneker, who impressed Jefferson even at a moment when he was increasingly invested in establishing Black racial inferiority. Tellingly, Jefferson chose not to revise his opinion of collective Black incapacity in the face of Banneker's example but instead to elevate him as a remarkable individual, the proverbial exception that proves the rule. Discussing Jefferson's response, Britt Rusert notes that "the language of the 'black genius' has, indeed, sometimes been used as a tool of surveillance and control by white Americans . . . containing and ignoring the specific interventions made by thinkers like Banneker . . . a silencing often performed *through* the recognition of 'genius.'"[53] Likewise, the criminal genius of this study ought not be conflated with the "Black avenger" trope brilliantly analyzed in a recent book by Gregory Pierrot. Although there is significant overlap with the formation I study here, the Black avenger is an individual figure whose purpose is "hiding collective action" and upholding a Western version of masculinity.[54] Retrospective assessments, to be sure, have often confused nineteenth-century instances of criminal genius with the masculinist exceptional individual, as in many portrayals of Nat Turner (most famously Nate Parker's disastrous 2016 film, *The Birth of a Nation*). Properly situated in its larger context, however, antebellum criminal genius operates in and through, and ultimately discloses, a larger collective of human, material, and environmental forces.

Thus, across these pages, I work to dismantle the premise that genius, insofar as it is universal, is unassimilable to Blackness.[55] Blackness is not a limit to humanity or aesthetic capacity, and criminal genius, while radical, implies neither pessimism nor optimism. In centering Blackness in a nineteenth-century study of aesthetics, this book owes much to Ivy G. Wilson's example.[56] As Wilson notes, the term "aesthetics" is often linked to formalism or to evaluative criticism, while later thinkers such as Jacques Rancière have instead insisted on "the necessity of reclaiming the aesthetic" so that it is no longer "disaggregated from examinations of the historical and political." Working in this vein, returning the aesthetic to its political and historical foundations, including, importantly, the tradition of the oppressed, Wilson brilliantly explicates "the meanings of black representation in politics, where blacks hovered in a state of political being marked as non-entities at worst and nominal subjects at best" in order to "offer a reading of a subversive black aesthetic" concerned with "the affective possibilities of aesthetics as a model and a means through which collectivities can fulfill the unfinished work of democracy." Wilson focuses on the visual and aural specters of Blackness in the American national project, what he calls "the politically nonmaterial elements of democracy."[57] Focalizing precisely the concurrent and excessive materiality that also marks Blackness, I expand on this work. Those aspects of collective agency that, often surprisingly, arise out of this same nexus are what constitute criminal genius.[58]

In the ensuing chapters, I detail iterations of criminal genius (zombie, convict, outlaw, and fugitive) to understand the varied "genres" of the human that diverse embodied and textual figures enacted in the United States prior to 1845. These alternative humanisms oppose white supremacist ontologies of "Man" as, per Wynter, the Western world's "referent-we," a cisgendered, heterosexual, white man standing in for an ostensibly universal humanity. The period under consideration, between the 1790s and the 1840s, coincides with the rise and consolidation of liberalism as the basis of US political identity and citizenship. Individual agency is intimately linked to Man's definition of the human: one possessing an individual will and the capacity to act according to that will and thereby, per Locke, to assert property ownership over the products of one's labor.

Following the terms of this definition, white supremacy calls Black humanity into question throughout US history. Yet my goal is not to recuperate humanity in the very liberal terms that have eclipsed so much Black experience. The false universals that undergird liberalism have exerted a stranglehold on the period's historiography. Working against this, I aim to expand the historiography of the period and bring into sharper view the distributed forms of agency, and indeed humanity, that liberalism both disavows and produces.

Thus I ask how and where Black experience has reclaimed oppressive forms of objectification and even dehumanization to produce radical alternatives to liberal humanism. Fred Moten's iconic opening of *In the Break* exemplifies this approach: "The history of blackness is testament to the fact that objects can and do resist."[59] To consider the "history of blackness" as proof of objects' agentic capacities is to embrace fugitive, creative, liberatory possibilities that have at times emerged from atrocity. Although many have, like Moten, framed them as *resistance*, I argue that a laser focus on resistance *alone* can obscure as much as it reveals. Criminal genius does not open onto claims for recognition or incorporation but offers instead a radical praxis of reimagining and remaking the world. This book uncovers a prehistory that unsettles today's popular notions of criminal genius, calcifications of late nineteenth-century criminology (which linked race, crime, and genius to degeneracy via eugenics), Victorian and modernist literature (with its criminal masterminds like Professor Moriarty and Fu Manchu), and mass culture (e.g., *Batman*'s Joker or *Breaking Bad*'s Walter White).[60] These later figures celebrate the individualism of a lone male figure malevolently standing against society; but in the period I attend to here, print culture developed a conjuncture of Blackness, crime, and genius that was collective, often feminized, and oriented toward an ethical horizon, albeit with frequently violent framings.

Attention to criminal genius in the figures of the zombie, the convict, the outlaw, and the fugitive uncovers a historically significant conception of agency that is racialized and distributed. This differs, however, from the various "posthuman" and "new materialist" agencies over which much ink has recently been spilled, such as Jane Bennett's "thing power" or the "effectivity of non-human or not-quite human things."[61] Bennet's theory purports to "give voice to a vitality intrinsic to materiality" and reveal "the world as a swarm of vibrant materials entering and leaving agentic assemblages."[62] Unlike this agentic "vibrant matter," the criminal genius exercises an agency that is not exclusively material but also, at the same time, voluntarist. This is a crucial distinction. In addition to the voluntarism that partially marks criminal genius, the formation I study here is also situated within histories of racialization. Contemporary posthumanists, by contrast, tend to work outside questions of history and of social and political domination. This is despite the fact that their theories emerge directly out of histories of racial domination and violence.

Long before posthumanism or the new materialisms, a long Black radical tradition, including contributions by Wynter, Fanon, and Aimé Césaire, has critiqued Western conceptions of the human and theorized the alternate agencies of those classed and treated as nonhuman.[63] Key recent scholars including Alexander Weheliye, Zakiyyah Iman Jackson, Cristin Ellis, and Kyla Wazana Tompkins have drawn our attention to the omission of this line of thinking in most posthumanist work. As Jackson writes, "The economies of value presumed in posthumanism and animal studies need to be historicized and transformed."[64] Likewise, Weheliye castigates posthuman extensions of agency: in failing "take into account race as a constitutive category in thinking about the parameters of humanity," they wind up "reinscrib[ing] the humanist subject . . . by insisting that this is the category to be overcome, rarely considering cultural and political formations . . . that might offer alternative versions of humanity."[65] Attention to early America's criminal genius helps accentuate the historical realities on which posthuman and new materialist theories ultimately depend. Criminal genius encompasses individual intentionality not in opposition to but alongside what Bennett calls "material recalcitrance" and other collective forces. Thereby it opens a view of the potentiality of this historical counter-formation of agency that is both materialist and voluntarist.

Although not all criminal genius figures are racialized as Black, I show how all accrue social force through the vectors that produce Black racialization, particularly those that racialize criminality as Black. Because racialization as Spillers famously outlined, builds on and extends a loss of gender difference, the criminal genius troubles colonial gender hierarchies and at times presents alternate *"representational* potentialities" for social subjects. Recovering these early instantiations of criminal genius, however they appear, therefore requires the lens of radical Black feminist politics. It is only through this lens that the real history of criminal genius becomes legible, because only Black radical thought can grasp racialized criminality as liberatory. As Barnor Hesse and Juliet Hooker write, "Delineating and contributing to a distinctive field of black political thought has always required that we recuperate conceptually the Western-attributed outlaw status of black politics."[66] Although the instances of criminal genius I discuss in this book are specifically US based and comprise both white and Black writers and actors, the racialized agency that criminal genius mobilizes is global in its history and reach.

All accounts of genius concede its transgressive elements. But where most genealogies situate genius within a Romanticism filtered through an institutionalized modernism, early American criminal genius developed in relation to linked struggles over racial slavery and crime in the new nation. Therefore, instead of the Romantic individual, this book centers the disenfranchised, disinherited, and incarcerated, as well enslaved and fugitive people, who, along with abolitionists and reformers, decried practices common on plantations and in the new nation's penitentiaries, as crimes against humanity. Figures I study here—including the largely forgotten white murderer Samuel Frost; the Black political writer David Walker; the insurgent Nat Turner and his no less radical mother, Nancy; and the often nameless but palpably present Dismal Swamp maroons—occupied the space of genius by transgressing law. In so doing, they drew on materialist and distributed agencies in addition to voluntarist forms, including the agency of print, of the natural environment, and even of the divine and thus upset the notion (still widely held) that individual agency adequately indexes humanity.

This study of criminal genius therefore challenges a central tenet of much historically oriented scholarship, which aims to "restore humanity" to the dispossessed by retroactively reincorporating those who were excluded into the realm of the liberal humanist subject. In these chapters I describe how disabled people, enslaved people, and free Black people mobilized criminal genius, manifesting social existence precisely where liberal citizenship would most seem to exclude them. Scholarly interventions meant to "give voice to the voiceless" miss something crucial: the distributed agencies always at play within and against liberal forms. Because there have been untold millions who neither sought nor gained liberal agency, I instead find genres of agency that emerge in more collective and distributed formations. The humanity of the dispossessed could never be restored by scholarship not only because scholars are not gods but also because it is only from a narrow liberal frame that humanity could ever seem eradicable. *Liberal* agency remained constitutively unavailable to countless individuals, but their humanness nonetheless persisted. In contrast to many recuperative histories, then, this study of aestheticized criminal genius allows us to read neglected, indeed sometimes unnamed, actors back into the historical record and, along with them, extralegal modes of subjectivity.

Work responsive to the now-familiar calls to "give agency" or, more commonly, "give voice" to the disenfranchised often exclusively takes the form of excavating instances of liberal agency,[67] frequently headed by overtly resistant figures like Nat Turner or, more palatably, Frederick Douglass. Douglass did not participate in collective armed resistance, but, of course, he left a rich body of work, one that has often been reduced to fit a narrowly progressivist narrative of US history. Turner's legacy is more contested, as the opaque central text on which Turner historiography remains centered, *The Confessions of Nat Turner*, is an "as told to" account. As I show in chapter 4, when we attempt to push past this complexity and limit the Southampton Insurgency to the story of an individual hero (even as it remains also that), we neglect the mobilization of distributed agency that makes the event's legacy so powerful. As Walter Johnson has argued, history approached "from the bottom up" has become problematically "compressed into the impulse to 'give them back their agency.'"[68] The outlaw, collectivist Black agency that the Southampton Insurgency exemplifies could never be "stripped" because it is not the exclusive property of a single individual. My intention across these pages is neither to deny nor minimize the struggles and successes of marginalized individuals—Turner being a quintessential example—who did achieve some measure of resistant, liberal agency or of the scholars who have directed our attention to them.[69] At the same time, when scholars understand the "human" exclusively as a liberal agent, ipso facto the only way to acknowledge the humanity of the enslaved is by seeking to reinstate their self-determination. To quote Johnson, "By applying the language of self-determination and choice to the historical condition of civil objectification and choicelessness, historians have ended up in a mess."[70] To adopt this position is to continue a misguided, centuries-long tradition of reinforcing the race and gender hierarchies we are setting out to critique. We must consider humanity differently.

In following chapters, I hew to this insight from the Black radical feminist tradition while employing literary studies methods, which, at one and the same time, center the voluntarism so closely associated with narrative plot and yet also, equally, allow for a reading of the unwritten or the ineffable that most often characterizes the experience of the dispossessed. Simultaneously, I draw on approaches from print and material culture studies, which trace printed matter's world-shaping potential. Edward Larkin had recently underscored agency's centrality to narratives of American individualism:

> Benjamin Franklin, of course, stands as the paragon of this new liberal subject endowed with agency and able to rise up from relatively modest beginnings to become a celebrated figure in politics and science through his intelligence, discipline,

and the force of his will. It's been a remarkable story that has taken hold across the political spectrum. In broad terms, liberals and conservatives alike have embraced this narrative. If scholars have debated the relative influence of liberalism and republicanism on the Revolution, there has been much less dispute about Revolutionary agency. The rise of American democracy has been tied to the rise of the agential subject.[71]

Yet agency was in fact a much more contested notion in the period than the literature generally acknowledges. Countering the view of agency as individual and autonomous, enacted by a universal abstract self, formations of Blackness growing out of the period reveal a fugitive agency at the intersection of crime and art. This agency, embedded, embodied, and collective, transgresses the borders of self and world policed by liberalism.

The impulse to elevate exceptional instances of individual agency as masculinist "genius" is a eugenicist outgrowth of white Enlightenment and Romantic philosophies. The lens of institutionalized modernism through which we tend to access those legacies has left our view overly narrow. We have largely forgotten that, in the late eighteenth and early nineteenth centuries, the discourse of genius was, at times, explicitly collectivist. Even elite white male characters most often noted as archetypes of lone individual genius, like Ahab, nevertheless are explicitly situated within larger networks. Scarred and disabled, Ahab could not pursue Moby Dick without the financial backing of New England shareholders (like Aunt Charity, who also helped outfit the ship) and merchants (who in turn derive their profits from slavery), a willing and experienced multiracial crew, and, indeed, that "not unintelligent agent" Moby Dick himself. Perhaps the most famous European commentator on genius was Kant, who captures this collectivity when he writes: "Genius actually consists in the happy relation—one that no science can teach and that cannot be learned by any diligence—allowing us, first, to discover ideas for a given concept and, second, to hit upon a way of *expressing* these ideas that enables us to communicate to others."[72] The aesthetic and political work of the Southampton Insurgency exemplifies this. It exceeds its extensive yet incomplete historical record but remains nevertheless overdetermined. In this wake, Turner emerged in story, song, and print culture as powerful, intelligent, ethical, enslaved, Black, and possibly divinely inspired. Turner becomes quintessential criminal genius, "daring," in amanuensis Thomas R. Gray's words, "to raise his manacled hands to heaven." As much aesthetic creation as a verifiable historical reality, criminal genius expanded the forms of life available to those who have been called socially dead.[73]

Engaging in the field of law and literature, the present study challenges the normativity of the assumption that the political subject is primarily a subject of law. Rather than disentangling race from crime, I demonstrate that racialization and criminalization are historically entwined categories, and I focus on cases, such as slavery, where legal issues are, or seem to be, outside the law and the possibility of redress lies in the aesthetic realm. Instead of exposing how the liberal state requires conceptions of negative personhood, as Colin Dayan has so compellingly done, this book discovers the positive potential that emerges from within the same bleak legal and cultural landscape. I argue for the forms of agency and collectivity available to late eighteenth- and early nineteenth-century criminals and enslaved peoples precisely insofar as they do not conform to abstract Enlightenment formations of the human.

To make this case, these chapters draw on both well-known material and archival research to map alternative constellations of agency across a range of cultural landscapes. They include the 1793 yellow fever epidemic, as documented by Benjamin Rush, Richard Allen, Absalom Jones, and Charles Brockden Brown; New England crime periodicals, in particular the cases of one white murderer, Samuel Frost, and one falsely accused Black man, Abraham Johnstone; David Walker's foundational contributions to African Atlantic political philosophy; a fugitive aesthetics enacted by Great Dismal Swamp maroons that shaped Edgar Allan Poe's aesthetic production; and enslaved insurgency considered, in line with Thomas De Quincey's aesthetic writings, as one of the fine arts. Weaving together theoretical, historical, aesthetic, and materialist approaches, I put pressure on a familiar understanding of agency as the exclusive property of the autonomous male liberal subject, depicted most notably as the Romantic individual, to show how different forms of subjectivity, especially those associated with the criminal, the disabled, the enslaved, or the nonhuman, offer counter-models of agency. Supplanting that self-reliant American individual who pulls himself up by his bootstraps, criminal genius represents an important fugitive legacy of the revolutionary Atlantic world.

The first chapter sets out this book's purpose: to rethink connections among Blackness, criminality, and genius in the United States before the Thirteenth Amendment. All three took shape in the revolutionary 1790s, when a rapidly changing Atlantic world muddled liberal notions of individual agency, even as an emerging US nationalist narrative seemed increasingly to rely on them. The chapter explains how the 1793 Philadelphia yellow fever epidemic generated new theories about Blackness, crime, and agency responsive to the racialized animacies of the figure of the criminal, of disease itself, and of the dead bodies it produced. Building on this foundation, chapter 2 centers on two late eighteenth-century executed convicts: Abraham Johnstone, a falsely accused free Black man found guilty of murder, and Samuel Frost, an unpropertied, young white man with a possible neurodevelopmental disability, who murdered his father and later his employer in late eighteenth-century Massachusetts. Johnstone used his criminal status to communicate his vision of collective Black thriving, exemplified by his relationship with his wife. Frost's case shows how criminalization came to entail racialization despite a white phenotype. Print culture constructs him as a criminal beyond reform, described in one broadside as "the connecting grade between the human and brutal creation." From the unsettled boundaries of the human within early American print culture, a racialized merger of print and personhood creates a "corpus" that forges connections among shifting collectivities extending across time and space.

Though among the earliest Black radical political publications, David Walker's *Appeal to the Coloured Citizens of the World* does not so much resist as occupy the twinned pathologies that captivate Black life and ground liberal individualism: criminality and death. Leaning into these racialized framings, chapter 3 identifies an alternative humanism in Walker's pamphlet. Asking in 1829, "What is the use of living, when in fact I am dead?" Walker cuts to the heart of a question that haunts US literature: How do the socially dead speak? His "demon-like production" responds by reconstructing Cartesian skepticism about the existence of the external world and refuting Jeffersonian doubts regarding Black humanity. Though potentially bloody, God's incipient justice exceeds doubt, and it is this horizon of justice, rather than Enlightenment reason, that secures universal humanity in the here and now. Calling for "coloured citizens" to "prepare the way" for divine retribution, Walker countermands Jefferson's virulent questioning of Black humanity and establishes criminal genius in its place.

Returning to the frame developed in my discussion of Abraham Johnstone and Samuel Frost, chapter 4 takes up another radical convict's corpus. Nat Turner is often singled out as an example of active rebellion against the institution of slavery. This is because self-directed, willed resistance is a familiar form of political agency. But the print archive offers limited access to any authentic Nat Turner. Rather than try to resolve long-standing disputes over the authenticity of the documents surrounding Turner, I place him in a collective Black genealogy that also includes his mother, Nancy. Decentering Turner and taking an aesthetic approach to the archive shows us that the events in Southampton are best understood not as a rebellion against unjust laws but rather an insurgency that reveals different genres of the human.

As noted earlier, the aestheticization of crime intensifies in the 1840s, in lockstep with debates over enslavement and Blackness. Chapter 5 turns to maroons in the natural and literary environment of the swamp, with particular attention to the poetry of perhaps the most infamous "genius" of American literature, Edgar Allan Poe. Rather than examine the legal subjectivities in Poe's tales, I focus on one of his most cited yet surprisingly little-studied poems, "Dream-Land" (1844), where the maroon in Virginia's Great Dismal Swamp doubles as Poe's "dark" genius. This foregrounding of associations between fugitivity, aesthetics, and the swamp's geographies of escape helps reorient mistaken white historiographies of genius and show their interrelation with Black cultural formations. Finally, the conclusion looks back at the early history of the criminal genius from the perspective of late nineteenth-century criminology and eugenics, with particular focus on the "American Lombroso," Arthur MacDonald. Despite criminal genius's importance throughout the eighteenth and nineteenth centuries, the term itself did not enter the lexicon until the end of the nineteenth century, when criminology, a new science, began to link genius to criminality through a discourse of degeneracy. Late-century scientific designations succeeded in dismantling genius's volatile minoritarian formation of aesthetic and political power.

Together, these chapters show how criminal genius designates racialized figures that exceed abstract notions of the liberal, isolated subject; cut against colonial gender hierarchies; and work instead more broadly through assemblages of print culture, human being, and the material world. Because protocols of New Historicism have often invisibly relied on a liberal view of agency (despite an ostensible stance against Cold War liberalism), its studies often implicitly or explicitly aim to recover and restore liberal agency to these excluded individuals. Referring to this "wide-ranging recuperative tendency" in early American studies, Ed White and Michael Drexler have observed that a "pedagogical emphasis on reading against the grain to recover unrepresented voices has become standard practice."[74] Criminal genius has been difficult to see in this milieu. Moreover, a false choice often constrains the reading practices of literary scholarship: either we must situate aesthetic productions in one or more contexts, or we must identify the heroic work of those productions themselves. Where the former shows the text as unsurprisingly shaped by its time and place, the latter reserves shaping agency for the text alone. Yet this apparent tension dissolves when we attend to genres of agency and humanity beyond the liberal subject. Criminality was linked with creative genius; creative genius, in turn, as we have seen, was strongly associated with Blackness and hence also cut against hegemonic constructions of gender. The frame of genius offers new perspectives not only on the racialization of criminality but, crucially, on associations between Blackness and criminality as sites of radical possibility in the late eighteenth- and early nineteenth-century United States.

Recovery histories showcasing enslaved people's individual agency are crucial. Instances of such agency were far more numerous than historians were, for centuries, willing to grant. Despite this willful legacy of misrecognition of enslaved people's resistance, the fact remains that there were multitudes who did not seek or gain the sorts of resistant, masculinist individual agency spotlighted in recovery scholarship. The figures I concentrate on here would be easy to incorporate into this heroic masculinist framework, but nuanced attention to their legacies points in a different direction. My interest in shifting this emphasis has been informed by David Kazanjian's critique of the "benevolent desire to impute a familiar political agency to the subaltern."[75] Instead, as Saidiya Hartman, M. NourbeSe Philip, and others have variously demonstrated, by attending more carefully to the gaps and fissures shot through historical records of enslavement, we can find new genres of agency, and indeed humanity, inherent in more collective and indeed extralegal modes of subjectivity. This work is fundamentally not about recognizing the claim of the oppressed to be admitted into an Enlightenment universalism that mistakenly excluded them; rather, by centering histories of racialization and enslavement, we glimpse alternate universalisms that, in straining the boundaries of legibility and law, may yet guide our unfinished projects of freedom.

CHAPTER ONE

Zombies of Civic Virtue

The summer of 1793 was hot and dry in Philadelphia, which was then the US capital, its most populous city, and home to the largest free Black community in the nation.[1] The year had been a profitable one, and many white people fleeing the Haitian Revolution arrived that summer to North America's busiest port hoping to remake their fortunes. Mosquitoes swarmed, especially near the docks. The heat lowered water levels, which provided a perfect insect breeding ground, giving rise to the conditions for one of the area's worst yellow fever outbreaks. A viral disease, yellow fever results in violent illness with highly visible, indeed terrifying, symptoms. Beginning with fever, nausea, and reddening of the eyes, face, or tongue, the disease then either resolves or moves into its toxic phase, which causes jaundice, hemorrhaging, multi-organ dysfunction (including heart, liver, and brain), coma, shock, and death. In 1790s Philadelphia, theories about the fever's origin broke into two camps: importationist and sanitationist. The importationists believed yellow fever was a contagious infection brought and spread by foreigners, while the sanitationists maintained that the fever was of local origin, caused by putrid air and preventable by maintaining hygienic conditions throughout the city. As we now know, it was actually mosquitoes that transmitted this gruesome and often fatal disease, which was common across the early Atlantic world's warmer climates.

    I begin my study of criminal genius with Philadelphia's 1793 yellow fever epidemic because the late eighteenth-century US capital was an important testing ground for early theories of scientific racism, and this Philadelphia summer played a key role in establishing criminal genius as a counter-formation of that history. As Robert Levine explains, "In the popular (white) imagination," the yellow fever epidemic was "linked to the revolutionary 'germs' spread by the contemporaneous black rebellion in Saint Domingue."[2] Congress was disbanded during the epidemic, because everyone with the means to do so had fled the city. "Of those who remained," Levine adds, "many shut themselves up in their houses, and were afraid to walk to streets."[3] The epidemic disproved a long-standing medical belief in Black immunity to the disease. Excess deaths, which numbered in the thousands, decreased the population by an estimated 10 percent, disproportionately affecting the poor and Black people who were unable to escape the city.

A whole cast of criminal genius figures emerged from the yellow fever epidemic. They include the (unidentified) virus itself, yellow fever corpses, assemblyman John Swanwick, and an anonymous figure whom printer Mathew Carey describes as a "master rogue." All were bad actors undermining self-interested civil society. Yet the epidemic also produced criminal geniuses who acted with good intent: physician Benjamin Rush, clergymen Absalom Jones and Richard Allen, and members of Philadelphia's larger Black community who served as nurses and undertakers, including convicted criminals given early release to help with relief efforts. Each of these benign actors, including the white individuals, found themselves racialized as Black and depicted as having maliciously set out to undermine white civil society, even or especially as that society's failures to care for its own come into sharp relief. Existing connections between Blackness and criminality are visible here, though these signifiers remain volatile. In this moment, an increasing racialization of enslavement also helped establish criminality's figurative Blackness. Yet, in contrast to later periods, this early Black criminality contained a radical potential for imagining and shaping the world otherwise. Crucially, this was before late nineteenth- and early twentieth-century sociological studies forged stultifying statistical linkages between Blackness and criminality. Since then, significant resources have been devoted to decoupling race and criminality and to showing how race and crime have shaped the modern United States. Because, as Khalil Gibran Muhammad emphasizes, "black criminality had become the most significant and durable signifier of black inferiority in white people's minds," influential figures including W. E. B. Du Bois and Ida B. Wells "labored tirelessly" beginning in the 1890s "to deracialize black criminality."[4] Such urgent efforts, from Wells to Muhammad, have had the unfortunate side effect of obscuring the fact that, in this earlier era, Black criminality did not readily index inferiority. Black criminality challenged both an emerging liberal individualism and race scientists' redoubled efforts to provide biological justifications for enslavement in the face of a growing international abolitionist movement.[5] Moreover, precisely insofar as criminal agency was the only agency that the law reliably accorded to Black people, it revealed the limitations of legal subjectivities and gave rise to extralegal genres of humanity.[6]

Enslaved and free Black people's legal status was notoriously nebulous: legal rights and privileges were not only few and far between but also highly mutable. Enslaved people could be held liable for transgressing the law but generally could not hold property, marry, serve as witnesses in a court of law, or sign legal documents. The Missouri freedom suits, by contrast, reveal instances where enslaved individuals exercised legal rights, to petition the courts for freedom. The mechanism by which they were able to do so was as follows. First, an enslaved person had to claim that they had been wrongfully assaulted or falsely imprisoned; when their enslaver maintained that they were a slave and therefore had not been falsely imprisoned or illegally assaulted, these individuals then had the opportunity to prove that they were in fact free.[7] This key example of enslaved people's access to legal avenues to challenge their enslavement highlights a baseline understanding of enslaved people's inherent criminality: all "imprisonment" of enslaved people was justified and could only be "false" if the party so "imprisoned" were not in fact a legal slave. The ongoing relevancy of the view of enslavement as punishment for a crime going back to Roman and Arabian law, which I discussed in the introduction, also extended to instances where enslaved people broke or were accused of breaking the law. Although such purported criminal activity often resulted in legal action, sometimes, in lieu, the consequence was sale. For example, Stephen Smith, described in the popular press as an "accomplished villain," experienced both. Born enslaved, Smith was sold, as punishment for theft, from Virginia to the West Indies. As he narrates in his dying confession, Smith later went (presumably self-emancipated, another act of "theft") to Canada. There he continued his career in crime, culminating with his execution for burglary and arson in Boston in 1797.[8] Smith traversed a path from enslavement to freedom and back again multiple times, under at least three discrete governments. The one relative constant across the mutable and pluralistic legal systems that spanned the early nineteenth-century Atlantic world, as Stephen Smith's life exemplifies, was that Black people could count on being held responsible for criminal activity.

In Boston, Black activist, businessman, and writer David Walker, the focus of chapter 3, describes the precarity of ostensible legal protections for non-enslaved Black people in the early nineteenth-century United States:

> I have known a poor man of colour, who laboured night and day, to acquire a little money, and having acquired it, he vested it in a small piece of land, and got him a house erected thereon, and having paid for the whole, he moved his family into it, where he was suffered to remain but nine months, when he was cheated out of his

> property by a white man, and driven out of door! And is not this the case generally? Can a man of colour buy a piece of land and keep it peaceably? Will not some white man try to get it from him, even if it is in a mud hole? I need not comment any farther on a subject, which all, both black and white, will readily admit. But I must, really, observe that in this very city, when a man of colour dies, if he owned any real estate it most generally falls into the hands of some white person. The wife and children of the deceased may weep and lament if they please, but the estate will be kept snug enough by its white possessor.

This sort of de facto disenfranchisement for Black people persisted across the United States until it was legally codified in the *Dred Scott* ruling in 1857. Until then, the status of free Black citizenship and attendant rights was, as Martha S. Jones elucidates, a story of "of how lawmakers and jurists fumbled, punted, confused, and otherwise failed to settle the question. Free black activists were generally of one mind. But even if they agreed that they were citizens, they did not agree about whether the state might affirm that fact."[9] Notoriously, Chief Justice Roger B. Taney's majority opinion, which settled the question for a time, held that under the law, Black people "are not included, and were not intended to be included, under the word 'citizens' in the Constitution." Although Taney's judgment would be nullified by the Fourteenth Amendment following the Civil War, it codified the view of earlier Black thinkers such as Walker regarding the political status of free Black people in the young United States. Surveying the history and precedent for his opinion, Taney notes that in the late 1780s, at the Constitution's framing, "the black man had no rights which the white man was bound to respect[,] ... was bought and sold, and treated as an ordinary article of merchandise and traffic, whenever a profit could be made by it. This opinion was at that time fixed and universal ... an axiom in morals as well as in politics, which no one thought of disputing, or supposed to be open to dispute." Taney here asserts directly what Walker had already recognized: that the white supremacist legal architecture of the United States held that Black rightlessness, alongside the sacrifice of Black lives and liberty "whenever a profit could be made by it," was not only justified politically but held as a *universal* moral axiom. Walker's 1820s Boston vouchsafed nothing in return for respectable, self-interested hard work when the industrious party was racialized as Black. Decades earlier, in 1790s Philadelphia, Absalom Jones, Richard Allen, Benjamin Rush, and Philadelphia's free Black community all learned this lesson the hard way, when the popular press represented their virtuous actions as evidence of their vice.

From such vantage points it becomes clear that "Black criminality" is a more-than-twice-told tale, with painful and destructive effects lasting over four hundred years. Associations of Blackness with criminality remain strong in the twenty-first century in such fields as neuro-criminology, which purports to be "post-racial" but in fact builds directly not only on discredited, racist pseudoscience but also on narratives about racial visibility, or what Fanon refers to as "epidermalization."[10] Like so many aspects of racism, the cultural and ostensibly "scientific" discourses that link Blackness with criminality have a protean quality, enabling this conjuncture to shape itself anew with each significant shift in the legal and political status of African Americans, from the Emancipation Proclamation to the Civil Rights Act. Antebellum African Americans who ran afoul of the law, like Stephen Smith, often stood out as "accomplished villains" and raised the possibility that the world might be radically reimagined and remade. Within Black art and politics, as Richard Iton has argued, "desires not to be excluded from the community of the 'normal' often underwritten by a particular form of vindicationist spirit . . . can translate into an avoidance of struggle and the abandonment of transformative possibilities."[11] Otherwise understandable desires to maintain respectability have obscured ways that less reputable forms may nevertheless have more capacity to make another world possible.

Over the course of the nineteenth century, Blackness and criminality came to be identified with one another, as white supremacist culture increasingly represented both as material facts. This conjuncture produced heightened, dynamic forms of oppression that drastically limited possibilities for Black life. The cultural forces that link Blackness to crime frequently do so via pathology or the logic of disease, as Dylan Rodriguez explains: "Criminalization . . . composes a form of normalized warfare against those (human) beings that embody the symbolic orders of death, pathology, and unassimilability into the order of Civilization, which itself thrives in the long historical disordering, immobilization, and/or (attempted) destruction of other human socialities."[12] Yet what Barnor Hesse and Juliet Hooker call Black "outlaw status," world shaping and world destroying, carries, precisely in its capacity to represent ways of being outside of Western hegemonic forms, the conditions of possibility for another, more equitable, more nourishing world.[13] We see these dynamics at play in 1793: yellow fever provoked a crisis for ideas of liberal agency when the experience of Philadelphia's free Black community, together with Rush's own experience, gave the lie to narratives of virtue rewarded. Over the course of the epidemic and in its immediate aftermath, the animacy of corpses and the disease itself, both ostensibly passive objects, likewise overtook Man's ingenuity and cleared space for criminal genius, which carved an alternative model of agency that exceeded abstract conceptions of personhood, including legal subjectivities.

"For the Honor of Human Nature"

The epidemic posed a crisis for the formations of liberal agency that were at the heart of developing conceptions of citizenship in the young polity and highlighted the potentiality of an alternative, collectivist agency that exceeded its racist, settler-colonialist origins. Crèvecoeur famously mythologized "America" as a place where "each person works for himself," where a diverse array of individuals receiving just reward for steady labor and virtuous living could find common cause.[14] But yellow fever deeply unsettled this idea of America, even as it underlined the ideologies of whiteness that it constructed and required. As Philadelphia printer Mathew Carey wrote in his history of the epidemic, *A Short Account of the Malignant Fever*, this was a period during which all the "'mild charities of social life' were suppressed by regard for self," as daily "frightful scenes were enacted, which seemed to indicate a total dissolution of the bonds of society in the nearest and dearest connexions."[15]

Providing examples of this dissolution, Carey describes "a husband deserting his wife, united to him perhaps for twenty years, in the last agony—a wife unfeelingly abandoning her husband on his death bed—parents forsaking their only children—children ungratefully flying from their parents, and resigning themselves to chance, often without an enquiry after their health or safety." He ends his sketch of the city's complete social unraveling with vignettes of "masters" evicting "faithful servants" and "servants abandoning tender and humane masters."[16] Carey's pamphlet circulated widely and went through multiple printings: in later editions, he pleads with readers not to judge the city by its worst moment. The plea itself demonstrates the point: the yellow fever epidemic threw an idealized republican citizenship, based on self-interest and "natural" bonds such as family and domestic service, into chaos. It revealed that the republican model of citizenship was not fit for purpose. The forms of sociality it fostered fell apart in the face of death and disease. Husbands and wives, parents and children, domestic servants and employers all abandoned one another. Corpses were left rotting in the streets, as individuals cast any collective good aside and strove to save themselves and themselves alone.

Or so at least in most official narratives. As Derrick Spires has shown, an important alternative account of the epidemic, written and published by Absalom Jones and Richard Allen, two members of Philadelphia's free Black community, exemplifies another conception of citizenship, which Spires terms "neighborly

A SHORT
ACCOUNT
OF THE
MALIGNANT FEVER,
LATELY PREVALENT IN
PHILADELPHIA:
WITH A STATEMENT OF THE
PROCEEDINGS
THAT TOOK PLACE ON THE SUBJECT IN DIFFERENT
PARTS OF THE
UNITED STATES.

BY MATHEW CAREY.

THIRD EDITION, IMPROVED.

PHILADELPHIA:
PRINTED BY THE AUTHOR.
November 30, 1793.

Title page from Mathew Carey, *A Short Account of the Malignant Fever* [. . .] (Philadelphia, 1793). Courtesy of the American Antiquarian Society citizenship," existing alongside more dominant models. Philadelphia's free Black community theorized and practiced this neighborly citizenship, which, crucially, did not dissolve but coalesced when faced with the challenges the fever presented. Jones and Allen were founding members of Philadelphia's Free African Society, a benevolent organization that later became the first Black episcopal church in the United States. Years later, Walker would memorialize Allen as follows: "Suffice it for me to say, that the name of this very man though now in obscurity and degradation, will notwithstanding, stand on the pages of history among the greatest divines who have lived since the apostolic age, and among the Africans, Bishop Allen's will be entirely pre-eminent."[17] In a 1794 pamphlet entitled *A Narrative of the Proceedings of the Black People, During the Late Awful Calamity in Philadelphia, in the Year 1793: And a Refutation of Some Censures, Thrown upon Them in Some Late Publications*, Allen and Jones seek to remind readers that Black Philadelphians organized to act as nurses and undertakers when no one else would.[18]

Early claims that Black people had a natural immunity to the fever's disastrous effects were quickly proved wrong, but Black Philadelphians continued their work. As Jones and Allen write, upon realizing the extent of the general distress, "We set out to see where we could be useful."[19] Their mobilization of the Black community helped fill a void created by liberal republican citizenship:

> A profligate abandoned set of nurses and attendants (hardly any of good character could at that time be procured,) rioted on the provisions and comforts, prepared for the sick, who (unless at the hours when the doctors attended) were left almost entirely destitute of every assistance. The dying and dead were indiscriminately mingled together. The ordure and other evacuations of the sick, were allowed to remain in the most offensive state imaginable. Not the smallest appearance of order or regularity existed. It was in fact a great human slaughter house, where numerous victims were immolated at the altar of intemperance.
>
> ... [A]lthough "hardly any of good character at that time could be procured" yet only two black women were at this time in the hospital, and they were retained and the others discharged, when it was reduced to order and good government.[20]

In an exceedingly poorly run hospital, the two Black women employed organized responsible care and provided relief for the sick and dying. At a moment when, citing Carey's widely circulated account, "hardly any of good character" were willing to step forward, Jones and Allen emphasize that these women stood out as compassionate conscripts in a thankless fight against a merciless disease. Jones and Allen's account is replete with such acts of Black kindness and compassion in the face of a truly horrendous epidemic. This was a moment when Black peo-

A
NARRATIVE
OF THE

PROCEEDINGS

OF THE

BLACK PEOPLE,

DURING THE LATE

Awful Calamity in Philadelphia,

IN THE YEAR 1793:

AND

A REFUTATION

OF SOME

CENSURES,

Thrown upon them in some late Publications.

BY A. J. AND R. A.

PHILADELPHIA: PRINTED FOR THE AUTHORS,
BY *WILLIAM W. WOODWARD, AT FRANKLIN's HEAD,*
NO. 41, CHESNUT-STREET.

1794.

Title page from Absalom Jones and Richard Allen, *A Narrative of the Proceedings of the Black People* [. . .] (Philadelphia, 1794). Courtesy of the American Antiquarian Society ple of their own free will worked for a common good, utilizing, as Spires has shown, an already-existing praxis of "neighborly citizenship" based on communitarian principles and hewing to the Christian parable of the good Samaritan.[21]

Where Carey grounds his account of the epidemic in liberal terms of vice/virtue and debt/reward, Jones and Allen describe the actions of the Black community as motivated by a more radical collectivity. In intensively economic terms, Carey extols the benefits of public praise for good action as a just payment for services rendered, and he criticizes his fellow citizens for being too stingy with praise and too generous with condemnation: "When the debt is great, and the only payment that can be made is applause, it is surely the worst species of avarice, to withhold it. We are always ready, too ready to bestow censure—and, as if anxious lest we should not give enough, we generally heap the measure."[22] By contrast, Jones and Allen describe the motivations of Black men and women, filling the roles of organizers, nurses, and undertakers, as aiming at nothing more or less than social good: "Our services were the production of real sensibility," they write. "We sought not fee nor reward."[23] Given Carey's insistence that Philadelphians ought to be as generous with public praise for virtue as they are with public rebuke for vice ("When we are so solicitous to deter by reproach from folly, vice, and crime, why not be equally disposed to stimulate virtue and heroism, by freely bestowing the well-earned plaudit?"),[24] it would be reasonable to expect such approval to be warmly heaped on the Black community following the epidemic. Any expectation of public reward for these good acts, however, was thwarted. Indeed, it was widespread condemnation of the Black community's role in the epidemic that spurred Jones and Allen to publish their *Narrative*.

Demonstrating still further the contortions of a polity grounded on the idea that "each person works for himself" in expectation of just reward, Carey and many other white Philadelphians thanked Black Philadelphians for their "real sensibility" with slanderous accusations of Black extortion, crime, and riot during the fever. Carey himself had fled the city during the epidemic and, as Jones and Allen themselves point out, made a tidy profit off the multiple printings of his pamphlet. Yet his account of the epidemic levels the charge of extortion against Philadelphia's Black community: "The great demand for nurses afforded an opportunity for imposition, which was eagerly seized by some of the vilest of the blacks. They extorted two, three, four, and even five dollars a night for attendance, which would have been well paid by a single dollar. Some of them were even detected in plundering the houses of the sick."[25] Answering such "censures," Jones and Allen assure the reading public that, while precious few white people stepped forward to lend a helping hand, "there were as many white as black people, detected in pilfering, although the number of the latter, employed as nurses, was twenty times as great as the former."[26]

Giving the lie to the charges he himself made, Carey goes on to pardon himself for his stinging accusation of Black extortion with words of praise singling out Jones and Allen: "But it is wrong to cast censure on the whole for this sort of conduct, as many people have done. The services of Jones, Allen, and Gray, and others of their color, have been very great, and demand public gratitude."[27] Jones and Allen's refutation of Carey's stinging "praise" highlights the complexities of race and citizenship in relation to disease and criminality at this time. They reject this ostensible olive branch of individual esteem to underline the collective harm that Carey's account perpetuates: "Mr. Carey pays William Gray and us a compliment; he says, our services and others of their colour, have been very great &c. By naming us, he leaves these others, in the hazardous state of being classed with those who are called the 'vilest.'"[28] Seeing power in collectivity, Jones and Allen refuse to be named along with William Gray, a fellow member of the Free African Society and a fruit vendor, as exceptional. Instead, they write, "we feel ourselves sensibly aggrieved by the censorious epithets of many, who did not render the least assistance in the time of necessity, yet are liberal of their censure of us."[29] Jones and Allen decline to be singled out as deserving public gratitude and instead align themselves with the broader "us" that suffered Carey's censure, "the vilest." The same "real sensibility" that induced Black Philadelphians to help, while white Philadelphians fled or hid, also motivates this complaint against libel. Being "sensibly aggrieved" alongside other community members, Jones and Allen diagnose Carey's desire to hold them apart not as mitigating, but rather as part of, the larger problem of dissolved sociality Carey himself impugns. Refusing Carey's poisoned peace offering, Jones and Allen remain on the offensive: "Is it a greater crime," they ask, implicating Carey and his profits gained from disaster journalism, "for a black to pilfer, than for a white to privateer?"[30] Minor Black misdeeds pale in comparison to exorbitant white criminality.

Jones and Allen's pamphlet, in addition to turning Carey's accusations of Black criminality back on profit-driven white people, also adds an important corrective to Carey's discussion of the role of released convicts in aiding the sick. In contrast to his denigration of Black people's humanitarian efforts, Carey effusively praises their work in liberal humanist terms:

> For the honor of human nature, it ought to be recorded, that some of the convicts in the jail, a part of the term of whose confinement had been remitted as a reward for their peaceable, orderly behavior, voluntarily offered themselves as nurses to

attend the sick at Bushhill, and have in that capacity conducted themselves with so much fidelity and tenderness, that they have had the repeated thanks of the managers. Among them are some who were formerly regarded, and with justice, as hardened abandoned villains, which the old system was calculated to make every tenant of a jail, who remained there a few weeks.[31]

Carey here aligns himself with penal reformers, aiming to restore criminals to useful citizenship. Noting these convicts' voluntarist offer of help, he lauds the initiative's restorative effect on "hardened abandoned villains." Yet in the very moment of adopting this progressive stance, he signally fails to note that a majority of these convicts were Black. Moreover, Carey occludes the African Methodist Episcopal Church's organizing role and instead praises "human nature" itself for the success of this early release plan. Jones and Allen correct the record:

Here it ought to be remarked (although Mr. Carey hath not done it) that two thirds of the persons, who rendered these essential services, were people of color, who, on the application of the elders of the African church, (who met to consider what they could do for the help of the sick) were liberated, on condition of their doing the duty of nurses at the hospital at Bush-hill; which they as voluntarily accepted to do, as they did faithfully discharge, this severe and disagreeable duty.—May the Lord reward them both temporally and spiritually.[32]

Emphasizing that a significant majority of the convicts thus released were "people of color," Allen and Jones are silent about any former depravity of the incarcerated. They instead refer to this early release as a "liberation." This is in keeping with their "real sensibility" and again contrasts Carey's description of this release as a "reward," which hews to the economic logic that governs self-interested citizenship. Where Carey seems to think that "repeated thanks" is sufficient payment for these formerly incarcerated Black people putting their lives on the line to care for the sick, Jones and Allen indicate the need for some more substantial remuneration. They pray that those liberated will receive "temporal" as well as eventual spiritual rewards.

Carey's sidelining of race in this context underscores a significant aspect of penal reform—namely, its primary orientation toward white offenders. As Jeannine Marie DeLombard has shown, for early penal reformers, inmates were normatively white, despite the fact that people of color have always been disproportionately incarcerated in the United States. Tellingly, the first inmate at Philadelphia's famed Eastern State Penitentiary in 1829, Charles Williams, was African American. Yet during the era of penal reform, in the first half of the nineteenth century, Northern African American inmates were "perceived to be ineligible for the carceral regeneration requisite to civic reintegration," and Southern Black people in this era continued to face corporal and capital punishment, as penal reforms there too were "effectively reserved for whites."[33] Penal reform efforts therefore helped forge the specific links between Blackness and criminality that would go on to shape modern history. The experience of Philadelphia's Black community during the yellow fever epidemic, from those accused of "vileness" and riot to the convicted criminals whose Blackness was whitewashed in Carey's widely circulated account, shows that the racialization of criminality thus encompasses whiteness. Liberal reform was effectively oriented around the assumption that where white criminality is environmental and therefore reformable, Black criminality is innate and immutable. Jones and Allen, and Philadelphia's Black community more broadly, were rightly concerned about the insidious turn that the epidemic marked in "progressive" reform discourse. Spires describes the Black community's "disillusionment upon realizing that, despite demonstrating their collective public spirit and responsibility in terms that their erstwhile white judges should have recognized and honored, no amount of 'proof' would be sufficient to overcome impediments that had nothing to do with black capacity and everything to do with white power."[34] The epidemic highlighted white authority's utter failure to distinguish vice and virtue when the actors involved were Black.

Demonstrating the limitations of self-determining, rights-bearing individuals to change their social standing through either good will or good works, the epidemic raised serious questions about the significance of vice and virtue and, more broadly, about the nature of human agency and will in general. Physician, politician, and penal reformer Benjamin Rush, who put his life at risk to stay and offer his services to Philadelphians during the epidemic, was also heavily abused afterward. Detractors labeled Rush a "poisonous trans-Atlantic quack" who "appointed two illiterate Negro men, and sent them into all the alleys and bye places in the city, with orders to bleed, and give his sweating purges to all they should find sick, and bloody and dirty work they made among the poor miserable creatures that fell in their way."[35] Rush, Jones, and Allen appear in such accounts as crazed, villainous, and bloodthirsty evildoers, rather than well-intentioned citizens and virtuous medical practitioners. To observers and participants like Jones, Allen, and Rush, yellow fever upset the ascendent notions of individual agency that an emerging US nationalist narrative increasingly required. As a result of the crisis to which the epidemic gave rise, an alternative, if long-buried, American legacy of collective agency develops. Crucially, this assemblage of actors—

print culture and, as we will see, the corpses of the epidemic's victims—goes hand in hand with a new conception of criminality as disease that undercuts any straightforward conflation of humanity with voluntarist agency.

"They Will and Prefer Nothing"

When voluntaristic avoidance of vice and embrace of virtue proves an ineffective path to social belonging, what fills this void? Criminal genius carves a model of agency and humanity out of a racialized landscape that exceeds abstract conceptions of personhood, including legal subjectivities. This agency, which is itself racialized as Black, encompasses what Mel Chen refers to as those "animacies" that traverse "insensate, immobile, deathly" matter.[36] Divisions between material and immaterial, bodily and spiritual, concrete and abstract dissolve to reveal "a richly affective territory of mediation between life and death, positivity and negativity, impulse and substance."[37] Animacy is a useful frame for understanding how criminal genius operates via an agency that is both materialist and racialized. In the case of the yellow fever epidemic, the figure of the criminal, the disease itself, and the corpses of yellow fever victims all evince embodied animacies. Human and nonhuman environments thus fuel a Black agency that encompasses, even as it eclipses, agency's liberal, voluntarist form, which is abstract and "free" insofar as it is ostensibly unmoored from the particularities of lived experience (race, gender, ethnicity, sexual orientation, disability, etc.). The evolution of Benjamin Rush's medical theory and practice exemplifies this dynamic and shows how an ungovernable, racialized materiality dismantles liberal agency, even for a practitioner like Rush who very much would have liked to place the material world in the service of that agency.

It was during the yellow fever outbreak of 1793 that Rush fully developed his unitary theory of disease, through which he began to explain all disorders as resulting from what he termed "capillary tension." Rush undertook his medical training in Edinburgh, where a Scottish Enlightenment curriculum drew on the work of English philosopher David Hartley and Dutch physician Hermann Boerhaave.[38] Hartley's 1749 *Observations on Man, his Frame, his Duty, and his Expectations* built upon a Newtonian understanding of mechanistic causes and effects, while Boerhaave saw pathologies as rooted in bodily processes, explicitly divorced from mind.[39] For Rush and others who had trained alongside him, mind and body were both fundamentally material. It was during 1793 that Rush moved this line of thinking still further and came to see all "disease" (yellow fever, criminality, revolt) not as individuated but as a type of fever or "morbid excitement" that required depletion to regain an equilibrium. Thus, Rush's treatment for yellow fever—the "heroic" treatment—involved extreme purging and bloodletting (depletion), with the idea that this would release tension in overstimulated bodies and allow a body to once again find balance. Because of its dangers, heroic treatment was controversial. But Rush believed that controlled yet significant bloodletting would not only cure the disease itself but also stand as a bulwark against social agitation and violence. Rush's medical and political activity fully intersected, per Jacquelyn C. Miller, coming to "imbue disease, medical therapeutics, and his patients' bodies with multifaceted political significance."[40] Rush's heroic treatment and his approach to penal reform and social order seamlessly blended the literal and figurative: the "methods he developed to deal with disorders in the somatic dimension of late-eighteenth-century American life reflect his simultaneous concern with maintaining the political health of the new American nation."[41] Thus although Rush disagreed with a widespread belief that yellow fever itself was imported from the Caribbean, he nevertheless shared adjacent concerns about the very real possibility that the region's revolutionary spirit might influence the political direction of the United States.

As a prophylactic, he believed that the heroic treatment would prevent social disruption on US soil as the Haitian and French Revolutions unfolded. Rush proclaims, "A great field [has been] opened for new means of curing moral and political maladies," and, more locally, he predicts that "bleeding would probably lessen the rage for altering the Constitution of Pennsylvania."[42] In his *Enquiry into the Origin of the late Epidemic Fever*, Rush acknowledges that his views were unpopular because they ascribed a native origin to the disease. Many feared that nativist theories would curtail travel to the port city still further and worsen the epidemic's already devastating economic impact. Rush counters that "Commerce can no more be endangered than Religion, by the publication of Philosophical truth."[43] He argues that the economy could only benefit if empirical facts held sway over the ever-threatening specter of superstition:

> On the contrary it [commerce] must suffer most by the adoption of the traditional error which I have endeavored to refute; for while the cause of a malignant fever is obvious to the senses, it will be easy to guard against it; but while it is believed that the disease may be imported, and no body know from what *place*, at what *time*, and in *what manner*; we shall not only be careless in the midst of filth and danger, but our city will always hold its character for health by a timid and precarious tenure.[44]

For Rush, the nation's economic well-being requires a clean explanatory model like the one he seeks to uncover, rather than series of nebulous, xenophobic what-ifs. Rush concludes his letter, "Medical, like religious superstition cleaves so closely to the human mind, that it often exists under new forms, and names, in spite of the cultivation and progress of reason: hence we find that malignant fevers, which in former ages were ascribed to celestial, planetary and demoniacal influence, are now with the same superstitious indolence, and with as little truth, ascribed to *importation*, or to an *unknown something* in the air."[45] Rush's mechanistic understanding of body and mind informed his theories that public health and national economy be guided by reason, lest superstition's "unknown somethings" take hold and agitate the body politic still further. This view likewise had implications for medical jurisprudence's treatment of race and the human will.

In an 1810 lecture on medical jurisprudence, Rush discusses how the *will* may be affected when "deranged" by disease. People suffering from a diseased will may, despite being in full possession of their reason, still commit acts that are beyond their control. Rush provides several examples, including an account of one woman who said she was possessed of "the best of husbands, and a family of promising children" as well as "the perfect exercise of my reason." Yet she sometimes found herself wishing "for an ax, that I might split open their heads, and lay them all dead at my feet."[46] Others who possess reason but suffer from a diseased will may find themselves with the irresistible desire to commit theft, for no profit or purpose. Still others, when in the grip of depressive states, like one man who said he sometimes felt so low that he "would not rise from his chair" to prevent his family "from being butchered before his eyes."[47] Extending this analysis in his 1812 *Medical Inquiries and Observations upon the Diseases of the Mind*, Rush emphasizes that the will may also be deranged by another, equally material cause: disuse. The *unexercised* will can "lose all sensibility" and come to resemble "a paralytic limb." This can happen to anyone but, he argues, is especially common among enslaved people.

Owing to the prolonged "habit" of acting only in accordance with the wishes of others, Rush writes, enslaved people frequently come to "*will* and prefer nothing." Rush's discussion of enslaved will-lessness calls to mind Herman Melville's eponymous short story about Bartleby, who could (or would) say nothing but "I would prefer not to." The question of whether Bartleby's preference is willful or whether it happens despite any intention Bartleby might have to the contrary, remains an open one. Presumably this question remains open for Rush's enslaved will-less people also. Where Bartleby, a white male waged worker, retains a preference, if only in the negative, the enslaved people Rush discusses have no preference at all. Rather, the maladies of the will he delineates more fully conjure up one of the period's most terrifying "superstitions": the zombie. Although today's familiar idea of the zombie, a revivified corpse lacking in all human spirit, was not yet extant in 1790s Philadelphia, the condition of zombification was becoming increasingly known in the United States in the wake of the Haitian Revolution. Although Rush is not explicit about any connection between his diagnosis of will-lessness and the animated corpses of Vaudou (Haitian) / Voodoo (US), both are linked to the condition of enslavement in the Americas. Just as Rush diagnoses will-lessness as resulting from enslaved people's prolonged "habit" of "preferring nothing," the zombie, or *zonbi*, metamorphosed West African understandings of various states of ensoulment and soullessness in the context of transatlantic enslavement. As Elizabeth McAlister explains, the zombie "originates from sensationalized descriptions of a set of Afro-Caribbean mystical arts."[48] Yet it is precisely these clear links with Afro-Caribbean religious and spiritual practices that relay the conditions of New World enslavement. As Stephan Palmié emphasizes, there is a direct relation between the Haitian *zonbi* and economic exploitation through capitalist regimes of enslavement: "The zonbi and the reduction of humans to commodified embodiments of labor power to which it speaks are experienced, chronicled, and analyzed by its victims in the form of phantasmagoric narratives about how even the bodies of the dead, bereft of their souls, do not escape conscription into capitalist social relations of production."[49] Zombification is the ultimate punishment for an enslaved person. Death is no liberation for the zombie, whose body is forced to linger in this world even after the soul departs.

The zombie, at the same time, exemplifies direct transgression of the bounded Enlightenment legal subject. Even as it mirrors and intensifies the condition of enslavement, the zombie, as the epitome of a human without will, deeply unsettles the Eurocentric, white supremacist frameworks that were constantly under construction to shore up racial slavery. Zombies, having no will, have no capacity to "resist" per se.[50] So too in Rush's view, humans whose will has atrophied are creatures that are first and foremost *economically* distinct from other humans: left to themselves, will-less individuals "neither buy nor sell, nor transact any kind of business." Enslaved people, having lost their will, become as "a paralytic limb." They do not buy or sell: they are bought and sold. In Rush's iteration, once cured of this malady, the will-less creature would once again become the fully human *Homo economicus*, transactional and voluntaristic. Insofar as the will-less merely perform those actions necessary to sustain animal life, however, they instantiate another genre of humanity not reducible to its economic function. Moreover, in fulfilling the conditions necessary for life, the zombie seeks to transform the rest of humanity, universalizing their condition. That is to say, the zombie or will-less person, having lost the capacity to resist, has gained the ability to imagine and shape humanity differently, beyond the bounds of economic, zero-sum logic that guides self-interested citizenship.

Indeed, humans with unexercised will in the first half of the long nineteenth century in the United States numbered in the millions. In addition, those whose will proved utterly incapable of producing the effects they desired in the world (as was Rush's, along with Jones and Allen's) were myriad. These facts alone roundly call into question any exclusive alignment of humanity with voluntarist agency. Many humans either do not have or cannot effectively exercise the liberal, individual agency of *Homo economicus*. Narratives that compellingly feature the existence of humans without will, from Rush's *Medical Inquiries* to tales of African American and Afro-Caribbean zombies, originate at this same late eighteenth-century moment when liberal agency was beset with contradictions in the face of the linked forces of racialization, criminalization, and enslavement. Reading the zombie as inextricably bound up with revolutionary struggle against enslavement, Sarah J. Lauro concludes, "There is a direct line that connects the metaphysical tactics of the Haitian revolutionary and the Vaudou zombie."[51] As with Haitian revolutionaries who were concurrently revising Enlightenment principles toward a more truly universal horizon, those operating beyond the clearly defined boundaries of voluntarist humanism in the new United States undermined self-interested citizenship and began to construct extralegal models of subjectivity, beyond forensic personhood. Ultimately, Rush's conclusions about people afflicted by will-lessness disturb any impulse to define the human itself as coextensive with the liberal agent, just as the fallout of the epidemic itself revealed sharp limitations in liberal conceptions of individual agency, whether manifested as criminal transgression or civic virtue.

"Reliques of the Deceased"

In an important counterpoint to the idea of a human without motive or will, yellow fever itself materialized for Rush and others as a conscious, determined actor: a formidable adversary with a will of its own. In reviewing contemporary medical, newspaper, and fictional descriptions of the fever's vicious will during Philadelphia's 1793 epidemic, we can see that racialized animacies characterized the figure of not only the criminal but also the disease itself. During the epidemic's early weeks, Rush initially recorded a sense of his own helplessness as he struggled to find a way to combat the disease. In a letter to his wife, dated August 25, 1793, Rush writes, "My Dear Julia, . . . the fever has assumed a most alarming appearance. It not only mocks in most instances the power of medicine, but has spread thro several parts of the city." On August 29, he tells her that "the disease has raged with great virulence." Frequently, Rush and many others designate the yellow fever as the "malignant disorder." This description likewise suggests that this disease possessed a vicious will and was set on reducing the city to chaos: *malignant-*, from the Latin, means "contriving maliciously." Rush goes still further: the malignant disorder, as he describes it, possesses motive and will. It attacks, it rages, it even mocks.

Racialized animacies also imbue dead bodies of yellow fever victims. Just as the disease itself has agency, the bodies of its victims enter public health debates in ways that not only highlight the intersections of medicine and imagination but also underscore the role of animacy at this moment. These animacies are aestheticized, and part of the work they perform is at the level of language and imagination. To take one key example: late in the year 1793, after the end of the yellow fever outbreak, John Swanwick, a Pennsylvania assemblyman, banker, and sometime poet who would soon be elected to the US Congress, published a letter in a Philadelphia newspaper arguing for the construction of a burial ground outside of the city limits. Swanwick lyrically describes the victims' corpses as "reliques of the deceased." He is especially concerned that an imagined, sentimental attachment to the dead might damage public health. Animating the lifeless corpses strewn about the city in the wake of the yellow fever epidemic with this evocative gothic phrase, Swanwick cautions Philadelphians, in future, not to let "tender attachment for the reliques of deceased relatives overcome that first of all principles: self-preservation." Rush shared Swanwick's sanitationist views and published an approving reply to the letter. Here they join many of their contemporaries, who believed that corpses threatened human life both mentally and physically by prolonging grief and, potentially, by transmitting disease. Deprived of all signs of life, including breath, pulse, and will, those who had once been honored friends and beloved family left behind "immense bodies of putrefying substances within the heart of the city . . . as it were at every man's door." Though will-less, these bodies, Swanwick and others fear, might still present a clear and present danger to living Philadelphians, thereby extending the pernicious influence of the animated fever itself. Their danger to human life, much like that of the Haitian zombie, manifested for Swanwick precisely as a threat to self-interested civil society.

Swanwick's letter raises key questions regarding agency when the will to self-preservation is threatened by the decomposing corpse. Corpses have agency without will; they infect without intention. In the face of their racialized animacy, those properly motivated by "self-preservation" find that their own voluntarist agency is unable to protect them. If the epidemic eventually spurred debate about proper treatment of corpses, it began with debates about how to treat the living bodies the disease attacked. Swanwick expressed his beliefs about how an Enlightened humanity ought to think about, and deal with, bodies, both before death and, indeed, after. In framing the body as a "relique," Swanwick suggests an unenlightened worldview that needs to be superseded by reason. This implicitly Africanist or Roman Catholic perspective holds the body and its traces as sacred or magical relics, which in turn pose a threat to civil society. Even so, for Swanwick, as for Rush, the corporeal form is more than "a body of putrefying substances." Although the desacralization of a "lifeless" corpse becomes, as Phillipe Ariès's famous study shows, a tenet of a modern, scientific view, the 1793 epidemic underscores the fact that the corpse's animacy cannot be fully restrained.[52] Thus, it is not a desacralized body that becomes, in Rush's later medical theory and practice, the site at which all disease emerges but rather the body conceived as agentic in its own right. Rush numbered among those eighteenth-century vital materialists who, as Monique Allewaert has demonstrated, held that "any part—whether a unit of matter or an organized form like a plant or an animal that contributes to some larger system—possesses agency and autonomy."[53] Rush does not bifurcate mind and body, as did many of his contemporaries, but conceives of both physical and mental illness as bodily. We have already seen how this played out in his discussion of maladies of the will. Through this lens, he likewise conceptualizes race (understood as skin color) and criminality under the umbrella of medical disorder. Rush, an influential penal reformer, argues that criminality is an affliction that could be both prevented and cured by the penitentiary's effects on human imagination. Likewise Blackness, or "negroidism," is for Rush a "skin disease." Noting the increasing virulence of racism during his lifetime, he calls upon "science and humanity" to "discover a remedy for it."[54] The "it" of course was not racism, white supremacy, or the criminalization of race but rather Blackness as skin color.

The belief that a corporealized imagination could shape and be shaped by the public good was widely shared. In addition to Rush and Swanwick, Adam Smith, in his analysis of sympathy's unruly nature, likewise highlights the period's racialized animacies. Though they believed corpses were vectors of disease, Rush and Swanwick saw reposeful nature as a healthful way to honor inevitable attachments to those who had been lost, as Smith has famously theorized. "We sympathize even with the dead," Smith argues, in spite of reason. Swanwick implores

Philadelphians to move the dead bodies outside the city's confines: "Let weeping willows, yew and cypress surround the mournful receptacle of the deceased . . . but let not some of the best squares of our city, in the most valuable parts, be occupied in a way so unwholesome and unsightly." Swanwick suggests that the garden cemetery can augment public health while serving sympathy's ends. Yet, as Smith also argues in *The Theory of Moral Sentiments*, sympathy with the dead can also produce more outré effects. Paradoxically, although corpses, by definition, do not feel, the living cannot help thinking about what it would *feel like* to be a corpse. Indeed, it is the very fact that the dead cannot feel makes the situation so unbearable: "That our sympathy can afford them no consolation seems to be an addition to their calamity."[55] In elaborating this paradox, Smith evokes a kind of counter-zombie. Sympathy with the dead produces, in a mirror image of a human without will, a lifeless body animated by a living spirt: "The idea of that dreary and endless melancholy, which the fancy naturally ascribes to their condition, arises altogether from our joining to the change which has been produced upon them, our own consciousness of that change, from our putting ourselves in their situation, and from our lodging, if I may be allowed to say so, our own living souls in their inanimate bodies, and thence conceiving what would be our emotions in this case."[56] Rush, Swanwick, and Smith all adopt a radical corporeality with fantasies of control, as when Rush maintains that everything his society views as undesirable is a material disease therefore susceptible to cure. Yet, even from their own words, it is clear that this corporeality and its hand-in-glove racialization are, inevitably, ungovernable. Swanwick himself provides a salient example: five short years after penning his letter, he died of yellow fever on his estate outside of Philadelphia. Between the time of this letter and his death, moreover, Swanwick was involved in serious financial scandals, accused of being a swindler and a forger.

In true gothic fashion, both crime and disease frequently figure in reform discourse as unwanted residues of a decaying and decrepit monarchical world. Doctors with modern training and new ideas are called in to excise or purge this remainder. When Swanwick talks about the corpses left in the wake of the yellow fever as "reliques of the deceased," he gestures at the fact that these traces do not disappear but compel our fascination. The racialized criminal genius, which develops out of this milieu, is precisely this kind of unruly remainder. From a bulwark of respectability, Swanwick himself, like Rush before him, wound up a criminal genius, disrupting social order by challenging the boundary between human and inhuman. Contemporaries describe him as "the greatest insurgent in the state," "slippery as an Eel," and "a contemptible creature."[57] These animalized descriptions of a civic leader show the ease with which criminal activity enabled one to pass into racialized territory. We see a similar racialization attaching to a criminal genius figure in Carey's pamphlet. In lauding Philadelphians for a relative lack of criminal activity during the epidemic, Carey presents the following an exception: "A hardened villain from a neighboring state, formed a plot with some negroes to plunder houses. He was a master rogue, had digested a complete system, and formed a large partnership for the most successful execution of his schemes. However he was soon seized, and the company dissolved."[58] This "master rogue" troubles a racial line: ostensibly white, he does not lead but rather "plot(s) with" negroes to create a "large partnership" of successful criminal activity.

Like Carey's "master rogue," and later Swanwick, Rush was racialized in slanderous accounts of his malevolence that ominously associate him with a band of Black people beset by "enthusiasm." Rush was "accused of profiteering . . . charged with acting precipitously and lethally, and with endangering the lives of Philadelphia's white citizens by employing uneducated blacks as his medical assistants."[59] A conservative English expatriate newspaper editor named William Cobbett, who objected strongly to Rush's abolitionism, published an account by a rival, Dr. Currie, who describes Rush as "elevated to a state of enthusiasm bordering on frenzy." One vignette accuses him as not only bloodthirstiness but also as transgressing racial boundaries in sitting too intimately "alongside" a Black man whom Currie describes as "his": "In passing through Kensington one day, with his black man on the seat of his chaise alongside of him, he cried out with vociferation, 'Bleed and purge all Kensington! Drive on, boy!'"[60] The racialized terror encoded in this image was not lost on Cobbett or his readers. The scene evokes the specter of Black revolution, coming just months after refugees from Haiti arrived on Philadelphia's shores to escape "bloodletting" at the hands of another "black man," Toussaint Louverture. Importantly, this same Cobbett represents Louverture as set on "destruction" of Saint-Domingue's "white inhabitants." Cobbett claims that Louverture sought Haiti's political independence from France not of his own free will but only after being incited by a white abolitionist, the French statesman Léger-Félicité Sonthonax.[61] These images of the revolution in Haiti formed part of the larger cultural imaginary Cobbett's readers brought to his account of Rush swaying another Black man, with whom he was overly familiar and whom he placed dangerously in charge of "bleeding" Philadelphia's white citizenry.

For these and other publications, notably one calling him a "potent quack,"

Rush filed a libel case against Cobbett. The court upheld the charge that Cobbett had set out to "blacken" Rush's reputation by calling him "a quack" and "charging him with murdering his patients."[62] Even having won the suit, in the epidemic's wake, Rush experienced extreme alienation. In a private letter in 1797, provoked by "a new wave of personal attacks" following another outbreak, Rush writes, "Ever since the year 1793 I have lived in Philadelphia as in a foreign country."[63] Here, Rush expresses, simply, pathos. Yet in public writing, notably his 1796 publication, *An Account of the Bilious Remitting Yellow Fever, as it Appeared in the City of Philadelphia, in the Year 1793*, Rush channels this sense of alienation into rhetorical aggression against Black people.

Rush, a staunch abolitionist who nevertheless pathologized Blackness in multiple ways over the course of his career, here describes Black contributions to yellow fever relief efforts in dehumanizing terms. He does not, like Carey, describe Black relief efforts as criminal. However, in his retrospective 1796 *Account*, Rush joins Carey in suggesting that Black nurses were not properly human.[64] Carey, in addition to insinuating "widespread black theft," writes that "many men of affluent fortunes . . . have been abandoned to the care of a negro." Such lines exemplify, per Spires, how "Blackness becomes Carey's marker for absence."[65] Yet Rush's explanation of why his medical treatment was not as successful as, in his view, it ought to have been, contains a still more blatant diminishment of Black humanity: "What medicine would act upon a patient who awoke in the night, and saw through the broken and faint light of a candle, no human creature, but a black nurse, perhaps asleep in a distant corner of the room."[66] Chillingly, Rush here draws a bright line between "human creatures" and "black nurses." This retrospective account contrasts with his earlier personal letters, where Rush describes African American nurses, with gratitude, as brothers: "My African brethren are extremely useful in attending the sick." Praising Black relief efforts, in one notable letter, Rush recounts to Julia an instance of his own self-identification as Black: "I met a good woman of their society a few days ago at the foot of a pair of stairs. 'Ha! Mama,' said I, '*we black* folks have come into demand at last.' She squeezed my hand, and we parted."[67] Rush's later shift is drastic. In his private correspondence at the peak of the crisis, he positions himself as a brother ("brethren") and son ("Mama") to Philadelphia's Black community. He even claims Blackness as his own at a moment when it seemed to have "come into demand." In the 1796 public account, he sharply, almost invisibly, asserts a cleavage between a "human creature" and a "black nurse." Samuel Otter suggests that the difference is attributable to Rush's sense of "private versus public discourse."[68] To publicly embrace Blackness, as Rush had painfully learned between the time he wrote this letter and the publication of his retrospective account of the epidemic, was to become alien in the land of one's birth and criminalized in the white public imagination.

"The Wretch, Whose Heart Still Quivered"

Bridging Jones and Allen's and Rush's shared (if divergent) concerns about the effects of journalistic libel, Charles Brockden Brown's novel *Arthur Mervyn, or Memoirs of the Year 1793* uses the tools of fiction to explore the role language, especially rumor, plays in the production and racialization of criminality vis-à-vis disease. The appeal worked in two directions, because by the late eighteenth century, disease, together with crime and race, had become a mainstay of US popular culture, comprising a triptych of sorts for racialized animacy. Thus, it was no surprise that yellow fever literature, and particularly Carey's pamphlet, circulated widely and sold well. Brockden Brown likewise drew on the epidemic in several of his novels, notably *Arthur Mervyn* and *Ormond*, which link crime and race to disease. Brown, like Rush with his heroic treatment and view of mind and body as one and the same, understands crime and disease as conjoined phenomena. And like Swanwick and Smith, Brown demonstrates the essential ungovernability of imagination, even as he underscores how central metonymic, fictive identification is to the structures of representative democracy. *Arthur Mervyn* explicitly figures a nexus of disease, crime, and self-making as mutually conjoined in the context of the early national public sphere. The novel underscores disease's capacity to expose the inhuman latent within the human: it can transform an individual into a corpse, a near-corpse, or, indeed, a criminal. But not only does *Arthur Mervyn* figure disease as a cause of criminality; it also emphasizes areas of commonality between crime and disease. An infected Arthur Mervyn appears in the opening pages of the novel as barely human, wraith-like, standing alone, obscured in the shadows. It is clear to the novel's frame narrator, Dr. Stevens, that Arthur has been "disabled by sickness," but he quickly finds he must also question whether Arthur is a criminal.

Upon its publication, *Arthur Mervyn* was praised for its realistic description of Philadelphia's response to the 1793 epidemic. Much of this realism circles around the havoc that yellow fever played on the imaginations of those in its grip. In his own recounting, yellow fever enters Arthur Mervyn's world in the form of a tale masterfully told, a "rumor which had gradually swelled to formidable dimensions" and "of a nature to absorb and suspend the whole soul."[69] The narrative that rumor weaves ultimately proves all too true; moreover, it emerges as a distraction from Arthur's own moralistic plot, derailing his intention to restore money to its rightful owner.

> The malady was malignant, and unsparing. The usual occupations and amusements of life were at an end. Terror had exterminated all the sentiments of nature. Wives were deserted by husbands, and children by parents. Some had shut themselves in their houses, and debarred themselves from all communication with the rest of mankind. The consternation of others had destroyed their understanding, and their misguided steps hurried them into the midst of the danger which they had previously laboured to shun. Men were seized by this disease in the streets; passengers fled from them; entrance to their own dwellings was denied to them; they perished in the public ways.
>
> The chambers of disease were deserted, and the sick left to die of negligence. None could be found to remove the life-less bodies. Their remains, suffered to decay by piece-meal, filled the air with deadly exhalations, and added tenfold to the devastation.[70]

Brown's own fiction becomes in and of itself another iteration of this rumor that can "absorb and suspend the whole soul." Readers are gripped with fear but, given our readerly remove from the fever itself, a fear of what? Exploring this question, James Dawes describes contagion "as a model for clarifying basic aspects of readerly experience." Noting the disease's "transformation of the body into a sign," he emphasizes that "disease is foremost an experience in irresistibility."[71] The novel highlights the fact that illness, like murder itself, can kill: reducing the human to mere body, a physical mass of potentially dangerous matter. But imagination itself played a central role in medical understandings of illness in the late eighteenth and early nineteenth centuries, as Sari Altschuler has capably demonstrated.[72] Similarly, Brian Waterman points to rumor's central place in medical thinking about yellow fever. Physician Elihu Hubbard Smith, Brown's close friend and one of Rush's students, figures rumor as akin to a physical malady, suggesting per Waterman "that words and imagination—the very stuff of fiction—can have physical effects and even do bodily damage."[73] Indeed, what most troubles Brown in *Arthur Mervyn* is disease's capacity, via imagination (fear), to turn ordinary citizens into criminals.

We find this vividly illustrated when Thetford decides to remove Arthur, infected with fever, to the hospital. Arthur responds by explicitly comparing Thetford's action to crime: "I heaped the bitterest execrations on my murderer."[74] In the grip of fever-fear, Thetford metamorphoses from a merchant into a criminal. The hospital indeed proves to be an odious place, where "dying groans were the only music, and livid corpses were the only spectacle," where disease devastates humanity.⁷⁵ Arthur's description is worth quoting at some length:

> You will scarcely believe that, in this scene of horrors, the sound of laughter should be overheard. While the upper rooms of this building are filled with the sick and the dying, the lower apartments are the scenes of carousals and mirth. The wretches who are hired, at enormous wages, to tend the sick and convey away the dead, neglect their duty and consume the cordials, which are provided for the patients, in debauchery and riot. A female visage, bloated with malignity and drunkenness, occasionally looked in. Dying eyes were cast upon her, invoking the boon, perhaps, of a drop of cold water, or her assistance to change a posture which compelled him to behold the ghastly writhings or deathful *smile* of his neighbour.
>
> The visitant had left the banquet for a moment, only to see who was dead. . . . Presently, she disappeared and others ascended the stair-case. A coffin was deposited at the door, the wretch, whose heart still quivered, was seized by rude hands, and dragged along the floor into the passage.⁷⁶

Terrifyingly, those hired to care for the sick and dying turn out to be "carousing" wretches who ultimately become their patients' executioners. Although Brown sidelines any direct discussion of race, this passage clearly cites Carey's well-known depiction of Bush Hill Hospital, as well as Jones and Allen's less widely read refutation of it. When Brown describes Bush Hill's nurses as drunken "wretches" engaging in "debauchery and riot" despite being "hired, at enormous wages," he exacerbates Carey's libel. *Arthur Mervyn* not only clearly references but indeed shamelessly embellishes Carey's accusations against Bush Hill's Black nurses. Particularly notable is Brown's rhetorical conflation of the nurse in this scene with the disease itself, "bloated with malignity."

The stuff of nightmares, the passage ends with a living patient, a "wretch, whose heart still quivered," seized and dragged toward his coffin. Our narrator here does not describe the patient being entombed alive but something almost worse: readers are left with this image of the nearly dead dragged mercilessly toward the coffin in which he will spend his final, tormented moments. The murderous agent here is strangely passive, racialized via its connection to Carey's account as well as that of Jones and Allen, a coffin "was deposited," by whom we do not know, to be filled by a barely or nonhuman animacy that the synecdoche "rude hands" conveys. The victim is dragged out of the hospital, off the page, and beyond our gaze yet seared into our imaginations.

It is in this very space between life and death that we find figures like the wrongly convicted Abraham Johnstone and the white murderer Samuel Frost, to whom we will turn in the next chapter. Both were executed for murder, both figured as diseased, deformed, and defamiliarized wretches who, beyond our sight, were dragged, still living, toward their graves only to be ensconced forever therein just beyond the printed page. I read the group of printed texts surrounding Johnstone's and Frost's cases as each forming a discrete "corpus," and in the final chapter on Nat Turner, I attempt something similar with a mode of reading that encompasses the historical person, his words, and the words of others. My suggestion is that we read "criminal" acts together with the body of print engendered by figures like Johnstone, Frost, and Turner as a unified—if not entirely coherent—corpus. Both Johnstone's and Frost's organic and print lives predate, though just barely, the nineteenth-century juristic phrase "corpus delicti," an assemblage of facts that show concrete evidence of a crime.

We begin to see criminal genius, a zombification of the voluntaristic liberal agent, poised between life and death and gripping a collective imagination, in the gaps and fissures of the historical record and in the slippage between lived experience and written memory. This is the lacuna of Brown's yellow fever victim, dragged by racializing animacies (figured by Brown as a Black nurse who is, like the fever itself, "malignant") to his grave while still living. Taken together, the proliferation of publications surrounding those convicted of murder in the late eighteenth century attempts to contain the criminal imaginatively at a time when convicts were not yet sequestered physically in the penitentiary—after the advent of penal reform as an idea but before wide implementation of those reforms. When criminals' physical bodies increasingly fade out of the public's gaze and into the penitentiary, an explosion of crime literature steps in to fill the void. In the nineteenth century, the penitentiary becomes firmly rooted in modern criminal justice, agitation for the abolition of the death penalty is strong, and punishment is privatized. As public executions fade from practice, printed matter moves into the foreground and feeds a strong public appetite for crime. Inexpensive and increasingly lurid descriptions of criminal lives, trial reports, and confessional narratives become ever more ubiquitous. The textual embodiment of marginal personalities like Johnstone and Frost becomes the condition of possibility for the disappearance of the criminal body from the public view and for criminality's racialization, which functions in excess of phenotype. Yet the material and imaginative space of criminal genius enables these convicts, poised on the edge of death, to produce an idiosyncratic ethics that, if only fleetingly, forges connections among shifting transracial and transtemporal collectives.

CHAPTER TWO

The Convict's Corpus

On July 7, 1797, Abraham (né Benjamin) Johnstone sat down to write one last letter to his wife, Sally. Despite his assurances of her safety, Sally refused to visit the New Jersey cell where Johnstone awaited execution the following day. Woodbury Jail lay just across the river from Philadelphia, and both Johnstone and his wife had survived the yellow fever epidemic of 1793, though he only barely. Recalling that time, Johnstone writes, "The flux was then prevalent in Woodbury (it being the time of the Philadelphia sickness) and I was taken very bad with it: people feared that it was the fever I had gotten."[1] Bedding was then in short supply, so Sally traded a promise of her future labor at a local lodging house for some old rugs that would serve the purpose. Abraham, who had adopted his brother's first name and abandoned his own when he moved north into ostensible freedom, soon became dangerously ill. Sally, intent on nursing him, stayed by his side until he was on the mend. But with so many fleeing the city and seeking lodging, the owner of the lodging house threatened to charge them both with theft if she did not abandon her husband's bedside to work for her. Sally refused, sacrificing her good name and his to attend to her ailing loved one. Sally and Abraham Johnstone denied the charge of theft, as indeed Abraham would deny the later charge of murder for which he was to hang. Yet it was to this original accusation, the alleged theft of rugs to serve as his sickbed, that he traced the unjust series of false accusations that would culminate in his capital conviction for the murder of Thomas Read, "a Guinea Negro."

If an act of care set this ball in motion, Johnstone maintains that it was his material success as a formerly enslaved Black man that provoked the murder charge. "Doing well for myself," he states, "made me an object of envy and hatred."[2] Likewise, Johnstone may, as Stephen J. Hartnett suggests, have angered powerful local individuals when he helped another enslaved man to freedom.[3]

As Jeannine DeLombard notes, "The only undisputed facts appear to be that Thomas Read, having previously sued Johnstone, went 'missing' and that the Delaware ex-slave was charged for and eventually convicted of the African's murder on the basis of circumstantial evidence in the form of testimony from his New Jersey neighbors, both black and white."[4] Although he was keenly aware that his biological life was shortly to end, Johnstone expected that the legacy of care that initiated his criminalization would continue. In his touching final missive to Sally, on the cusp of his entry into eternity, Johnstone conjures his own ghost: "Should my spirit ever present itself to your view, be not afraid Sally it will be . . . on the watch to shield and defend you from any impending danger."[5]

Four years prior, a markedly divergent set of circumstances attended another man who also was soon to face execution. On July 16, 1793, a half moon, midway on its journey across the sky, became visible in the Massachusetts twilight. Samuel Frost, a white man, had escaped by day. He hid now in the underbrush just outside of town, likely haunted by two very different ghosts, the ghosts of his victims. Ten years before, Frost had murdered his father by smashing his head in with a lever, and earlier that day he killed his employer, Elisha Allen. Recreating the murder of his father, Frost beat Allen's brains out with a garden hoe. According to the documents that would be printed in the days and months to come, this young man, like the moon in the sky that night, was half formed. Frost, twice a murderer, was racialized in contemporary depictions as a dark figure, halfway between human and animal. If, as Johnstone lamented, Black people in the late eighteenth century were frequently "looked on as a different species,"[6] so too Frost, as a racialized criminal, represented "the connecting grade between the human and brutal creation."[7] Johnstone's status as Black and free criminalized him, and Frost's violent retributive murders racialized him. Their respective convictions placed them both beyond the pale of liberal human sociality.

Unlike Johnstone, Frost was clearly responsible for murdering both his father and Allen, yet because of his neurodivergence, he struggled to have the law acknowledge his agency as a murderer. In 1783, Frost was acquitted of his father's murder on grounds of insanity, but—at his own insistence—his murder of Allen finally produced the death sentence. He was apprehended a few days after the latter crime, on July 20. On All Hallows Eve in 1793, Samuel Frost died at a well-attended public hanging in Worcester. He had to fight for the right to be charged with murder, thereby folded into a community that sought to exclude him. Johnstone, excluded as a free Black man, also found that his sentence of guilt (albeit one he denied) offered him a place of belonging. While maintaining his innocence of the crime for which he was to hang, Johnstone, like Frost, was able to imagine a reconstructed sociality from the law's scaffold: "Death shall give sanction to my assertions," Johnstone proclaims, "assertions that shall be sealed with my life, which the law claims forfeit and which to the law I give up as an atonement for any offence I may have been guilty of."[8] Frost, white, guilty of the crime of which he was convicted, and also guilty of the prior crime of murdering his father (of which he was not), found community within the rituals of execution. Johnstone, Black and innocent of the crime of which he was convicted, answered law's agency with his own and pointed to the limitations of legal subjectivities. When law claimed his life unjustly, he handed over that selfsame life to atone for those past acts of wrongdoing that were beyond the law's purview.

The historical records relating to both Frost and Johnstone are limited but highly suggestive printed materials that are relatively accessible in archives both physical and digital.[9] Johnstone, a Black man convicted of murdering another Black man, left an archive more restricted than Frost, a white man who murdered two other, older white men. Johnstone's archive comprises "The Address of Abraham Johnstone . . . to the People of Colour," "The Dying Words of Abraham Johnstone," and a final "Letter to his Wife," along with a third person note, "To the Public," all of which were printed in a single edition "for the purchasers" in Philadelphia in 1797 shortly after his execution and included no illustrations (fig. 2.1). Frost's more extensive archive comprises an execution sermon preached just before his hanging and published as a pamphlet shortly after; several brief, syndicated newspaper articles; and four broadsides (two offered for sale on execution day) that include various combinations of a third-person account of Frost, his last words or "dying" confession, a poem reflecting on the "solemn occasion" of his execution, and, finally, advertisements for these broadsides (fig. 2.2).

The Frost publications fit seamlessly into the American gallows print tradition, while the Johnstone materials stretch its limits. From the first publication of a North American execution sermon in 1674 to the rise of the popular press in the nineteenth century, readers in the colonies and the new nation consumed hundreds of books, pamphlets, broadsides, and poems describing the lives, and often the deaths, of convicted criminals.[10] And in the late eighteenth century, as Karen Halttunen has demonstrated, such publications increasingly describe criminals as animal or otherwise inhuman, just as they do in Frost's case.[11] Johnstone's pamphlet, by contrast, stands not only as "the single overtly antislavery eighteenth-century black crime narrative" but also as the only narrative in which a condemned Black person claims innocence.[12]

This chapter looks to these two figures to understand how late eighteenth-

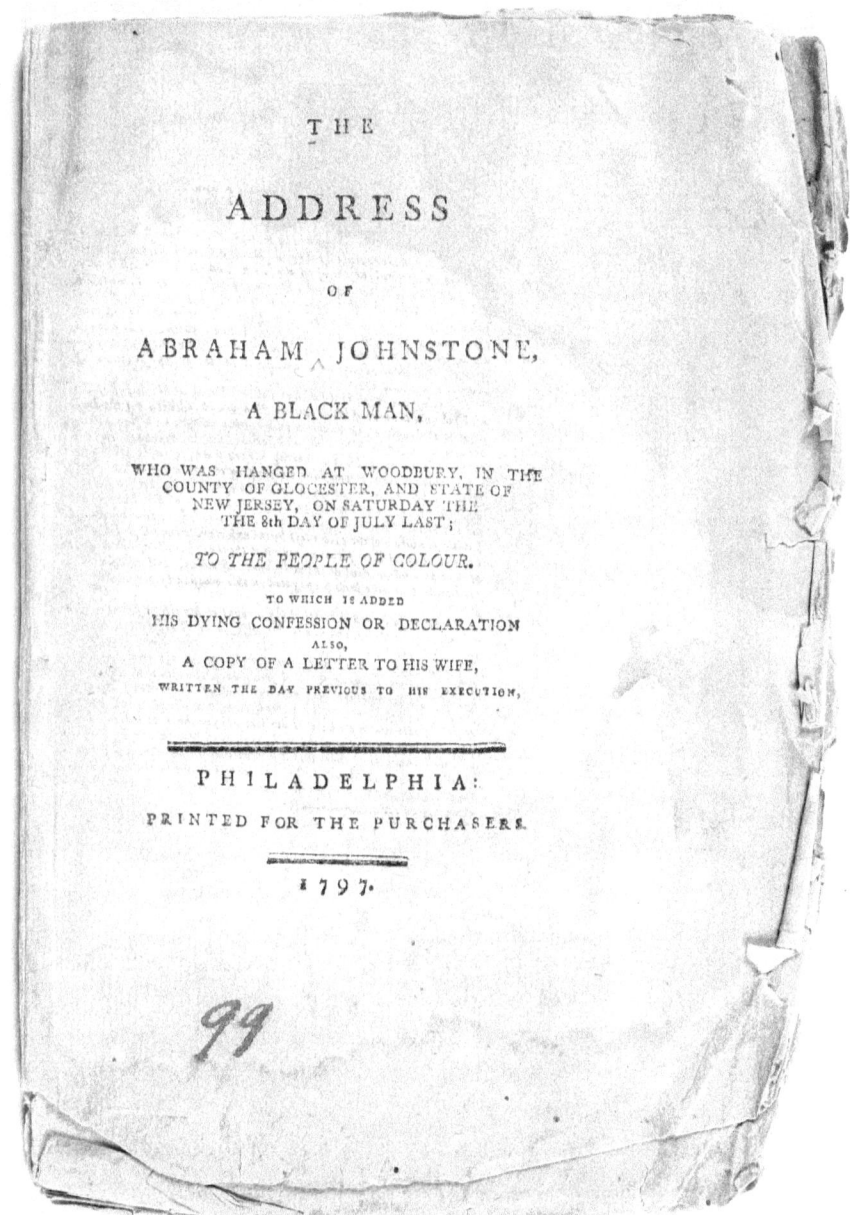

Title page from Abraham Johnstone, *The Address of Abraham Johnstone* [. . .] (Philadelphia, 1791). Courtesy of the American Antiquarian Society

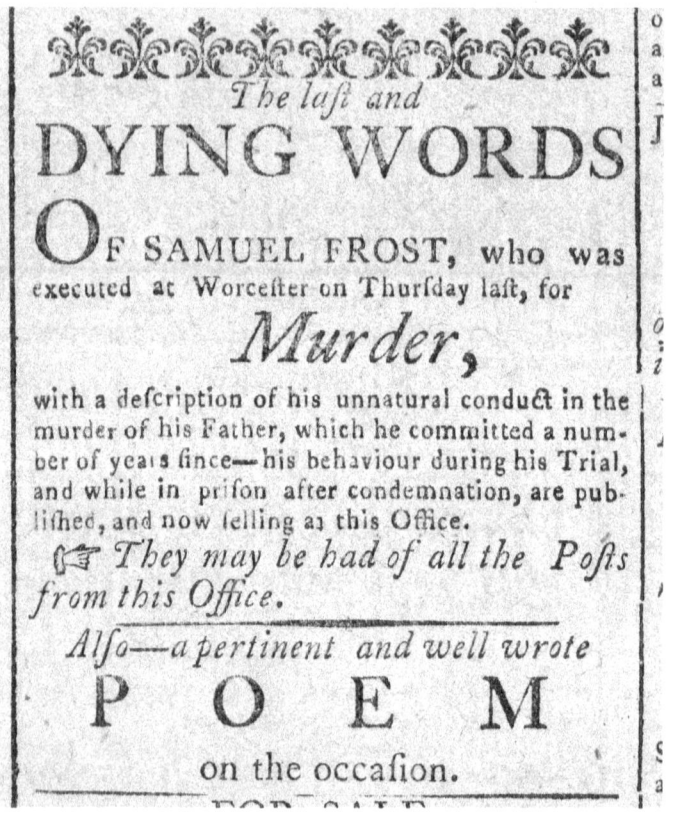

Advertisement for Frost's confession. *The Federal Spy and Springfield Advertiser* 1, no. 47 (November 5, 1793): 3, col. 3. Courtesy of the American Antiquarian Society

century criminal genius emerges from the print record's fissures and contradictions. Reading these two executed convicts alongside one another also helps us understand the relationship between criminalization and racialization in this period, as Northern states moved toward emancipation. Abraham Johnstone was a materially successful, falsely accused free Black man wrongly found guilty of murder, while Samuel Frost was a young white man with a possible neurodevelopmental disability who insisted on his guilt after murdering his father and his employer in late eighteenth-century Massachusetts. For both Frost and Johnstone, however paradoxically, it is the fact of their conviction that makes palpable the unsettled boundaries of the forensic person, which, as we have seen, underpinned individual identity for Locke and other Enlightenment thinkers.

Both Johnstone's and Frost's organic and print lives predate, though just barely, the nineteenth-century juristic phrase "corpus delicti," "the body of the crime," which refers to an assemblage of facts showing concrete evidence that a crime has been committed. Such evidence became codified to prevent the arbitrary exercise of power: to convict a person of a crime, it must first be established that the crime actually happened. Moving from here into the specificity of conviction itself, I propose a framework that we might term *corpus convicti*, "the body of the convict." This approach allows us read actual lives lived in tandem with printed representations of those lives, to acknowledge limitations on establishing authentic historical personhood without abandoning our search for meaning in the past altogether. It focalizes the real social fact of conviction, beyond the juridical question of guilt or innocence. *Corpus convicti* helps us see how the agency of the criminal genius is neither purely voluntaristic (and linked to law) nor purely material (and incapable of being held to ethical standards) but both. Johnstone used his conviction to communicate a vision of collective Black thriving, exemplified by his relationship with his wife, Sally. As a white man, Frost insisted that he be convicted for the crime he committed, despite judicial efforts to declare him mentally unsound. The two cases together help us see how criminalization came to entail racialization beyond phenotype and how conviction, ironically, has at times offered a view of the human that exceeds legal subjectivity.

"Admit Them to Be Human"

The publications surrounding Frost are consistent with the historical development of the American gallows print tradition, while those surrounding Johnstone deviate from the genre in ways that highlight how criminality was racialized in the period. Both Frost's life and Johnstone's are thus legible in relation to the social configurations of the emerging racial liberal state.[13] Frost was a dispossessed young man who may also have suffered from what we would today call a neurodevelopmental disability. Johnstone purchased his way out of enslavement into not only nominal freedom but also material security in New Jersey, only to be dogged by the specter of criminality. Although it may be tempting to resurrect them both as forgotten iterations of the remarkable American individual (lost avatars of Benjamin Franklin),[14] Frost and Johnstone were just two of many who were constitutively excluded from liberal citizenship. As Immanuel Wallerstein has argued, "The other face of the inclusiveness of citizenship was exclusion," because from its very beginnings, the liberal state has denied active citizenship to those deemed as lacking in virtue or intellectual capacity.[15]

Since the late eighteenth century, the list of those liberalism excluded has comprised not only criminals, people with disabilities (like Frost), and enslaved or free Black people (like Johnstone), but also women, Indigenous people, people of color, children, nonbinary people, and so many others.[16] A major aim of much historically oriented scholarship in the past several decades has been to restore humanity to the dispossessed by belatedly integrating excluded individuals into the ranks of liberal humanist subjectivity. Yet this is more easily said than done, because, as Charles Mills demonstrated across his career, "the same developments of modernity that brought liberalism into existence as a supposedly general set of political norms also brought race into existence as a set of restrictions and entitlements governing the application of those norms."[17] In other words, racial liberalism is liberalism itself, "the actual liberalism that has been historically dominant since modernity."[18] And, since agency in the liberal tradition is intimately linked to the definition of "the human" itself, on this view, to be human is to possess an individual will and the capacity to act according to that will.[19] This equation would hold that the (degendered, racial) slave functioned as the determining other to the (white, male) human. But the cases of both Johnstone and Frost show that self-determination and humanity are by no means coextensive. The publications that describe Frost repeatedly call his humanity into question, and, as Ajay Kumar Batra notes, the publications surrounding Johnstone "amount to a catalogue of injustices [that] . . . crowds out of view virtually all there is to know about his life" and renders historical access to his authentic existence "an archival dead end."[20] Rather than recuperating their humanity in liberal terms, however, I show that reading their lives in relation to the publications that represented those lives brings the collective agency of the criminal genius into view.

Both Frost and Johnstone express quite a different perspective on what constitutes the human than the liberal tradition, though Johnstone is more explicit than Frost. For Johnstone, the human is defined primarily by a shared capacity for love, care, and community. Just as David Walker would some thirty years later, Johnstone takes Black humanity as self-evident through a reductio ad absurdum that also castigates white depravity: "Such persons whose ungovernable passions hurries [sic] them to the gratification of their gross apetites [sic] by a promiscuous intercourse, and carnal knowledge of the bodies of blacks, must either admit them to be human or themselves to be guilty of the most odious and enormous of all crimes, a crime that I blush to name—therefore shall leave it to your imaginations to supply."[21] Cognizant of ongoing attempts to classify racialized peoples as different in species and with a keen awareness of racialized sexual violence and exploitation, Johnstone finds that the category of the human either applies to Black people, or it criminalizes white people. For if Black people are not human, then white people are precisely that "most odious" criminal, the bestialist, that itself blurs a distinction between the human and the animal. In pointing out that any reasoning white person must either "admit them [Black people] to be human or themselves guilty," Johnstone shows that the pseudoscientific "question" of Black humanity is in fact a question not about humanity at all but rather about criminality: the criminality of those who would seek to exclude Blackness from the realm of the human.

Johnstone does not need twenty-first-century historians to establish his humanity. The question that arises for the modern scholar, then, is this: How can we account for the lives of convicts like Frost and Johnstone without invisibly relying on racial liberalism's own tool kit, without recovering or belatedly recognizing the masculinist individual agency of figures constitutively excluded from liberal society? "Admit them to be human" in all the messiness that category entails, rather than recuperate a (liberal) humanity denied? I propose the *corpus convicti* as one answer to this question. We sidestep the problematic of the authentic innocent/guilty subject as the sine qua non of humanity when we analyze convicts' lives and deeds (real or fabricated) as they appear in relation to the late eighteenth-century print culture that represented, judged, aestheticized, or moralized on that life and those deeds. Later chapters, in particular my study of the gallows publications surrounding Nat Turner in chapter 4, will build on this approach, looking at how cases where the person and the publication become indistinguishable show agency as both voluntarist and material.

The "convict's corpus" reveals a collective agency that liberalism both disavows and produces. Though Frost and Johnstone may have written or collaborated on their printed accounts with unnamed amanuenses (this historical record is uncertain in this regard), we can nevertheless read them as creators who quite literally left themselves in their works. Such works need not be poems, paintings, or autobiographies: they may instead be deeds, like murder (Frost) or material economic advancement (Johnstone), or even affective states, the gestures at empathy we find in accounts of Frost or the acts of love and care we find in Johnstone's "Letter." A reading of the early US convict as corpus incorporates this insight by analyzing text, human doing, and human being in vital relation. This approach stands opposed to more familiar interpretive responses, for example, understanding Frost or Johnstone as purely textual beings (such as Roland Barthes's "paper beings," which vest agency in the critic as the producer of meaning and elide any historical person), or looking to the historical record to establish the contours of Frost's and Johnstone's authentic existence (and thereby attempt to ground claims for their individual liberal agency). The *corpus convicti* is simultaneously materialist and linguistic, and it therefore challenges the new materialisms, which promote a "material turn" precisely to counter a prior "linguistic turn" and "retrieve the body from discourse."[22] Where new materialisms attend to material agency, they siphon it off from history and textuality and thereby idealize it. My approach instead seeks to understand materiality in dynamic relation to historically situated voluntarist agency.

The rest of this chapter moves through readings Johnstone's "Address," "Confession," and "Letter to his Wife," as well as Frost's execution sermon, broadsides, execution poem, and the newspaper coverage of his trial and hanging. These readings show Frost and Johnstone emerging in the interrelation of their works: Frost's murder of Allen and of his own father, his escape and confession, and the print culture to which these actions gave rise; and Johnstone's attempts to build and maintain community, first in enslavement then in supposed freedom, thwarted by exclusion, criminalization, and ultimately the execution that, horrifically, was also what enabled him to convey his radical vision. The documents under consideration here are themselves material artifacts. Like the individuals they represent, these printed ephemera are conflicted and contradictory. In a sermon preached at Frost's execution, Massachusetts minister Aaron Bancroft depicts Frost as execrable. But elsewhere Frost appears oddly sympathetic and even capable of radical empathy, as when the "Account of Samuel Frost" explains that he was found banging his head against the prison wall to understand how his victims felt in their final moments. Similarly, Johnstone's "Address," "Confession," and "Letter to his Wife" all theorize an alternative understanding of the human at odds with self-interested liberal individualism and possessive personhood, while, at least superficially, ascribing to a politics of respectability, castigating his Black audience for attending "frolics" and attachment to drink. Looking at the push-pull of these publications in tandem with one another and with the individuals they represent, we find neither a unified Frost nor a unified Johnstone—real or imagined. Instead, we see that in both cases the very contradictions that the *corpus convicti* conveys help explode the ideal of autonomous agent as the human par excellence.[23]

Frost's murders and Johnstone's accusation of murder coincided with the ascendancy of liberal humanism, which was consolidated as the basis of US identity and citizenship in the late eighteenth and early nineteenth centuries. Yet the convict's corpus each left behind undermined liberalism's fundamental premise, that agency and humanity are coextensive and the exclusive property of the white man.[24] Countering racial liberal's view of agency as enacted by an individual, abstract, "human" self, the *corpus convicti* displays a racialized agency is that simultaneously voluntaristic, collective, and material. This approach reads print, embodied action, and larger institutional structures relationally. Rather than recognizing Frost or Johnstone's humanity through a heroic critical intervention that would somehow restore their status as liberal agents or "make them men," we find a collective agency that emerges in the publications surrounding their lives and deeds.

"With Becoming Detestation"

In his 1793 execution sermon for Frost, Bancroft encouraged his audience to feel disgust for this "pest of society."[25] The sermon's implicit definition of humanity is predicated on the exclusion of criminals like Frost as inhuman and therefore outside the bounds of community. Bancroft's execution sermon is consistent with a late eighteenth-century shift toward conceiving of criminality as a counter to liberalism, an "other-than-human" subjectivity. This was a shift enacted largely via print. The fact that there was no execution sermon preached for Johnstone is a lack laden with meaning. Black convicts facing execution drew comparatively little ministerial attention in this period. That this was particularly true when the alleged victims were also Black testifies to a devaluation of Black life that increased over the course of the eighteenth century. The absence of an execution sermon for Johnstone indexes a disregard for both his life as a free Black man and the life of the man whom he was convicted of murdering, "Thomas Reade, a Guinea negro." When we read Frost's execution sermon alongside the absence of a sermon for Johnstone, we can see how, in the late eighteenth century, the execution sermon as a form was adapted to index the phenotypically white criminal as Black.

The earliest examples of colonial execution sermons presented a Calvinistic view of criminality resulting from divine retraction of restraining grace. By the 1790s, however, in line with criminality's growing racialization, the convict represented in these sermons metamorphosed from an ordinary sinner into a creature at once powerfully other and decidedly man made. Although narratives of sin and punishment remained important to crime literature in the early nineteenth century, identifying individual deviance and explaining its origins in the story of an individual life began to take precedence. Execution sermons were preached either the Sunday before the execution or on execution day. The criminal was usually present, and these US sermons—preached by leading ministers rather than, as in England, minor clergy—drew large crowds. By all accounts nearly as many people heard the sermons as were present at the executions themselves, and these sermons then were among the first to reach more extended audiences via print.[26]

Before 1800, at least eight sermons were preached and printed at the executions of Black individuals, all of whom, except one, were convicted of a serious crime against a white person, either murder or rape. They were "a young girl" (executed for the murder of her enslaver's child in 1751), Bristol (convicted of the murder of his enslaver's child in 1764), Arthur (convicted of the rape of a white woman in 1768), Hannah Ocuish (convicted of the murder of a six-year-old white girl in 1787), Joseph Mountain (convicted of the rape of a white woman in 1790), Thomas Powers (convicted of the rape of a white woman in 1796), and Anthony (convicted of the rape of a white woman in 1798). By contrast, of the nine first-person biographies of African American criminals published in the United States before 1800, only four were from the pens or mouths of convicts who also received execution sermons (Bristol, Arthur, Joseph Mountain, and Thomas Powers); and, of the further five, only one, Pomp (1795), stood accused of a crime whose victim was white, "his cruel master." In addition to Abraham Johnstone, these first-person biographies were of Fortune Price, convicted of arson in 1762; Johnson Green, convicted of burglary in 1786; and Stephen Smith, convicted of burglary in 1797. The only execution sermon preached for a Black person convicted of a crime against another Black person was also the earliest. In 1721, Cotton Mather preached a sermon before Joseph Hanno's hanging. Hanno was convicted of the murder of his wife, "Nanny Negro," in 1721. Yet as Richard Slotkin points out, this sermon was "similar in its theological presumptions and rhetorical aims to those preached for white miscreants, and Mather frequently reminds his audience of this kinship in sin (both Original and habitual)."[27] Even the most tensely racialist and potentially dehumanizing moments in Mather's sermon point back to a fundamental commonality between convict and audience, as when he asks, "But, is the Black Thing that you have in Irons here before you, the only One that may be charged with Murdering his Wife among us?"[28] Mather, propounding that cruel and callous husbandly behavior regularly "hastens" wives to early graves, presses against his audience's racial prejudice to encourage identification. Thus, where the earliest examples of colonial execution sermons view criminality as retraction of restraining grace, Mather's sermon for Hanno stands squarely in this tradition.[29]

Late eighteenth-century execution sermons, however, displayed humanist, Enlightenment concerns and convictions as readily as they evinced the theological underpinnings of earlier sermons. A tale of individual self-fashioning replaced the traditional drama about the fate of the criminal's soul, and rather than being encouraged to see themselves in the condemned, audiences were encouraged to cultivate detestation for the criminal. Thus, as one might expect from a religious form with increasingly secular content, Bancroft's execution sermon for Frost was an internally conflicted document. In form and function it was very much in line with earlier execution sermons, yet whereas earlier American execution sermons centered on the soul of the condemned, Bancroft's focused on fashioning the liberal subject, precisely through its concurrent construction of the convict as a racialized other.

Bancroft's theme was not only how Frost turned into the kind of being who could commit the crime of murder but also how his audience might make themselves differently.[30] Attention to changes in the titles of execution sermons underscores this shift. Where early examples were given titles like "Speedy Repentance Urged" (1690, Cotton Mather), "The Folly of Sinning, Opened & Applyed" (1699, Increase Mather), and "Death the Certain Wages of Sin" (1701, John Rogers), Bancroft's 1793 sermon was titled "The Importance of a Religious Education Illustrated and Enforced" (fig. 2.3).[31] Similar in length and size to its precursors, Bancroft's sermon was printed and sold as a twenty-four-page pamphlet. Unlike many earlier execution sermons, however, Bancroft's text does not discuss Christ and the penitent thief, nor does it draw on salvationist language from the books of Job or Isaiah. He reads instead from 1 Samuel 3:13: "His sons made themselves vile, and he restrained them not." There were some later execution sermons, particularly after the Second Great Awakening, that continued the earlier tradition's emphasis on the criminal as representative of the miraculous possibility of divine mercy. But Bancroft's sermon, in its aim of exhorting good parenting through sound secular and religious training, participated instead in the period's widespread emphasis on the importance of education and care for youth.[32]

Working within the generic conventions of the American execution sermon, Bancroft goes through the list of "gateway" sins that might have set him on the slippery slope toward murder, only to conclude that this traditional explanation could not account for Frost's inhumanity: "He never mixed in those scenes of intemperance and dissipation, which frequently corrupt the moral powers of men. . . . [T]he temptations of ambition and avarice had no influence; yet in a country, where all men enjoy those advantages for moral and religious improvement . . . we behold him a savage, possessed of the most malignant and revengeful passions."[33] Minor sins did not set Frost up for a later fall. Rather, those sins were conspicuously absent. Frost figures here not as a typical sinner but as "a savage, possessed of the most malignant . . . passions." As a free white man in

Title page from Aaron Bancroft, *The Importance of a Religious Education Illustrated and Enforced* (Worcester, MA, 1793). Courtesy of the American Antiquarian Society

the newly formed United States, he had access to "advantages for moral and religious improvement," but they proved useless.

Bancroft eschews standard explanations for crime in the early American gallows tradition. Instead, he draws on a secular mode of personal history to account for how Frost, whom he characterizes as a "pest," came to infect society. Though he claims reluctance "to open the graves of the dead, and to expose to publick view the faults of those who have passed," Bancroft nevertheless says that "the father of this unhappy man was greatly deficient.... [T]he example set before him was impious, cruel, and barbarous. In this school the son was but too ready to learn."[34] The word of God recedes as Bancroft applies his "doctrine," from 1 Samuel, to Samuel Frost. An example of the results of bad parenting, Frost presents "a striking instance of the fatal effects of the neglect of early education."[35] Applying a Lockean paradigm to Frost's upbringing, Bancroft (who would himself shortly become the father of famed historian and statesman George Bancroft) stresses the importance of the strong, unshakeable influence on the mind of the child of early impressions, which take hold before reasoning capacity is fully formed.[36] Despite foregrounding "early education" and parental responsibilities, Bancroft nowhere acknowledges the fact that Frost had murdered his father, an omission I will discuss in more detail shortly.

Bancroft constructs the specter of inhumanity from the events of Frost's life not to save souls but to inspire successful self-fashioning of the liberal subject. Telling his audience to "aspire to the true dignity of your natures," he encourages them to distance themselves from Frost by cultivating feelings of disgust for him. Bancroft places Frost outside the sphere of white, male, rights-based belonging.[37] Instead of offering Frost spiritual counsel, Bancroft praises his audience for reviling him: "With becoming detestation and abhorrence, you contemplate the action which brought him to this untimely end."[38] He figures this disgust as attractive or "becoming" to his auditors: "Were you thought capable of his crime, you would exclaim, 'Are we dogs, that we should do this thing?' We believe you incapable of the crime of murder.... The path of honour and distinction in this world lies before you, to animate your minds to virtuous pursuits."[39] Bancroft lauds the imaginative limits that prevent his audience from questioning their own human belonging ("Are we dogs?"). Bancroft here references 1 Samuel 17:43: "And the Philistine said unto David, 'Am I a dog, that thou comest to me with staves?' And the Philistine cursed David by his gods," and 2 Kings 8:13, "But what, is thy servant a dog, that he should do this great thing?" For Bancroft, although "we" are not dogs, Frost implicitly is. In this separation of a white criminal from his larger community, enacted via the material, spoken, and print media of the execution sermon, we see an important dynamic in liberalism's construction.

At this moment in the sermon, we see that the racialization of liberalism that Mills has analyzed dovetails with criminality's racialization. When he finally addresses Frost directly, Bancroft retains his larger emphasis on self-making: "You are to be taken away from among the living, because you have made yourself vile, and are become unworthy longer to be a member of the community."[40] Insofar as he has "made [him]self vile," Frost enables Bancroft's audience to become properly human by cultivating disgust for those "unworthy" of being members of the community. Criminals like Frost are not ordinary sinners in whom the community must see themselves; rather, they are part of what must be excluded to shore up a racialized rights-based polity, in which humanity itself becomes something to which one aspires ("aspire to the true dignity of your natures").[41] Elizabeth Maddock Dillon offers a particularly lucid explanation of the seeming paradox of liberalism's inclusive exclusions: "This exclusion can be reversed in dialectical terms: that is, it is demonstrably the case that this exclusion includes white women and African Americans in an externalized—but foundational—position."[42] The antinomies of the liberal worldview likewise created a new kind of racialized criminal, a subject who, through an alchemy of environment and volition, exists outside the boundaries of the liberal human. When the "natural" becomes aspirational and disgust becomes an admirable affect, the racialized criminal, we might say, is un-self-fashioned.

As an example of what can easily happen to any "ordinary sinner" who has let down their guard, the executed convict of the traditional execution sermon becomes an object lesson and warning for other members of the community: there but for the grace of God go I. In contrast to these earlier sermons that worked to draw the convict back into the fold of sociality, including Black convicts like Joseph Hanno, late eighteenth-century sermons like Bancroft's, along with absent sermons like the one that was not preached for Johnstone, establish criminality's racialization. To assign the criminal subhuman status flirts with the absurd. Bancroft bumps up against this when he states, "We behold a human being, apparently devoid of all social affection and sense of moral obligation . . . [who] is now with ignominy to lose his life, as a pest of society." Frost's "apparent" lack of moral obligation renders him, impossibly, both "a human being" and "a pest." Johnstone directly discusses the contradictions of racial liberal thinking in his castigation of Europeans, who when they "discovered . . . that part of Africa called Guinea" were quick to criticize cruelties transpiring there but themselves "did not hesitate to barter and traffic for [Africans], as for other animals."[43] Of their descendants, contemporary US enslavers, he writes, "How preposterously absurd must an impartial observer think the man whom he sees one moment declaring with a most incredibly volubility in favour of natural right and general freedom, and the next moment with his own hands for some very trivial offence infecting the cruel and ignominious stripes of slavery and riveting its shackles."[44] As Johnstone establishes the self-evidence of Black humanity in the face of such stark contradiction, so too does Bancroft both admit and deny the criminal's humanity. The result, racialized criminality included as an exclusion, carries a potent charge.

Without doubt, Bancroft's sermon objectifies Frost, just as the absence of a sermon for Johnstone exemplifies disregard of his life as a free Black man, already excluded and objectified. But it is precisely through this objectification and diminishment that the convict's corpus as a whole (including the sermon, present and absent) attains agency. In contrast to liberal agency, which posits a freedom based on an abstract universality that is ostensibly unmoored from the particularities of lived experience (e.g., race, gender, ethnicity, class, sexual orientation, and disability), the agency of the *corpus convicti* is embodied and particularized.[45] Attempting to restore the convict's humanity would efface the space between liberal humans and "pests" or beings "of a different species," a space that liberalism itself constructed. This erasure would be a mistake because it is precisely from this space that the Frost broadsides and Johnstone's writings generate forms of connection and belonging that are not predicated on exclusion, abstraction, or transcendence.

"Creatures Formed to Live in a Mutual State of Dependence"

Reading the execution sermon, and lack thereof, in tandem with the other print documents surrounding Johnstone and Frost, we can see a theory and praxis that encompasses more expansive modes of belonging. The "Note to the Public" that introduces Johnstone's "Address," "Confession," and "Letter to his Wife" suggests that these assembled documents, particularly the "Letter," can offer a window into Johnstone himself, beyond the racialized criminalization that dogged him from freedom to the grave: "The copy of his letter to his wife is inserted merely to gratify the reader's curiosity, and that by his having the whole of the pieces left by the unfortunate convict, before him, he may be enabled to form an opinion of the true character, and guilt of the man independent of the malignant assertions, and innumerable falsehoods that have been propagated on this occasion by prejudiced persons."[46] Likewise, each of the Frost broadsides assumed a readership interested in attempting to understand his life, which appears by turns fascinating and repellent. Isaiah Thomas printed the first, *The Confession and Dying Words of Samuel Frost*, in Worcester (fig. 2.4). It was sold on execution day, along with a separate broadside, also printed by Thomas, which includes "A Poem on the Execution of Samuel Frost" (fig. 2.5). Both execution-day broadsides contain the same woodcut engraving, which shows a man hanging from a gallows in front of a large crowd. An official with a gun stands in the foreground on a horse-drawn death cart, and men with guns seem to surround the crowd from behind.

The two subsequent variations of this broadside reprinted the same confession and "Account of Samuel Frost," which also includes the poem. One gives the poem a different title, "A Poem on the Solemn Occasion." Sold by Jonathan Plummer, a traveling trader who dealt in, and sometimes authored, criminal broadsides and other popular pamphlets, *Last Words and Dying Confession of Samuel Frost* was printed in Boston, most likely by E. Russell.[47] It features eight woodcut engravings, making it the most visually arresting of the broadsides, as well as a brief description of Frost's behavior at the execution itself in the lower right-hand corner (fig. 2.6). The other post-execution broadside, printed by Henry Blake & Co. in Keene, New Hampshire, uses the same titles as the execution-day broadsides, though with different line breaks for the poem, and it has no engravings (see fig. 2.7). On execution day, the poem was published in a separate broadside that could be purchased at the same time as the broadside containing the "Account" and "Confession"; the two subsequent Frost broadsides incorporate all three texts. On each the typography is dynamic, with many words appearing either in bold, capitals, italics, or various combinations thereof. Sensational language is accompanied by accusing manicules, admonitory skull and crossbones, exclamation points, and gallows scenes. Exerting a material agency, such typography encourages readers to imagine the man and events presented as similarly captivating. Even the headline of the relatively spare Keene broadside offers a good example of this dynamism, with its combination of all capitals, boldface type, and italics.

Print documents like Johnstone's "Confession" and the Frost broadsides, which include first-person statements of convicts condemned to execution, had a history stretching back nearly as far as execution sermons.[48] Because many of the condemned could not write, convict confession as a genre troubles a concept closely linked to liberal concepts of agency in this period: authorship. Although confessions penned by amanuenses were purportedly "taken from the mouth" of the convict, it seems reasonable to imagine that Frost and Johnstone did write their own confessions. The "Account of Samuel Frost" indicated that "he could

The Confession and DYING WORDS of SAMUEL FROST,
Who is to be Executed this Day, October 31, 1793, for the
Horrid Crime of MURDER.

Samuel Frost et al., *The Confession and Dying Words of Samuel Frost* (Worcester, MA, October 1793). Courtesy of the American Antiquarian Society

A POEM.

On the EXECUTION of

SAMUEL FROST,

Who is to be Executed this Day, October 31, 1793, for the Murder of Capt. ELISHA ALLEN, of Princeton, Massachusetts.

"Learn to be wise from others harm,
"And you shall do full well."

REVIEW each ACT, on LIFE's important stage,
In every CLIMATE and through every AGE;
And still we find each passing scene will shew,
"That VIRTUE only, is our bliss below."
VICE for a while, with dazzling form may please,
Assume the borrow'd smile of careless EASE,
Display the charms of pleasure's roseate BOWERS,
Her gay ATTENDANTS and her happy hours;
But yet ere long shall TRUTH expose the CHEAT,
Her weak delusions and her foul deceit,
The hidden poison of her BREAST reveal,
And paint the terrors which her smiles conceal.
This day, my FRIENDS, exhibits to MANKIND
Th' effects which follow from a VICIOUS MIND;
Denounc'd by JUSTICE, in life's early bloom,
A WRETCH misguided seeks the silent tomb.
In tender AGE, when softer passions glow,
When PITY moistens at the tale of woe,

Deaf to her cry, HIS ARM, on malice bent,
To shades of DEATH, an aged PARENT sent:
Yet here his ART eluded JUSTICE' claim,
He knew the MANIAC or the FOOL to feign,
Impos'd on CANDOR, with a vague pretence,
And MERCY wink'd upon the black offence.
Ten YEARS revolv'd, when lo! by ANGER driven,
Again he breaks the great command of HEAVEN;
Again the MURDERER lifts his vengeful hand,
And aims the deadly weapon at his FRIEND.
Thus by his arm the FATHER, PATRON, dy'd,
At once the TRAITOR and the PARRICIDE.
Insulted JUSTICE now the WRETCH demands,
And sentenc'd DEATH awaits her stern commands.
Ye YOUTH who view the sadly solemn scene,
Learn hence the laws of VIRTUE to esteem,
Learn hence that HE who from his DUTY swerves
Will one day meet the VENGEANCE he deserves:
Ne'er let the flowery paths of VICE delude,
Nor let REVENGE upon your thoughts intrude.

"A Poem on the Execution of Samuel Frost" (Worcester, MA, 1793). Courtesy of the American Antiquarian Society

Last Words and Dying Confession

OF

SAMUEL FROST,

Who was Executed at WORCESTER, on *Thursday* the Thirty-first Day of *October*, 179[3] for the inhuman and cruel MURDER of Captain *ELISHA* [AL]LEN, of *Princeton*, who was his Guardian and Friend; which *horrid Crime* was committed on the Sixteenth Day of *July*, 1793.

☞ Said *FROST* [also] MURDERED his *OWN FATHER* on the 23d *September*, [178]3! For which *shocking Crime* he was tried and acquitted.

GENESIS, iv. 10.

"*The voice of thy*
"*Brother's blood cri-*
"*eth unto me from*
"*the ground.*"

Worcester-Goal, Octo. 30, 1793.

WAS born at *Princeton*, in the County of *Worcester*, (*Massachusetts*) *Jan.* 14, 1765. My Father's name was *John Frost*; he had 4 sons, the eldest died when he was 19; 2 of my Brothers are yet living. My Mother is dead; I always regarded her, and ever tho't my Father had no affection for her, and that he used her ill, this induced me to kill him, which deed I executed *Sept.* 23, 1783, as we were digging a ditch together; I knocked him down with a handspike, and then beat his brains out. Was apprehended, committed to goal in *Worcester*, and tried before the *Hon. Supreme Court*, and was acquitted contrary to my expectations.

My Mother died when I was about 14 years old, and I always supposed her death was occasioned by the bad treatment she received from my Father. He was very churlish, and void of all affection for his family.

After I was acquitted and got released from goal, I went and lived with Mr. *George Parkis*, afterwards with Mr. *John Gleason*, then with Mr. *Phinehas Gregory*; then went to live with Mr. *Ezekiel Sawin*: Went a second time to Mr. *Parkis*; after this I lived with Mr. *Jesse Fisher*; then with Mr. *Rice*. All these people lived in *Princeton*. Whilst I lived with Mr. *Rice* I arrived at 21 years of age; I left Mr. *Rice* and went to live with a relation, Mr. *Benjamin Wilson*, where I tarried about 3 weeks, and then went to Capt. *Elisha Allen's*, where I lodged one night. From Capt. *Allen's* I went and lived with Mr. *Solomon Parker*, and several others, but was only a little time with each—then I went to live with Mr. *Ephraim Osgood*; I left him and went to the house where I formerly lived with my Father, and tarried there five months in the year 1786; but receiving an affront, being told to do something against my inclination, I went off without taking leave, and took to the woods; I wandered 3 days and nights; in the day-time I kept in the woods, and at nights went to farms and lodged in barns, unperceived. In the woods I got and eat berries, and gathered apples in orchards, and on them I lived during the time.

Being tired of the woods, I went to *Fitzwilliam*, to Mr. *Wilson's*, my relation beforementioned, who had removed from *Princeton* to that place. I arrived there on the 22d of *Aug.* 1786, at breakfast time; I was very hungry and eat heartily—I tarried here 'til the 5th of *Sept.*

Soon after this a number of people were going to *Worcester*, to stop the sitting of the Court; they asked me to go with them, and treated me. I wanted to see what they would do; and went with them as far as *Holden*—at this place stopping at *Davis's* tavern, I went out to pick some apples to eat; after which I laid on the ground and went to sleep—when I awoke, I tho't I was doing wrong to go with those people to stop the Court, and would go no further. I left them and went to *Princeton*; there I met with more people going to *Worcester* for the like purpose—they gave me some drink. I left them and went to Mr. *Stephen Merrick's*, where I lodged that night. I then worked for several persons a few days; and in *Sept.* 1786, I went and lived with Capt *Elisha Allen*, who took me because it was the desire of a number of people. It was town-meeting day, and I went to the meeting.

I lived with Mr. *Allen* sometime, when chusing to go away, I went off at a time when I was sent to pasture with the cows; I was gone almost three days, living as I could; I spent three coppers while I was gone, and went almost as far as *Boston*—then I returned to Capt. *Allen's*. I went off several times afterwards, and was absent sometimes a longer and sometimes a shorter time, but got nothing by going away but flogging when I returned. Considering myself a slave, I tho't I had as well die as live as I did.—I had a small estate and wanted to work on that, but could not.—Mr. *Allen* had the care of my estate, and I supposed was paid for my living with him out of it. I thought several times I would kill him, and then tho't I would not.—At length, on the sixteenth of *July* 1793, I effected it thus—Capt. *Allen* was going to set out cabbage-plants, and ordered me to go with him, and to get a hoe; he went to the spot for planting, and I after the hoe; when I returned with the hoe, I found him stooping to fix a plant—I then thought it would be a good time to put my design in execution, and accordingly went up to him and gave him a blow with the hoe on the head, and repeated it. When I was about giving the third blow, he said, '*Forbear* Sam, *you have done enough.*' I made no reply, but continued repeating the blows til I supposed he was dead. I had beaten his head so as it had made a large hole in the ground and his brains came out. After I had finished him, I went into the woods not far distant, where I remained 4 days, living on berries, &c. While there I heard the voice of the people who I supposed were after me, I heard them call me, but they did not find me; at length I was tired of being in the woods, as it was hard fare—came and loitered about a house where I had formerly lived, and was discovered by some of the family, who took me into the house, gave me some victuals and secured me. I was then bro't to *Worcester* gaol again, and now shall certainly be hanged.——I declare that I ever had a great aversion to stealing and telling lies, and think them to be great crimes.—I always meant to tell truth, and never stole, except taking a few apples from orchards may be called so.——[*The foregoing* Account *was taken from the mouth of* Samuel Frost, *in prison.*

[AC]*COUNT of SAMUEL FROST.*

SAMUEL FROST was certainly an extraordinary character—his mind was evidently not formed altogether like others; he tho't it no great crime to kill such as he supposed treated him very ill, and did not appear to have a just conception of the heinous crime of MURDER.—His education appears to be very indifferent, but his natural capacity in man[y r]espects seemed to be equal to persons in gene[ral] whose minds have not been cultivated. He [had hig]h notions of honesty, and appear[ed o]ffended when it was suspected. He app[ears t]o have been a person who regarded truth [and] valued himself upon his probity and sincerity.—One striking proof of his dislike to falshood appeared when he was indicted before the *Hon. Court*—he plead guilty—he was told he might [ple]ad not guilty, was urged so to do, and was re[ma]nded to prison, in order that he might consider of the plea he had made, and retract it, &c. Yet notwithstanding, on his being again bro't into Court, he persisted in pleading guilty. He was sensible of favors granted him and expressed his gratitude for them, yet he had a most savage heart, which nothing could meliorate, an[d he wo]uld talk with the same calmness and composure of the *horrid Murders* he had committed, as tho' the persons who fell a sacrifice to his fury had been of the brutal creation. He could read and write, and often was found, while in prison, reading in the Bible; yet he shewed no sign of contrition especially for the *unnatural Murder* of his Father. Notwithstanding he read the Bible, he was not fond of conversing with the Clergy, and in general of the many who visited him, few of them could get him to talk with them. He went two Sundays to meeting after his sentence, but more thro' persuasion than inclination; and tho' urged refused to go again. On the first Sabbath he attended divine service, he appeared to be offended with the Minister because he mentioned the Murder of his Father. *Frost* said he did not like to be twitted of that—that [was an] old matter, and was settled long since. [Bein]g asked by the High-Sheriff if he [wi]shed to have a sermon preached on the day of execution, he said he did not care any thing about it—but would attend to the Sermon, on condition of not being brought back to prison, but be carried from the meeting to the place of execution.—He said, his killing Capt. *Allen* was rather more than he ought to have done, and would, if it was not done, stay 7 years first. He was a most dangerous person to society.—Being asked if he had his liberty, if he would kill any other person, he said there was one more he believed he should. He told some persons who visited him, one day, that he believed his Father and *Allen* had a very tough time of it. Being asked why he thought so, he said he had been beating his [h]and against the walls of the prison, in order to [kn]ow how they felt while he was killing [them]. He appeared to have a very confused idea of a future state—supposed he should go to purgatory—said he believed the devils wore large black wigs—and many other such chimerical expressions of folly and absurdity he uttered respecting a future existence. He did not appear pleased that the time of his execution was fixed at so distant a period; he wished, he said, to have it over a fortnight sooner. On the whole, as a man, he was savage—void of all the finer feelings of the soul, destitute of filial love and gratitude. He appears to have been a being cast in a different mould from those of mankind in general, and to be the connecting grade between the human and brutal creation.——The above will enable the Reader to form some idea of his rational faculties.——He was about five feet four inches high, rather slenderly built, and very strong. He had a peculiar way of tossing or twitching his head, and his countenance was very unpleasant.

A POEM on the solemn Occasion.

"*Learn to be wise from others harms,*
"*And you shall do full well.*"

REview each act on life's important stage,
In every climate and thro' every age;
And still we find each passing scene will shew
"That virtue only, is our bliss below."
Vice for a while with dazzling form may please,
Assume the borrow'd smile of careless ease,
Display the charms of pleasure's roseate bowers,
Her gay attendants and her happy hours;
But yet e'er long shall truth expose the cheat,
Her weak delusions and her foul deceit,
The hidden poison of her breast reveal,
And paint the terrors which her smiles conceal.
This day, my Friends, exhibits to mankind
Th' effects which follow from a vicious mind;
Denounc'd by justice, in life's early bloom,
A wretch misguided seeks the silent tomb.
In tender age, when softer passions glow,
When pity moistens at the tale of woe,
Deaf to her cry, his arm, on malice bent,
To shades of death an aged Parent sent:
Yet here his art eluded justice' claim,
He knew the maniac or the fool to feign,
Impos'd on candor with a vague pretence,
And mercy wink'd upon the black offence.
Ten years revolv'd, when lo! by anger driven,
Again he breaks the great command of heaven;
Again the *Murderer* lifts his vengeful hand,
And aims the deadly weapon at his Friend,
Thus by his arm the Father, Patron, dy'd,
At once the traitor and the paracide.
Insulted justice now the wretch demands,
And sentenc'd death awaits her stern commands.
Ye YOUTH who view the sadly solemn scene,
Learn hence the laws of virtue to esteem,
Learn hence that he who from his duty swerves
Will one day meet the vengeance he deserves;
Ne'er let the flowery paths of vice delude,
Nor let revenge upon your thoughts intrude.

☞ *The curious Reader may wish to know how* FROST *behaved, on the Stage, in his last moments; and as an intelligent Person, who was present at his Execution, has favored the Publisher with the following Particulars, he readily inserts them, which are as follow.*

"AT the place of Execution he behaved much as he had done in prison, and did not change his countenance or gesture until the cap was pulled over his face; at which he shewed some signs of his approaching dissolution:—Previous to which he spake a few words to the vast Multitude, assembled from *Worcester*, &c. on the melancholy occasion, which were—"*That he would not wish* YOUNG PEOPLE *should follow his steps.*"—FROST requested no prayer from the Clergyman who attended him; neither did he pray himself."

Sold by JONATHAN PLUMER, Travelling-Trader, in *Newbury*.—Price SIX PENCE single.

Samuel Frost et al., *Last Words and Dying Confession of Samuel Frost* (Boston, 1793). Courtesy of the American Antiquarian Society

The Confession and Dying Words of
SAMUEL FROST,

WHO WAS EXECUTED AT WORCESTER, THE 31st DAY OF OCTOBER, 1793, FOR THE

Horrid Crime of *MURDER*.

I WAS born at Princeton, in the County of Worcester, and Commonwealth of Massachusetts on the 24th day of January, 1765. My father's name was John Frost, he had four sons, of which when he was about fourteen years of age his brothers are living. My mother is dead; I always respected her, and ever thought my father had no affection for her, and that he did hate her till; this induced me to kill him, which deed I executed on the 23d of September, 1783, as we were digging a ditch together; I knocked him down with a handspike, and then beat his brains out. I was apprehended and committed to gaol in Worcester, and tried before the Supreme Court, and was acquitted contrary to my expectations.

My mother died when I was about fourteen years old, and I always supposed her death was occasioned by the bad treatment she received from my father. He was very churlish, and void of all affection for his family.

After I was acquitted, and got released from gaol, I went and lived with Mr. George Parkis; afterwards with Mr. John Gleason, then with Mr. Palethas Gregory; after living with them, I went and lived with Mr. Ezekiel Sawin, then went a second time to Mr. Parkis, after this I lived with Mr. Job Fisher, and then with Mr. Rice. All these people lived in Princeton. Whilst I lived with Mr. Rice I arrived at twenty-one years of age; I left Mr. Rice, and went to live with a relation, Mr. Benjamin Wilson, where I tarried about two or three weeks, and then went to Capt. Eliaha Allen's, where I lodged one night. From Capt. Allen's I went and lived a little time with Mr. Solomon Parker, and then with several other persons, but was only a little time with each—when I went to live with Mr. Ephraim Olgood; I left him and went to the house where I formerly lived with my father, and tarried there about five months, in the year 1786; but receiving no reward, being void to do something against my inclination, I went off without taking leave, and took to the woods—I wandered about for three days and nights: In the day time I kept in the woods, and at nights went to farms and lodged in barns, unperceived. I lived mostly on green berries, and gathered apples in orchards, and on them I lived during the three days and nights.

Being tired of living in the woods, I went to Princetown, to the house of Benjamin Wilson, my relation, before mentioned, who had removed from Princeton to that place. I arrived there on the 21st day of August, 1786, at breakfast time. I was very hungry and eat heartily—I tarried here until the 5th day of September, the same year.

Soon after this time a number of people were going to Worcester, to stop the sitting of the Court—they asked me to go with them, and promised me. I went to see what they would do, and went with them as far as Holden—at this place, stopping at Davis's tavern, I went out to pick some apples to eat; after which I laid down on the ground and went to sleep—when I awoke, I thought I was doing wrong to go with these people to stop the Court and would not go with them any further. I left them and went to Princetown—there I met with more people going to Worcester for the like purpose—they gave me some drink. I left them and went to Mr. Stephen Marcies's where I tarried that night. I then worked for several persons a few days; and on the 11th day of September 1786, I went and lived with Capt. Elisha Allen—who took me because it was the design of a number of people. It was then morning day, and I went to the meeting.

I lived with Mr. Allen sometimes—when choosing to go away—I went off at a time when I was first to pasture with the oxen—I was gone almost three days, living as I could—I spent three coppers which I was gone, and went almost as far as Boston—then I returned to Capt. Allen's again. I went off several times afterwards, and was often sometimes a longer and sometimes a shorter time, but did not get anything by going away but flogging when I returned. Considering myself as a slave, I have thought I had as well die as live as I did.—I had a small estate and wanted to work at that, but I could not—Mr. Allen had the care of my estate, and I supposed was paid for my living with him out of it. I thought several times I would kill him, and then thought I would not.—At length, on the 16th day of July, 1793, I resolved it then—Capt. Allen was going to his out cabbage plants, and desired me to go with him, and to get a hoe; he went to the spot for planting, and I after the hoe; when I returned with the hoe, I found him hoeing to fix a point—I then thought it would be a good time to put my design in execution, and accordingly went up to him and gave him a blow with the hoe on his head, and repeated it. When I was about to give the third blow, he said, "Forbear Sam, you have done enough." I made no reply, but continued repeating the blows until I supposed he was dead. I had beaten his head so as he had made a large hole in the ground and his brains came out. After I had finished him, I went into the woods and far distant, where I remained four days, living on berries, &c. Whilst I was in the woods, I heard the voices of the people who I supposed were after me; I heard them call me—but they did not see me, at length I was tired of being in the woods, as it was hard fare—came and loitered about a house where I had formerly lived, and was discovered by one of the family, who took me into the house and gave me some victuals and secured me. I was then brought to Worcester gaol again, and now the fate may be hanged.

I declare that I had always a great aversion to stealing and telling lies, and think them to be great crimes,—I always meant to tell the truth, and never stole, excepting taking a few apples from orchards may be called theft.

The foregoing account was taken from the mouth of Samuel Frost's pride.

ACCOUNT of SAMUEL FROST.

SAMUEL FROST was certainly an extraordinary character—his mind was evidently not formed altogether like that of other persons.—He thought it no great crime to kill such as he supposed treated him very ill—and did not appear to have a just conception of the heinous crime of Murder—His education appears to have been very indifferent, but his natural capacity in many respects seemed to be equal to persons in general, whose minds have not been cultivated. He had high notions of honesty, and appeared much offended when he honestly was suspected.—He appears also to have been a person who regarded truth; and he valued himself upon his probity and sincerity.—One striking proof of his dislike to falsehood appeared when he was incident before the Court—he plead guilty—he was told that he might plead not guilty, and was contained to prison, in order that he might consider of his plea he had made, and retract it, &c. yet notwithstanding to the being again brought into Court, he persisted in pleading guilty. He was sensible of whatever grieved him, and expressed his gratitude for them—Yet he had a most savage heart which nothing could mellow, and he would talk with the same calmness and composure of the horrid Murders he had committed, as though he performed a most meritorious act of heroism, and been of the bravest creature. He said he read and write, and often was found, whilst in prison, reading in the Bible—yet he showed no signs of contrition effectually for the unnatural murder of his father. Notwithstanding he read the Bible, he was not fond of conversing with the Clergy, and in general of the many who visited him, few of them could get him to talk with them. He went too fondly to evening after his sentence, but more through persuasion than inclination; and though urged refused to go again.—On the first Sabbath after his attended divine service he appeared to be disturbed with the minister, because he mentioned the murder of his father—Frost told he did not like to be twitted of it; it did not do all matter, and was settled long since.—On being asked by the High Sheriff if he wished to have a sermon preached, on the day of his Execution, he answered that he did not care by trying about it—he felt he would attend to the sermon on condition that he might not be brought back to prison, but be carried from the meeting house to the place of execution.

He had been known so far, that his killing Capt. Allen was rather more than he ought to have known—that he would, if it was not done, they (seven years first). He was a most dangerous person to society—On being asked if he had his liberty, if he would kill any other person, he answered there was one more he believed he should. He told some persons who visited him one day, that he believed his father and Allen had a very rough time of it—Being asked why he thought so, he said he had been beating his head against the walls of prison, in order to know how they felt which he was killing them.

It appeared to have a very confused idea of a future state—supposed he should go to purgatory—which he believed the Devils were large black angels—many other such abstracted expressions of folly and absurdity, he uttered respecting a future existence. He did not appear pleased that the time of his execution was fixed—to die died a penalty—he wished, he said, to have it over a fortnight sooner. On the whole, as a man, he was a savage—void of all the finer feelings of the soul, and destitute of the tender emotions of filial love and gratitude—He appears to have been a being and in a different mould from those of mankind in general; and to be the connecting grade between the human and brutal creation.

He was about five feet four inches high, rather slenderly built, and very strong. He had a peculiar way of resting or twitching his head, and his countenance was always unpleasant.

A POEM,
ON THE EXECUTION OF SAMUEL FROST.

"*Leave to the wife few other boons,*
And you will do full well."

REVIEW each act, of LIFE's
  important stage,
In every CLIMATE and through every
  AGE;
And still we find each passing scene will
  show,
"That VIRTUE only, is our bliss
  below."
VICE for a while, with dazzling form
  may please,
Assume the borrow'd smile of careless
  ease,
Display the charms of pleasure's ruddy
  BOWER,
Ever gay ATTENDANTS and her happy
  hour;
But yet ere long shall TRUTH expose
  the CHEAT,
Her weak delusions and her foul deceit,
The hidden poison of her DREARY re-
  veal,
And paint the terrors which her smiles
  conceal.
This day, my FRIENDS, exhibits to
  MANKIND
Th' effects which follow from a VI-
  CIOUS MIND;
Denounc'd by JUSTICE, in life's early
  bloom,
A WRETCH misguided seeks the silent
  tomb.
In tender AGE, when softer passions
  glow,
When PITY moistens at the tale of woe,
Deaf to her cry, HIS ARM, on ruthless
  bent,

To shades of DEATH, and aged PA-
  RENT sent:
Yet here his ART eluded JUSTICE'
  claim,
He knew the MANIAC or the FOOL to
  feign,
Impos'd on CANDOUR with a vague pre-
  tence,
And MERCY wink'd upon the blank of-
  fence.
Ten years revolv'd, where lo! by an-
  other blow,
Again he breaks the great command of
  HEAV'N ;
Again the MURDERER lifts his venge-
  ful hand,
And aims the deadly weapon at his
  PATRON,
That by his arm the PATRON PATRON
  died,
At once the TRAITOR and the PARRI-
  CIDE,
Infected JUSTICE now the WRETCH
  demands,
And sentenc'd DEATH awaits her stern
  commands.
Ye YOUTH, who view the sadly solem
  scene,
Learn hence the laws of VIRTUE to es-
  teem,
Learn hence that HE who from his PIE-
  TY swerves
Will one day meet the VENGEANCE he
  deserves :
Ne'er let the flow'ry paths of VICE de-
  lude,
Nor let REVENGE upon your thoughts
  intrude.

PRINTED AND SOLD BY HENRY BLAKE & Co.—KEENE, STATE OF NEW-HAMPSHIRE.

Samuel Frost et al., *The Confession and Dying Words of Samuel Frost* (Keene, NH, 1793). Courtesy of the American Antiquarian Society read and write." In Johnstone's case, Hartnett contends that Quaker abolitionists played a key authorial role; however, DeLombard affirms that "the circumstances of the *Address's* authorship, editing, publication, and circulation remain a mystery."[49] The status of authorship, crucial for reading these individuals as liberal agents, remains secondary to a theorization of the collective, racialized agency of the *corpus convicti*. The early eighteenth century saw an increased interest in the criminal's voice; by the mid-eighteenth century, dying-words broadsides had largely replaced an earlier genre of criminal conversion narratives and pious confessions. In older confessions, a third-person commentator often sketches the final moments of the condemned and evaluates the likelihood that the malefactor would reach heaven. In the Frost broadsides, an anonymous "Account of Samuel Frost" functions as a sort of gloss to the confession, an almost social-scientific apparatus that might help readers assess Frost's multiple, contradictory aspects. Late eighteenth-century confessions were often more sensational than their predecessors, offered more explicit details about the crime, and, in line with liberalism's emphasis on the individual, were increasingly concerned with unusual "characters" rather than the archetypal sinner.[50]

Countering the disregard indexed by Johnstone's lack of an execution sermon, Johnstone himself carefully cultivates an expanded community in his "Address," carrying his message to a broad public made available through the fact of his conviction. Likewise, in sharp contrast to Bancroft's disgust, the Frost broadsides encourage a direct engagement with Frost's very strangeness. As forms of connection that disavow themselves, both disregard and disgust are affects useful for cultivating liberalism's abstract, rights-based modes of citizenship. Yet both are fully capable of pushing in the other direction by revealing liberal humanism's contradictions. Envisaging the human far more expansively, both Johnstone's "Address" and the Frost broadsides stake material claims of belonging in the bedrock of disgust and disregard.

The experience of disgust is predicated on the most visceral forms of relation, whether a bad taste on the tongue or a monster in our midst.[51] Thus, it is unsurprising that the ability of the Frost corpus to engage readers is not limited to disgust. When we look at Frost's dying confession or at the "Account of Samuel Frost" published alongside it, we find an intricate imaginative economy of affect, which Bancroft's staid injunction of abhorrence does not erase but in fact enables. Crucially, this is not despite but intimately linked with descriptions of Frost's "inhumanity." Affective engagement increases in proportion to Frost's purported monstrosity, with readers fascinated by this "creature" existing "between the human and brutal creation." Disavowal itself creates the invitation to connection.

Likewise, Johnstone channels the disregard indexed by his absent execution sermon into his own "Address." In tone and substance, he uses the fact of his capital conviction to take on the authority of a religious figure like Bancroft. This is a public platform that becomes available to him because of the same racialization of criminality that we saw in Bancroft's sermon. As DeLombard notes, "Johnstone, assenting to his conviction, affirms his punitive, retroactive entry into the social contract."[52] Being Black and free, Johnstone was presumed criminal and found himself on a "slippery slope" not of actual malefaction but of accusation, starting small (theft) but culminating in a murder accusation. It is owing to the agency of the form of gallows literature itself that this ultimate crime comes to vest Johnstone with public authority. Once he ascends that platform, rather than preaching retribution or disgust, he shapes the form to his own ends, to model profound forgiveness and admonish society for its narrow vision. In the face of criminality's racialization, Johnstone implores his community to enhance forms of love and connection.

Johnstone opens with this explicit fear that his conviction will strengthen the ties between criminalization and racialization, "throw[ing] a shade over ... all those of our colour." His warm words regarding Northern states' recent moves toward emancipation transition directly to concern that his conviction "will be made a handle of" to impugn Black emancipation: "My unfortunate unhappy fate however unmerited or undeserved, may by some ungenerous and illiberal minded persons, but particularly by those who appose [sic] the emancipation of those of our brethern [sic] who as yet are in slavery, be made a handle of in order to throw a shade over or cast a general reflection on all those of our colour."[53] Johnstone, as most commentators emphasize, responds to this fear by enjoining his Black audience to court polite society. Per Batra, Johnstone "anticipates what we might now term a black politics of respectability: a collective effort to accord individual behaviors and attitudes with the dominant society's norms as a means of contesting the logic of racial subordination."[54] Thus, his *corpus convicti* is peppered with notably conservative advice to the Black community, such as, "be diligent and industrious in all your callings, manners of business and stations in life, be punctual, upright and just in all your contracts, engagements and dealings of what kind or nature soever."[55]

Yet Johnstone's approach should not be mistaken for mere accommodation to white values and belief systems. Instead, he radicalizes what would come to be called "respectability politics" outward, beyond accommodation and toward an ethic of communal interdependence and care. Thus, when he writes, "ripen that good disposition ... by so doing you will make yourself not only respectable but beloved,"⁵⁶ it is not respectability per se nor "contesting the logic of racial subordination" that motivates Johnstone. Rather, he directly aims at the possibility of creating a beloved community. Across "The Address," "Confession," and "Letter to his Wife," Johnstone is not only making the case for legal emancipation. He is not merely trying to move his community toward conditions that would help bring about this statutory end. Looking past reform, he is theorizing a duty of care that, for him, is fundamental to the human condition. The beloved community Johnstone speaks of is not retributive. It is "founded on a love of virtue" and, crucially, "on a sense . . . of those obligations which creatures formed to live in a mutual state of dependence on one another lie under."⁵⁷ Johnstone leverages the disregard indexed by his absent execution sermon to take on a ministerial mantle, essentially co-opting the platform of criminal confession.⁵⁸ In doing so, he philosophizes the human condition very differently than an Enlightenment thinker like Bancroft does. To be human is to be mutually dependent and therefore obligated to love and nurture other creatures so formed.

Johnstone traces both his liberatory vision of communal care *and* the atmosphere of racialized disregard to the formation of the United States as a sovereign nation founded on Enlightenment principles. "It was then," he writes, "that the prospect of total emancipation from slavery which now begins to brighten upon us had birth, it was then that freedom, liberty, and the natural rights of mankind ennobled every sentiment . . . expanded the heart with every thing great noble and beneficent."⁵⁹ At this moment of upswelling fellow feeling, Johnstone notes, "Every bosom glowed with an emanated ardour emulative of its noble and exalted source." Yet Johnstone is awake to the underside of this universal wave of Enlightenment: "Still my dear brethren we were forgotten, or we were not conceived worthy their regard or attention."⁶⁰ It is particularly this failure of "regard" and "attention" to which Johnstone attends. Those "great noble and beneficent" minds awakened by the revolutionary spirit were grounded by a bedrock of disregard for racialized people.

Johnstone emphasizes that the studied "forgetting" of Black people's worthiness of Enlightenment's emancipatory project was shot through with contradiction. "How preposterously absurd must an impartial observer think the man whom he sees one moment declaring with a most incredibly volubility in favour of natural right and general freedom, and the next moment with his own hands for some very trivial offence infecting the cruel and ignominious stripes of slavery and riveting it's [sic] shackles."⁶¹ The justification for such a bald-faced contradiction was, per Johnstone, that with US nationhood came a rise in Black people "being looked on as a different species."⁶² In the context of ennobled sentiment, to exclude Black people from emancipation required more than mere disregard. The justification is thin, however, and Johnstone easily dismisses specious arguments about fundamental human difference. Envisioning other courageous souls following after his death, Johnstone builds from a wrongheaded racialized humanism to another, radically inclusive, communitarian, and materialist vision of human being and doing.

The obligations of creatures formed for mutual care extend to forwarding arguments against racialization, even when what is required is more bravery than brilliance:

> It is but a very few years since any body could be found that had courage enough to step out of the common road of thinking and object to the insufficient unsatisfactory and unsubstantial arguments used against us, and tho' some probably might have thought on the subject, and could have urged weighty and substantial ones in our favour, yet they were deterred possibly by private consideration and interested motives, and probably by a fear of encountring [sic] popular and vulgar prejudice, from saying anything on a subject that required to be treated with so much circumspection and caution; but thank God in this enlightened age there will not be wanting men of genius, spirit and candour, who will have courage enough to step out of the common road of thinking.[63]

Where Enlightenment philosophy and burgeoning race science purport to great intellectual achievements, Johnstone points out the obvious truth that it requires no great intellect to disprove their "unsubstantial arguments." It was not any scientific or ethical challenge that hindered refutation but a failure of courage to speak truth to power, to "step out of the common road" in the face of "popular and vulgar prejudice." It is not so much that it would take a white genius to state what every Black person knows, but that any individual stepping forward must also have the "spirit and candour" required for truth telling. This indeed is the criminal genius of Johnstone's *corpus convicti*: Johnstone's conviction enabled a merger of print and person with a collective agency capable of marshaling words and deeds to expand narrow conceptions of the human beyond the legal subject.

Looking beyond the Bancroft sermon, Frost's larger *corpus convicti* reveals a similarly expansive sense of what it means to be human. His confession and "The Account of Samuel Frost" evince the sensationalism common in gallows literature of the late eighteenth century. In the Frost broadsides, this manifests via typography as well as through foregrounding a set of concerns, including radical, anti-patriarchal violence, which link Frost to the larger revolutionary Atlantic world. In the confession, Frost suggests that Allen's murder is justified by his de facto enslavement to him:

> I went off several times . . . but did not get any thing by going away but a flogging when I returned. Considering myself as a slave, I have thought I had as well die as live as I did.—I had a small estate and wanted to work on that, but I could not—Mr. Allen had the care of my estate, and I supposed was paid for my living with him out of it. I thought several times I would kill him, and then thought I would not.

After being acquitted of his father's murder in 1783, Frost lived with a series of men until, in 1786, he "went and lived with Capt. Elisha Allen—who took me in because it was the desire of a number of people." Frost saw Allen as an enslaver because he restricted his movement and access to property. Allen subjected Frost's body to punishment while compelling him to work on his land, even though Frost supposed he was paying out of his own estate the expenses Allen incurred by having taken him in. For these reasons, the "Account of Samuel Frost" indicates, "he thought it no great crime to kill such as he supposed treated him very ill." Like so many in the late eighteenth century, Frost saw his violent acts as according with a revolutionary ethic of justice.

Frost's identification with the condition of the enslaved takes up a metaphorics of enslavement that circulated promiscuously and often disturbingly across the revolutionary Atlantic. Frost of course was not enslaved, and in fact he held property (though he was restricted from accessing it). Yet although Frost's identification with enslaved persons was limited and problematic, it bears a marked difference from what we saw in the previous chapter, in Benjamin Rush's contemporary self-identification with "we black folks" having come "in demand." Rush's desire to take on Blackness in a moment of perceived exaltation is proto-minstrel. It contrasts sharply with Frost's material identification with enslavement, which he perceived as a racialized condition of social death: "Considering myself as a slave, I have thought I had as well die as live as I did." Like free Black writers David Walker, who asks, "What is the point of living when in fact I am dead?" and Maria Stewart, who asks, "Why sit ye here and die?" Frost identifies a state of death interchangeable with the disenfranchised, oppressive life conditions of enslavement.

Various publications, including Frost's execution sermon, likewise represent his physical appearance in racialized and ableist terms: he was "dark" and moved his body in nonnormative ways. *The State Gazette of South Carolina* reported that Frost was "a short man, of a dark complection [sic], short black hair . . . easily known by his constantly shrugging up his shoulders, stretching out his arms, and shaking his head," while "The Account" describes Frost as "about five feet four inches high, rather slenderly built, and very strong. He had a peculiar way of tossing or twitching his head, and his countenance was very unpleasant."[64] The Boston broadside includes a woodcut engraving that seems to have been meant to represent Frost that shows him glancing sideways at the reader.

In 1793, the year Frost murdered Allen, the French and Haitian Revolutions gathered momentum, with Louis XVI executed in January and slavery abolished in Haiti later that year. These currents are clearly on display in Frost's confession, with its emphasis on enslavement as a justification for violence and its own local history of revolt. Western Massachusetts had witnessed Shays's Rebellion in 1786–87, and in his confession, Frost details his decision to join, and subsequently abandon, the Shaysites. Many Shaysites were war veterans, and those Frost joined marched to oppose the state government by stopping the court at Worcester.[65] Frost accompanied the rebels "as far as Holden—at this place, stopping at Davis's tavern, I went out to pick some apples to eat; after which I laid down on the ground and went to sleep—when I awoke, I thought I was doing wrong to go with those people to stop the Court, and would not go with them any further."[66] Although Frost chose not to pursue economic justice alongside these revolutionaries, in the confession he returns to this revolutionary moment to explain his journey to seek justice through his murder of Allen on the basis of economic and personal oppression at his hands. The court the Shaysites set out to close was indeed the same court at Worcester that would ultimately sentence Frost to die for his crime.

The solar calendar in the 1793 *Worcester Almanack*, which, like the first Frost broadside, was printed by Thomas, further connects Frost to revolutionary sensibilities through its references to the French Revolution (fig. 2.8). Frost murdered Allen on July 16, 1793. The *Almanack* enthusiastically marks July 14 as the fourth anniversary of "the glorious revolution in France," and marks July 16 with "Ça Ira! Ça Ira! Ça Ira!"[67] Translating roughly to "It'll Be Okay," the most popular song of the French Revolution expressed violently democratic sentiment:

> Ah! ça ira, ça ira, ça ira,
> Les aristocrates on les pendra!
> Le despotisme expirera,
> La liberté triomphera.
> (Oh! It'll be okay, be okay, be okay,
> The aristocrats, we'll hang 'em all.

Despotism will breathe its last,
Liberty will take the day.)

The revolutionary atmosphere was palpable. It influenced not only Frost's murders but also the affective responses they generated. In addition to his murder of Allen, a patriarchal guardian figure, Frost was also guilty of literal patricide ten years prior. The Frost broadsides make much of this, with a manicule at the top of the Boston version emphasizing the fact front and center. Frost committed this "shocking Crime" at a time when Britain had been styled (by Thomas Paine and others) as the "bad" parent from which a now-grown America had righteously severed itself. We might reasonably speculate that, three short years after Cornwallis's surrender, Frost was acquitted partly because of the larger political and military landscape of the 1780s. And even amid uprisings by the Shaysites and others, the escalation of violence in Haiti and France, and the move toward a stronger centralized government in the United States between 1784 and 1793, Frost had to insist that his murder of a second patriarchal figure, Allen, produce the sentence of death.

Frost begins his confession with a brief personal history and genealogy of his living and dead relations. He relates that while laboring beside his father ten years before, "I knocked him down with a handspike, and then beat his brains out" because of his ill treatment of Frost's mother. Frost's direct ownership of these deeds, as well as his claim that he murdered Allen because he saw himself as enslaved, are the most voluntaristic moments in the Frost corpus. Unlike the broadsides, Bancroft's sermon avoids the potentially dangerous idea that Frost's crimes may have been motivated by anti-patriarchal impulses.[68] Bancroft's aim is to separate Frost from the community through disgust, and so he studiously avoids connecting Frost to a revolutionary narrative. The "Account" indicates that Frost had attended Sunday meeting twice after his sentence: he had been offended by the minister for mentioning his murder of his father. He "said he did not like to be twitted of that—that it was an old matter, and was settled long since" (col. 4). It is possible that this minister was Bancroft, who consequently did not mention this murder on execution day out of respect for Frost's wishes. The content of the sermon, however—in particular, Bancroft's disdain for Frost—suggests otherwise. Even if Bancroft were the minister mentioned in the "Account," the execution sermon's audience, whom Bancroft was at pains to distance from Frost, would have been a much larger crowd, and that much more potentially unruly, and that much more potentially sympathetic to Frost. The broadsides expand on this potential for sympathy with their suggestions that these murders

JULY begins on *Monday*, hath xxxi Days.

THE grand ethereal bow its tints displays,
The various colours of the Solar rays:
Descending drops ting'd with the grateful light,
Compose th' extended arch to charm the sight.

SOLAR CALCULATIONS, &c.

Days.	☉	Days.	☉	Days.	☉
1	♋ 10 7	13	♋ 21 33	25	♌ 3 2
3	12 2	15	23 27	27	4 56
5	13 56	17	25 22	29	6 51
7	15 50	19	27 17	31	8 46
9	17 45	21	29 12		
11	19 39	23	♋ 1 7		

d	d	Calendar, remarkable days, observations, &c.	☉ rise	☉ sets	L. D. H. M	☉ S	7*s rise
1	2	*Governments should*	4 28	7 32	15 4	3	1 21
2	3	Visitation of Vir. Mary.	4 28	7 32	15 4	3	1 17
3	4	*be supported for*	4 29	7 31	15 2	4	1 13
4	5	American Ind. 1776.	4 29	7 31	15 2	4	1 10
5	6	*the good of the*	4 30	7 30	15 0	4	1 6
6	7	*governed; not*	4 30	7 30	15 0	4	1 2
7	F	6th Sund. past Trinity.	4 31	7 29	14 58	4	0 58
8	2	*for the emolument*	4 31	7 29	14 58	4	0 54
9	3	*of the governours.*	4 32	7 28	14 56	5	0 50
10	4	Columbus born in France,	4 32	7 28	14 56	5	0 46
11	5	(and lived 59 years.	4 33	7 27	14 54	5	0 42
12	6	*The man who injures*	4 33	7 27	14 54	5	0 38
13	7	*no person, nor proper-*	4 34	7 26	14 52	5	0 34
14	F	Anniverf. of the glorious	4 35	7 25	14 50	5	0 30
15	2	(revolution of France.	4 35	7 25	14 50	5	0 26
16	3	Ca Ira! Ca Ira! Ca Ira!	4 36	7 24	14 48	5	0 21
17	4	Com. Camb. Mahomet	4 37	7 23	14 46	6	0 17
18	5	(died, 634, aged 64.	4 38	7 22	14 44	6	0 12
19	6	*ty, nor good name,*	4 38	7 22	14 44	6	0 8
20	7	St. Margar. and Bridget.	4 39	7 21	14 42	6	0 4
21	F	8th Sund. past Trinity.	4 40	7 20	14 40	6	eve.
22	2	St. Mary Magdalene.	4 41	7 19	14 38	6	11 52
23	3	*ought not to be*	4 42	7 18	14 36	6	11 48
24	4	*molested by society,*	4 43	7 17	14 34	6	11 44
25	5	Dog Days begin and Cai	4 45	7 15	14 30	6	11 40
26	6	St. Ann. (nights.	4 46	7 14	14 28	6	11 36
27	7	*nor any individual,*	4 47	7 13	14 26	6	11 32
28	F	9th Sund. p. Trin. St.	4 48	7 12	14 24	6	11 28
29	2	(Joseph. *on account of*	4 49	7 11	14 22	6	11 24
30	3	St. Martha, Virgin.	4 50	7 10	14 20	6	11 20
31	4	*his opinion.*	4 51	7 9	14 18	6	11 17

"July," *Thomas's Massachusetts, Connecticut, Rhode Island, New Hampshire & Vermont Almanack, with an Ephemeris, for the Year of Our Lord 1793* (Worcester, MA, 1792). Courtesy of the American Antiquarian Society were, at least in part, a result of a radical struggle for some more equitable mode of belonging.

Importantly, the basis of this belonging is both material and affective. The broadsides represent Frost's actions as unnervingly consistent not only with a radical, violent politics but also with an enumeration of Frost's own valuation of honesty and attempts at sympathy. Inhuman and cold hearted, Frost in the "Account" nevertheless expresses an uncanny desire to share his victims' experiences: "He told some persons who visited him one day, that he believed his father and Allen had a very tough time of it—Being asked why he thought so, he said he had been beating his head against the walls of the prison, in order to know how they felt whilst he was killing them." Here, Frost demonstrates a startling capacity for intersubjective imagination. In beating his head against the prison wall in order to occupy the position of his victims, Frost channels liberal moral philosophers of his day like Adam Smith, who argued that since we "have no immediate experience of what other men feel," the only way to have an idea of how others are affected is "by bringing the case home to [one]self."[69] Taking this idea to an extreme of literality, Frost reminds readers that he is a body to be punished as much as a mind to be puzzled over. Indeed, we see in Frost's actions an implicit revision of Smith. Unlike Smith's liberal abstractions, the theory of sympathy suggested in Frost's *corpus convicti* suggests the necessity of embodiment for intersubjective imagination.[70] Frost's visceral display insists on sympathetic connection as an embodied phenomenon.

"Launched into Eternity"

In facing the end of his biological life, Johnstone emerges as a figure in print espousing an expansive vision of the human as based not in forensic personhood but in a sense of mutual obligation and radical care. And in banging his head against the prison walls as he awaited his own execution, Frost illustrates that physical embodiment, rather than abstract sympathy, generates the affective connections that ground community. In these two late eighteenth-century historical figures, we have two exemplifications of the *corpus convicti* showing humanity as exceeding the bounded subject of law via the agency of print and affective engagement. Around the same time that Johnstone and Frost lived, entered the print record, and died, Immanuel Kant was developing a metaphysical system in which the materiality inherent in embodiment likewise informed what he called *sensus communis* (common sense), the basis for which was the aesthetic. Most critical discussion of the aesthetic since has emphasized transcendence and purity. But for Kant and other late eighteenth-century thinkers, the aesthetic assures connection between humans and the world we perceive: it creates connections via materiality between human and nonhuman bodies. As Edward Cahill has noted, many contemporary writers on the aesthetic were invested in "linking the sensory perception of objects to the processes of association" and easily assimilated the "proximity of the material and the ideal."[71] Like those excluded from liberalism's abstract modes of belonging, the aesthetic in late eighteenth-century philosophy also occupied the space between human and nonhuman.

It thus should not be a surprise that in the execution poem for Frost, as in Johnstone's "Address" and "Letter," we glimpse the convict as creative genius, whose agency emerges out of and exceeds liberalism's exclusions.[72] The aesthetic assumes a quasi-sacred role in the eighteenth and nineteenth centuries, as that which bridges the otherwise irreducible divide between appearances and reality. Yet at the same time, art also becomes increasingly marginal to social and political life. As part of this process, an overdetermined liminality comes to define crime, art, and Blackness as alienated and abject. The racialized criminal is thus carefully excluded from the liberal realm of consensus and self-governance. Racialized criminality emerges in tandem with, but is not reducible to, liberal humanism. In this final section, I trace how execution underwrites Johnstone's emphasis on the power of language in making, and breaking, the bonds of sociality. His "Letter to his Wife" continues to privilege reputation and reciprocal human kindness, while owning the missteps that accompany all such efforts. Paradoxically, racialized criminalization enables Johnstone to embody this message. Likewise, the very inhumanity that Bancroft constructs in his sermon merges with the aesthetic in the execution poem to present Frost as a nascent criminal genius.[73]

The thirty-eight-line "Poem on the Execution of Samuel Frost" was printed and offered for sale as a separate broadside on execution day and later appended to the two post-execution broadside editions of the account and confession.[74] It begins with an injunction very much in line with an older model of gallows literature: "Learn to be wise from others harms, / And you shall do full well." Highly moralistic, the theme is virtue rewarded and vice punished, as the poem's quotation from Alexander Pope's *Essay on Man*, "That virtue only, is our bliss below," indicates. The poem suggests that Frost, "At once the traitor and the patricide," is being executed not only for murdering his "patron" Allen but also as punishment for the murder of his father and, the word "traitor" suggests, perhaps also for his brief alignment with the Shaysites. These rhymed pentameter couplets depict Frost as having counterfeited insanity to escape punishment for that initial crime of patricide:

> Yet here his art eluded justice' claim,
> He knew the maniac or the fool to feign,
> Impos'd on candor with a vague pretence,
> And mercy wink'd upon the black offence.

The poem reinscribes a more traditional perspective on crime in its emphasis on Frost's guilt. But it offers a crucial and eminently modern twist: Frost is not just guilty but artful. Through performance, feigning the maniac or the fool, he slips through the cracks of human justice.

The poem works to correct this loophole and hold Frost fully to account. Like older gallows publications, it attempts to repurpose Frost's act as a specifically moral lesson. Unlike the warnings of an earlier period, however, the slippery-slope moral as applied to Frost's case is nonsensical:

> Ye youth who view the sadly solemn scene,
> Learn hence the laws of virtue to esteem,
> Learn hence that he who from his duty swerves,
> Will one day meet the vengeance he deserves:
> Ne'er let the flowery paths of vice delude,
> Nor let revenge upon your thoughts intrude.

Wayward youth ought to take care, the poem suggests, lest they be tempted onto the path of viciousness and wind up on the gallows. Yet Frost had not followed any "flowery paths of vice": drinking, lust, lying, or any of the "gateway" sins of traditional gallows literature. In Frost's case, the temptation the poem warns against is nothing less extreme than parricide itself, since this is the very first act in which Frost's own "duty swerve[d]."

Like Bancroft's sermon, then, the execution poem distinguishes Frost from ordinary sinners and places him beyond the pale of the liberal citizen. But where the sermon makes Frost explicitly brute and inhuman, he emerges in the poem instead as a criminal genius. Artful and full of "vague pretence," he appears as a deceiver uniquely guilty and incapable of being accounted for by older execution rituals and publications. The inhuman space created for the racialized criminal in Bancroft's sermon reappears in the poem as the more capacious, mediated space of the aesthetic. In the sermon Frost is included in an emerging liberal society as who, or what, is excluded. He is the figure of negative personhood by which members of this society can recognize their own belonging, denied even the capacity for true guilt. On this view, Frost's crimes are not even crimes but merely the result of deficient education and upbringing. In contrast, when the poem finds itself incapable of accounting for Frost in the terms of a society that has faded, he emerges as an aesthetic agent, a genius exceeding the role of excluded other to which Bancroft's liberal stance would like to restrict him. Frost's guilt is greater than that of the everyday sinner, because he is responsible not only for the crimes he has committed but also for the design employed in their execution and cover-up. Where the gambit of the sermon is to make Frost inhuman, the poem intensifies this maneuver: it makes him an artist.

As Daniel A. Cohen has argued, we can trace the origins of American popular culture to the tradition of gallows literature. In the late eighteenth and early nineteenth centuries, the popular press irresistibly performed a double abjection, of the aesthetic and of the criminal, that readers voraciously consumed and disparaged. As changes in print technology allowed for cheaper and more lavishly illustrated representations of the criminal, the increasingly sensationalized popular press filled its pages with shocking details of far more outrageous crimes than Frost's or Johnstone's. Sensationalized confessions, criminal pamphlets, criminal biographies, and trial transcripts eventually came to stand in for the convict's fleshly body as it was locked within the inscrutable walls of the penitentiary. Although neither Johnstone nor Frost experienced incarceration in a penitentiary system, experiments with private punishment were already underway during their lifetime.[75] Setting the stage for a nearly total eclipse of the criminal's physical body by a body of print, 1790s print culture had begun to represent the real or purported deeds of convicts in ways that an earlier gallows tradition never imagined.[76] Colin Dayan's discussion of the racial dimensions of the twenty-first-century incarceration explosion is also salient here: "The prediction for future ex-criminal disenfranchisement rates suggests how black citizens in the United States, once convicted of crime, will be indefinitely excluded from the society in which they live."[77] This shift also set the stage for the emergence of the collective agency that I have been tracing in the *corpus convicti*.

The newspaper coverage of Frost's crimes, trials, and finally his public execution helps bring into view this merger of material and voluntarist agencies. In the pages of a 1783 issue of the *Massachusetts Spy*, "a person by the name of Samuel Frost" made his first appearance in print (fig. 2.9). This account is all the print world saw of Frost until his trial was briefly mentioned in the *Salem Gazette* and the *Vermont Gazette* in May 1784: "Samuel Frost, a minor, for the murder of his father. The jury after being together eighteen hours, acquited [*sic*]

> WORCESTER, October 2.
>
> On Wednesday afternoon, last week, was committed to gaol in this town, a person by the name of Samuel Frost, for the murder of his father, which he effected by knocking him down, and then beating his brains out with a lever, as they were at work together digging a ditch. He is a young man of about eighteen years of age, and belonged to Princeton.
>
> On Tuesday evening, last week, a gentleman, in passing a street at the north end of Boston, in the evening, was knocked down by some person unknown, and robbed of about twenty guineas.
>
> The next evening a store was broken open in Boston, and goods were stolen to a large amount.
>
> It is said that there have been upwards of thirteen hundred deaths in Boston, within ten months past.
>
> In the ship General Washington, arrived at Philadelphia, came passenger the Baron de Beelen, with his suite, from Brussels, who, it is conjectured, will be constituted Ambassador from the Imperial Court.

"Worcester, October 2," *Massachusetts Spy: Or, Worcester Gazette*, 8, no. 649 (October 2, 1783): 3, col. 4.

him on account of Insanity."[78] Judging from the "Account" and from the much more widespread newspaper coverage of Frost's 1793 murder trial, there seems to have been every opportunity for Frost to have renewed the insanity defense through which he was acquitted of his father's murder in 1784. But Frost persisted in his plea of guilty and even, according to the reportage, "demanded to be hung."[79] A number of newspapers printed one of two identical accounts of Frost's 1793 trial.[80] All affirm that Frost was indeed "a person of sufficient understanding" to be "properly guilty" (and hence executable), yet this decision stands in tension with what these same accounts describe as his "apparent hardened insensibility and stupid indifference, which prove him destitute of every social principle, and of all proper sense of the enormity of the crime."[81] In keeping with the contradictions of liberal humanism, Frost's callousness and incapacity for sociality appear in the news coverage as both the very reasons to execute (his indifference exacerbating the heinousness of his crime, a view we see in the sermon and poem) and the reasons to acquit once again (his inadequate understanding of wrongdoing, a view also put forward in the sermon). Failing to evince full humanity, the criminal is here a liminal creature beholden to and produced by man rather than God, "properly guilty" yet "destitute of every social principle." By insisting that he be tried and hanged, Frost refuses liberalism's exclusion and claims his existence as part of a larger collective. Like banging his head against the prison wall to understand how his victims felt, Frost's demand to be punished in his body, according to the letter of the law, is an assertion of belonging. But what kind of belonging is this?

In the newspaper coverage, the fact that Frost's disregard for life extended even to his own is taken to heighten his inhumanity and affirm the propriety of his exclusion from liberal society, which, as Michel Foucault emphasizes, places a premium on biological life. Frost stridently refuses to be incorporated into the liberal sphere as an insane person, though the newspaper accounts suggest this was the path he was most encouraged to take. The so-called wild-beast test, which dated from Henry de Bracton's thirteenth-century work *Of the Laws and Customs of England*, had long guided application of the insanity defense. Bracton's insane criminal was "not much above the beasts, who lack reason."[82] A plea of insanity would have kept him alive but also under the control of another patriarchal custodian like Allen. By contrast, the public display and punishment of his body would have secured him—in an earlier day—a place among a community of other sinners. The premodern community he may have been seeking to join through the judicial or religious ritual of public execution had all but disappeared by 1793. Instead, at the time he was tried, his crimes, execution, and the surrounding print materials "launch" him into a different mode of belonging: a collective, mediated existence that extends beyond biological death yet remains linked with materiality.

By December 1793, more than half a dozen papers across the country had covered Frost's execution, including the *Massachusetts Spy*, the *Concord Herald*, the *Columbian Sentinel*, the *Independent Chronicle*, the *Oracle of the Day*, the *Essex Journal*, the *New Hampshire Journal*, the *Daily Advertiser*, the *Impartial Herald*, the *Weekly Register*, the *New Hampshire Gazette*, and the *Baltimore Daily Intelligencer*. Many of them also excerpted large portions of "The Account of Samuel Frost." The following account appeared in several (fig. 2.10), including the issue of *Dunlap's Daily Advertiser* that carried Swanwick's and Rush's recommendations for how to handle Philadelphia's yellow fever corpses:

> WORCESTER, Nov 6.
>
> On Thursday last, Samuel Frost was executed in this town, pursuant to his sentence, for the murder of Capt. Elisha Allen, of Princeton, on the 16th day of July last. This man, just ten years before he murdered Capt. Allen, killed his father, for which horrid crime he was tried, but acquitted by the jury, who supposed him insane. Before execution, a Sermon was preached by the Rev. Aaron Bancroft, to a very large audience. The criminal was present. After which he was carried to the place of execution. He shewed few or no signs of penitence. On being asked by the High Sheriff if he wished to say any thing to the spectators, he answered that he had not much to say—he would not have them follow him.— The High Sheriff repeatedly asked him if he wished his execution delayed? He answered, as often as asked, No!— as he was to go, (that was his expression) it had better be soon over. The scaffold dropped, and this uncommon murderer was launched into eternity. It is thought the number of spectators present were about 2000.

"Worcester, Nov 6," *Essex Journal & New Hampshire Packet*, no. 491 (November 13, 1793): 3, col. 3. Courtesy of the American Antiquarian Society

In the 30th ult, Samuel Frost was executed in Worcester, pursuant to his sentence, for the murder of capt. Elisha Allen, of Princeton, on the 16th day of July last. This man, just ten years before he murdered capt. Allen, killed his father, for which horrid crime he was tried, but acquitted by the jury, who supposed him insane. Before execution, a sermon was preached by the rev. A. Bancroft, to a very large audience. The criminal was present—After which he was carried to the place of execution. He shewed few or no signs of penitence. On being asked by the high

> sheriff, if he wished to say any thing to the spectators, he answered, that he had not much to say—he would not have them follow him. The sheriff repeatedly asked him if he wished his execution delayed? He answered as often as asked, no! as he was to go (that was his expression) it had better be soon over. The scaffold dropped, and this uncommon murderer was launched into eternity. It is thought the number of spectators present, was about 2000.[83]

After hearing the sermon, Frost indicates he has nothing to say and is ready to be hanged. Ready "to go," he was surrounded by a large group of spectators that included vendors selling copies of the first broadside containing his confession and the "Account" or the broadside "Poem on the Execution of Samuel Frost." The newspaper coverage describing Frost's behavior at his execution contrasts with the brief "eyewitness" account given in column 4 of Jonathan Plummer's Boston broadside (fig. 2.6); here Frost reportedly says "that he would not wish YOUNG PEOPLE should follow his steps." It is possible that Plummer is the author of this account of Frost's final moments, since it contrasts with the newspaper coverage yet aligns with traditional "last words" accounts.[84]

Johnstone's death by execution was, by contrast, not considered newsworthy. Just as his purported murder of a Black man did not garner enough attention to warrant an execution sermon, so too the fact that his hanging was not covered by the press further indexes the devaluation of Black life. Frost, white, when actually guilty of his father's murder, entered a racialized space of non-belonging and non-conviction. Rebelling against this living death, he murdered again, and this time he insisted on conviction and gained a certain kind of belonging and a distributed agency. Johnstone, Black and formerly enslaved, existing already in a racialized space, was criminalized and convicted despite his innocence. Out of this conviction, he too gained a certain belonging and agency, a platform from which he theorized another form of human being. The gallows tradition accorded Johnstone, racialized from the start of his life, a platform less far-reaching than Frost's. Yet Johnstone was, as we have seen, keenly aware of the power conviction accorded, proclaiming, "Death shall give sanction to my assertions."[85] His conviction enables him to communicate an expansive vision of human being, a vision that also allows him to move gracefully toward a death that also entails social belonging. He writes, "Yes, dear brethren with joy will I rush into the presence of my God."[86] And this is because of his certainty of salvation. For Johnstone, to be human is to be savable. Against spurious racialized arguments to the contrary, Johnstone insists that humanity is coextensive with susceptibility to salvation, which he refers to as the "right to saving grace." This merger of theology with the language of rights is characteristic of Johnstone's revisioning of the human, against the secular push toward exclusion. The "undoubted right as human beings to salvation," he writes, was never "questioned until the subtlety of after ages, in order to gloss their diabolical and inhuman traffick."[87]

Where the execution poem figures Frost as an artist, Johnstone's "Address" and "Letter to his Wife" reveal his own understanding of the power of language. In particular, he dwells on the power of lies. Lies, in the form of false witness, of course, are what landed Johnstone on the gallows. They are for Johnstone the ultimate malignity and reveal the underside of human interdependence: the power humans, as "creatures formed to live in a mutual state of dependence," have over one another. Protecting one's own name, particularly under the conditions of racialization, is impossible:

> We can lock up from a thief, but cannot from a liar, for by this you rob a man of what is out of his power to lock up; his good name, and it would be far better for a man to lose all his money than his good name; for, in taking his money, we only take what others had before him, and what he might reinstate by industry, but robbing a man of his good name, ye do not, cannot enrich yourselves, and you thereby make him poor indeed, for every effort he can use cannot reinstate his good name, which is dearer to every good man than life.[88]

Reputation, not property, is the essential currency in Johnstone's view. Property and money can be protected in a way that reputation cannot: to protect one's good name requires a society founded upon the recognition of reciprocal duties: "To receive and communicate assistance, constitutes the happiness of human life—man may indeed preserve his existence in solitude, but can only enjoy it in society."[89] Just as a good name was more important, and more vulnerable to malefaction, than moveable property, so too Johnstone here emphasizes the value of sociality in living a good and joyful life. The sustenance of mere biological life is possible for the unsupported individual, but the capacity to take pleasure in that life requires company.

In the most radical moment across his writings, Johnstone expands on this sense that mutual obligation, not accumulation of knowledge or property, forms the basis of the good life: "The greatest understanding of an individual, doomed to procure food and raiment for himself, will barely supply him with expedients to keep off death from day to day; but as one of a large community, performing only his share of the common business, he gains instruction and leisure for intellectual pleasures, and enjoys the happiness of reason and reflection, and the supreme felicity of rendering himself useful to his fellow creatures in a greater or lesser degree according to his ability."[90] Where each individual could in theory sustain life on their own, the task would be arduous, all consuming, and spiritually bereft. Working in concert with others, however, and contributing what they are most suited to contribute, brings not only material well-being but also, more importantly, time for leisure, education, and, the greatest good of all, "the supreme felicity of rendering himself useful to fellow creatures." In this moment, Johnstone anticipates Karl Marx's slogan, "From each according to ability; to each according to need," nearly verbatim, by nearly a century.

Repeatedly, Johnstone returns to this bedrock of human sociality, with all its vulnerabilities and flaws. In the "Letter to his Wife," Johnstone laments the fact that Sally will not come visit him in prison for fear for her own safety as a Black woman in such a place. Johnstone admits his own shortcomings. "I went astray and lusted after other women," he confesses, and readers get the sense that just resentment at Johnstone's betrayal may have played some role in keeping Sally away. Even so, Johnstone's declarations of the enduring strength of his love, even or especially in the face of his own faults and transgressions, are compelling: "My true and fond heart rested with you, and love for you always brought your wanderer back: you were to me, my all! my everything dear and beloved." The bond between Abraham and Sally proved more potent than the temptation to sever that bond, such that even as he otherwise would embrace imminent death, his connection to Sally holds him back: "All that seems terrible in death is the parting from you."[91] With greater concern for Sally's well-being than his own potential jealousy, Abraham enjoins her to find another husband, with care to select someone "that will love and protect you . . . rather than a pretty baby to look at who might . . . break your heart." And as noted previously, he warns her not to be alarmed if she finds that his spirit remains by her side, "hovering on the watch to shield and defend you from any impending danger."[92]

Johnstone closes with two actions that highlight the merger of material with spiritual care. He leaves Sally a treasured possession: "My white Hat, that you were so fond of, I leave you with this injunction that you wear it yourself while it lasts and give it, to no other person." Although the white hat came to symbolize the heroic rescuer only in the visual medium of twentieth-century cinema, there is a sense here that this particular bequest is rich with meaning. Abraham encourages Sally to give herself to another but asks that she keep his white hat, an item already dear to her, for herself alone, not to share it with anyone else. And, in signing off, Johnstone leaves another material trace of his physical being. He instructs the bit of paper on which he writes to continue his good work in the world: "I've kissed this paper—and bid it convey the kiss to you my love: And now my dear Sally, I bid you... an eternal Farewel [sic]."[93] Johnstone conjures his own ghost to care for her when he is gone, he engages in a poetics of property in leaving Sally his white hat, and finally he entrusts mere paper to convey some remnant of his physical being or "true character" after he is gone, his loving kiss. Across each of these acts, we see Johnstone imagining that what constitutes the good of human life, "to receive and communicate assistance," may well continue even after death "ushers" him "into an endless eternity."[94]

By insisting on execution, or at least avoiding a verdict of not guilty by reason of insanity, Frost in some degree directed his own destiny. Likewise, Johnstone is at pains to accept the law's pronouncement despite his insistence on his innocence, largely because it offered a rare opportunity to exercise his will and convey his views for a better society, and for the potential to continue life's happiness beyond the grave. Yet the *corpus convicti* has agency not only because of such instances of voluntarism, or solely as a result of the enduring materiality of print itself, but also because of its rhetorical, taxonomic, historical, and imaginative existence at the limits of liberal humanism. I want to distinguish the *corpus convicti* from Jane Bennett's theorization of matter as "vital" and agency as distributed across human and nonhuman actors. The collective agency I analyze here includes, but is not limited to, individual agency: it retains the link between agency and subjectivity that Sharon Krause has argued is necessary for democratic politics: "In denying the link between agency and a subjectivity that is reflexive and individuated, albeit not sovereign, the new materialism threatens to eviscerate the grounds for holding persons responsible. Consequently, it cannot sustain a model of agency that is viable for democratic politics."[95] The mediated collectivity of the *corpus convicti* is entirely missed by a reading that relies on liberal norms of agency as operating directly, via intention and consciousness. Its agency exists only in the space between reality and representation, the space of racialized criminality. The *corpus convicti* includes key voluntaristic moments, but it is not wholly the property of Johnstone or Frost as individual subjects, nor is it primarily oppositional; it is, instead, situated between "between the human and brutal creation."[96] From the unsettled boundaries of the human within early American print culture, a racialized merger of print and personhood creates a "corpus" that forges connections among shifting collectivities extending across time and space.

In the cases of Abraham Johnstone, Samuel Frost, and other marginalized figures of the long nineteenth century, scholars can offer more adequate accounts by literally re-membering the bodies of writing that sprung up in response to their lives, deeds, and confrontations with the law, because in so many cases recovering authentic, forgotten, or maligned voices remains impossible. Strengthened rather than limited by materiality, the agency of these excluded figures becomes most efficacious when the boundaries of the liberal human are most unsettled. Returning to the archive to account for those enigmatic figures like Johnstone and Frost who inhabit liberalism's antinomies, we can reopen the possibility of a more truly inclusive polity, which was at once promised and foreclosed by humanism. Developing and leaning into the racialized framings of crime and genius submerged in the convict's corpus, the next chapter identifies an alternative Black humanism in David Walker's 1829 *Appeal*.

CHAPTER THREE

Outlaw Humanism

Walker's *Appeal, in Four Articles; Together with a Preamble, to the Coloured Citizens of the World, but in Particular, and Very Expressly, to Those of the United States of America* (1829), flashed across the Atlantic world in three editions between 1829 and 1830. Its appearance was stunning, yet the *Appeal* was not, as it is often taken to be, precisely exceptional: like a comet, however brilliant, the orbit it traced was both eccentric and recursive. The criminal genius animating Walker's *Appeal* was not singular but of a piece with the zombification of moral agency in fever-ridden Philadelphia, the racialized disenfranchisement of an innocent Black man and a neurodivergent white man in the late eighteenth-century Northeast, the insurgency in Southampton Virginia that conjures the name Nat Turner, and the fugitive genius of the Great Dismal Swamp maroons.

Walker knew he was stretching the boundaries of law and taking his life in his hands in circulating his radical, collectivist vision of fully realized justice across the Atlantic.[1] Walker's words found their way from the Boston printshop likely belonging to two white Bostonian printers, David Hooton and Matthew Teprell, to the slaveholding Southern states of his birth, and they even circulated internationally.[2] Publishing under his own name, Walker distributed the *Appeal* every way he could imagine: by enlisting the aid of sympathetic (or naive) white people, mailing it through the US postal system, and sewing copies of the pamphlet into sailors' clothing to be smuggled, illegally, into Southern states.[3] Attempts to legislate this outlaw document immediately ensued. As Black abolitionist Henry Highland Garnet wrote in 1848, "This little book produced more commotion among slaveholders than any volume of its size that was ever issued from an American press."[4] In South Carolina, a white steward named Edward Smith was arrested for possessing and distributing these "pamphlets of a very seditious & inflammatory character." In Georgia, two missionaries to the Cherokees and a printer were arrested for possession of copies of the *Appeal*.[5] The pamphlet's appearance in Virginia and Louisiana incited severe legislative action against enslaved and free Black people and spurred lawmakers to intensify penalties for white people teaching Black people to read or write, while North Carolina pursued legal action against a free Black agent found to have been working with Walker and an "incendiary preacher" galvanized by the *Appeal*.[6] The pamphlet also circulated widely via numerous reprintings, a number of which were unattributed. As Lori Leavell has shown, the *Appeal* appeared in numerous forms in the antebellum years, beyond the pamphlet itself. These recirculations included Garnet's 1848 reprinting, as well as lengthy "appropriations in fellow abolitionists' texts, including those that failed to identify Walker as the author," and even very brief "excerpts and references in periodicals," including numerous circum-Atlantic newspapers. Moreover, the *Appeal* appears in the period's fiction, including extensive, if indirect and unattributed, reference in Robert Montgomery Bird's popular 1836 novel *Sheppard Lee*.[7]

Although scholars are still unpacking the *Appeal*'s full literary and textual impact, the political and economic threat it posed, as well as the threat to individual safety of white Southerners, was clear immediately.[8] The editor of the Boston *Columbian Centinel* pronounced the *Appeal* "one of the most wicked and inflammatory productions that every issued from the press."[9] And Georgia's governor called it "danger in a new shape."[10] Of course, what looked like danger to a white Southerner signified quite differently for free and enslaved Black Southerners, as Cheryl Wall writes: Walker's "call for blacks to take up arms to end slavery incited bravery among blacks who heard it and put fear in the hearts of slaveholders, who quickly banned the publication in the southern United States."[11] Following the *Appeal*'s first edition, death threats poured in, as Southern white leaders called for Walker's arrest. While Massachusetts governor Harrison Gray Otis "condemned Walker's project," he refused to comply with Southern governors' calls to apprehend Walker, since he had not violated state law. After the third edition and within a year, Walker, age thirty-three, was found dead at his home. While recent historians cite tuberculosis as his cause of death, popular memory has not been able to resist conjuring foul play. W. E. B. Du Bois, for instance, wrote that the *Appeal* resulted "very possibly in the murder of the author."[12] Often referred to as "the father of Black nationalism," a murdered Walker would stand first in a tragically long line of African American male leaders who met a violent end in early adulthood: Medgar Evers, Martin Luther King Jr., Malcolm X.[13]

Yet whether a result of direct political violence or not, Walker's dying was overdetermined. Whether via retributive violence or via disparate exposure to tuberculosis, called "Negro Consumption" by antebellum physicians in its acute form, death was coming for Walker.[14] Bringing Ruth Wilson Gilmore's valuable definition to bear, that racism is the "production and exploitation of group-differentiated vulnerability to premature death," we can see that Walker's death via pathogen was, like retaliatory assassination, racially driven.[15] This is not abstract theory but a material fact, and one of which Walker himself was well aware. Walker's death by tuberculosis does not indemnify white supremacist malefaction, but it does place Walker in company as much with twenty-first-century Black victims of public health failings as with the elite twentieth-century Black male leaders with whom he is more often aligned.

Across nearly two hundred years, Walker stands in dialogue with contemporary scholar Christina Sharpe. Both address the monstrous history of premature deaths that generated the modern world. Sharpe queries, "In the midst of so much death and the fact of Black life as proximate to death, how do we attend to physical, social, and figurative death and also to the largeness that is Black life, Black life insisted from death?"[16] Sharpe's question is poignant and productive. Likewise, in answer to whether he feared for his life having published this incendiary critique of white supremacy, Walker frames a question of his own: "What is the use of living, when in fact I am dead?" Here Walker anticipates Sharpe, suggesting that Black life, which is to say life lived by people of African origin in the world of European colonialism and its aftermath, has always exceeded the frameworks of death that simultaneously condition its existence. Sharpe's "fact" (that Black life exists "as proximate to" death) accepts a division between the literal and the figurative that Walker's earlier "fact" (the transtemporal reality of his own death, "What is the use of living when in fact I am dead?") disavows. Yet both share the key insight that Black life, like Black death, exceeds its own negation.

To *insist* Black life from death, a transaction Sharpe marks as ongoing, is to render transitive what is normatively intransitive. Because Blackness and being misalign, as in Fanon's zone of nonbeing, or Spillers's flesh, it takes inordinate effort to produce and, more to Sharpe's point, to reproduce Black life. Sharpe's grammatical play in the phrase "Black life insisted from death" (with its contrast to more syntactically normative phrasing like "insisting on Black life under threat of death") captures a phenomenology of Blackness, a lived experience that is at once painful and joyous and never meets the threshold of an uncontested *being*. As Sharpe explains, she is not interested in "seeking resolution to blackness's ongoing and irresolvable abjection" but rather in uncovering "what, if anything, survives this insistent Black exclusion, this ontological negation, and [asking] how do literature, performance, and visual culture observe and mediate this un/survival."[17] The furor that the straightforward statement "Black lives matter" can produce, four hundred years after enslaved Africans first arrived in British North America, shows that merely *insisting on* Black life (in all its grammatical normativity) remains a revolutionary effort in a world that, from the seventeenth century to the present day, has never stopped working to maintain premature Black death as ordinary.[18]

Understandably, the struggle against the white supremacy that underwrote this exploitation is often framed as a fight against *dehumanization*. For example, Alicia Garza writes, "We were forced to . . . build a country that never truly considered us human and still refuses to honor our humanity."[19] This perspective assumes that the horrors of racial slavery and its legacies require profound othering. By contrast, both Sharpe and Walker refuse the fight for humanity by framing the terrain otherwise. Sharpe's grammar of Black life *insisted from* death shifts away from a humanist framing and eclipses white supremacy's blood-soaked normativity. Looking back down the centuries, Sharpe, Walker, and a host of Black radical thinkers in between have resolutely maintained that Black people have always *insisted* life from death, that Black humanity is a fact so palpable it need not be argued. Yet the agent of this insisting, the "who" that insists, transgresses liberal humanist bounds and exercises an agency that, as in the *corpus convicti* theorized in the previous chapter, is fluid and multimodal, connecting individual voluntarism with collective effort. This is the frame this book develops around the "criminal genius," yet, as Walker's case exemplifies, to center this history of distributed agency in Black history is to walk a tightrope, sidestepping otherwise crucial frameworks of civil resistance to ask what they overlook. If Sharpe's syntax focalizes a slippage between Black life and its attendant forms of death, it is important to note that this slippage is ontological as well as grammatical.

While it is perhaps the earliest Black radical print publication, Walker's *Appeal*, which one contemporary reader described as a "demon-like production," does not so much resist as occupy the twinned pathologies captivating Black life: criminality and death.[20] As we have seen, Walker explicitly frames himself as a dead man. At the same time, he is also a writer, public speaker, husband, father, businessman, and activist.[21] Living is useless to one who is dead, a fact that renders death threats entirely immaterial. Notably, Walker does not argue for his own humanity: this is as obvious as his own death. Rather than compile evidentiary support for Black humanity, Walker jumps straight into identifying "coloured citizens" as a global political class with common interests, justified in employing any means necessary to protect those interests.²² He directly broke the law by circulating the *Appeal* and inciting revolt. The *Appeal* galvanized Southern lawmakers to enhance existing legislation "to control and prevent black literacy" and to enact significant "anti-free-black legislation," for example, in Louisiana, where the legislature voted to expel "all free blacks who had entered the state after 1825."²³ As the litany of legislative response to Walker's unprecedented publication indicates, what Walker did was, fundamentally, violate the social and legal cornerstone of the United States, racial enslavement, by both theorizing and embodying an outlaw Black humanism.

When he asked in 1829, "What is the use of living, when in fact I am dead?" Walker cut to the heart of the question haunting the nineteenth-century United States: How do the socially dead speak? Provocatively, the *Appeal* responds by reconstructing skepticism about the existence of the external world, while simultaneously refuting supposed doubts regarding Black humanity. Though potentially bloody, God's incipient justice exceeds doubt, and it is this horizon of justice, rather than abstract thought, that secures universal humanity in the here and now. Calling for "coloured citizens" to "prepare the way" for divine retribution, Walker militates against the supposed "question" of Black humanity. As one who thinks and writes while "in fact" dead, Walker's reality is not separate from but intertwined with the speculative and the fantastical. This chapter argues that an aesthetic and philosophical approach is key to understanding Walker's emancipatory agenda, which neither begins with resistance nor ends with recognition of Black humanity. Instead, the *Appeal* enacts an outlaw humanism, calling into question the very existence of the world in order to limn the possibility of another world where justice is restored. As Melvin L. Rogers has argued, Walker's insistence on using the word "citizen," to which he had no legal claim in the United States, "calls out a form of political activity that is not itself dependent on the juridical framework from which blacks were excluded" to show that "blacks constituted themselves as political actors at the very moment their ability to do so was called into question or denied."²⁴ Walker's political intervention was thus concrete and speculative at one and the same time.

Most twenty-first-century readers readily acknowledge the validity of Walker's claims to justice. Yet at the same time, Walker's intellectual and creative contributions remain underexamined.²⁵ Drawing on deep learning and significant theoretical as well as practical grounding, Walker insists on justice as a material force. "Unquestionably," as Elizabeth McHenry notes, "the *Appeal* was the product of an educated and active mind,"²⁶ and among the clearest indications of this learning is Walker's direct engagement with Thomas Jefferson's virulent questioning of Black humanity. For this reason, Walker's responses to Jefferson have garnered the lion's share of critical attention in studies of the *Appeal*, particularly those studies that look to its political and cultural interventions. However, I demonstrate here that, to ground his critique of Jefferson, Walker had to reach further back, to the founding of modern philosophy in the work of René Descartes. Though previous scholars seem to have overlooked his connection to Descartes, Walker was one of the shrewdest commentators on the Cartesian dilemma, and the *Appeal* stands as perhaps the period's most innovative exploration of how an embodied humanity might navigate an uncertain world. For Walker and those other "degraded, wretched, and abject" individuals whom he addresses as "coloured citizens," the possibility of the world's nonexistence is not tragic but utopian, as it opens the doors of possibility for another world where Black lives matter. Walker's speculative reworking of the Cartesian cogito constitutes an outlaw humanism, produced by one who lived and wrote while "in fact dead."

"Such Hellish Cruelties"

Though Walker and many of his associates were free according to the letter of the law, Walker knew that its spirit tended toward Black bondage and perpetual liability to premature death. Without the rights protections that the state afforded citizens, or even reliable legal recognition, the condition of unenslaved Blackness was often, Walker understood, the condition of outlawry.[27] As Terri L. Snyder writes, "Across the Anglo-American colonies, lawmakers altered the legal category of the outlaw in order to fit the goals of a growing slave society. Their actions reflect the ways in which the legalities of slavery and criminal justice were powerfully intertwined, particularly but not exclusively in the southern colonies."[28] Like outlaws, free Black people remained subject to arbitrary violence and ever proximate to social, civil, and indeed biological death.[29] Born around 1796 in North Carolina, most likely to an enslaved father and free mother, Walker was raised in the South and traveled the United States extensively before settling in Boston, where he ran a used clothing shop and became active in the Black community, helping to found and then selling subscriptions to *Freedom's Journal*, the first Black-owned and operated newspaper in the United States. Between 1826 and 1828, Walker was instrumental in establishing the Massachusetts General Coloured Association to, in his own words, "unite the coloured population ... forming societies, opening, extending, and keeping up correspondences, and not withholding anything which may have the least tendency to meliorate *our* miserable condition."[30] Walker's *Appeal* was the first publication to assail anti-Black racism directly (fig. 3.1). It is often mischaracterized as an abolitionist

WALKER'S

APPEAL,

IN FOUR ARTICLES;

TOGETHER WITH

A PREAMBLE,

TO THE

COLOURED CITIZENS OF THE WORLD,

BUT IN PARTICULAR, AND VERY EXPRESSLY, TO THOSE OF

THE UNITED STATES OF AMERICA,

WRITTEN IN BOSTON, STATE OF MASSACHUSETTS,
SEPTEMBER 28, 1829.

THIRD AND LAST EDITION,
WITH ADDITIONAL NOTES, CORRECTIONS, &c.

Boston:
REVISED AND PUBLISHED BY DAVID WALKER.

1830.

Title page from David Walker, *Walker's Appeal, in Four Articles* (Boston, 1829). Courtesy of the American Antiquarian Society pamphlet, when in fact it is much more than that. Walker aims not simply to end racial slavery but to bring about racial justice writ large. He advocates increasing access to education, rebuilding American Christianity, and redistributing wealth such that Black people reap the "gold and silver" that their sweat, blood, and tears had brought to America. As W. E. B. Du Bois wrote in 1940, Walker's *Appeal* proposes no less than a "program of organized opposition to the action and attitude of the dominant white group. . . . It involves the use of force of every sort."[31] Walker's recognition of Blackness as a type of criminality enabled him to make the conjuncture of Black life with death explicit within both US philosophical frameworks and European antecedents.

Walker stakes his radical emancipatory agenda on aesthetic and philosophical terrain, and these are the lenses through which we must view his legacy, rather than the affective and political frames that have much more often been brought to bear in studies of the *Appeal*. The matter Walker's readers have tended to find most salient regarding this text is its anger. Despite Walker's patent philosophical commitments, it is the *Appeal*'s affective register, an anger approaching rage, that garners most interest, then and now. Walker's contemporaries as well as later readers have all remarked on the emotionality of the *Appeal*, often to the exclusion of the text's philosophical considerations of Black life and its interrelation with Black death. In this vein, literary scholar Ian Finseth remarks that the *Appeal* is "a scorching denunciation of slavery and hypocrisy; its anger, indeed, is the quality that has always evoked the strongest responses."[32] Similarly, historian and biographer Peter P. Hinks claims that Walker's "vehemence and outrage" is "unprecedented among contemporary African American authors."[33] Indeed, anger screams from the pages of this short denunciation of racism worldwide, which also marshals an attendant irony, indignation, and reprobation, especially in its attack on how Enlightenment ideals of equality and freedom ironically authorize the institution of slavery.

A few outliers, including McHenry, Marcy Dinius, and, earlier, Herbert Aptheker, place the spotlight elsewhere. While McHenry describes the *Appeal* as "a furious indictment of American slavery," she also notes that its arguments for "violent resistance" have been "overemphasized," and Dinius foregrounds the "deeply textual" nature of Walker's intervention, arguing that its most "immediate, concrete, and significant impact" was its effects on Black and Indigenous authors, not its anger and violence.[34] Crucially, Aptheker remarks that Walker's religiosity, not his outrage, is the *Appeal*'s most noteworthy feature: "If there is any one characteristic in the Walker work that is clearer and sharper than any other, it is its religiosity; of course this sense in no way contradicts Walker's equally passionate sense of wrong, rather, it complements and defines it."[35] Like Aptheker, I want to direct our attention away from Walker's "passionate sense of wrong" and toward the horizon of justice onto which his anger opens and that conceptions of genius make more visible.[36] Although Walker's passion is crucial, the narrow focus thereon too often repeats epistemic violence that in its more virulent forms stereotypes Black people as emotional rather than rational or, in a more recent transmogrification only more ostensibly benign, as moral guides rather than cogent thinkers. Bringing the framework of genius to bear on Walker's work helps us see its intellectual and aesthetic aspects alongside important emotional and theological elements.

Walker marshals justified rage and religiosity to dismiss the notion that mind(/soul) and body are separate or even separable entities. These aspects of human experience complement one another in Walker's view. Religious, emotional, and intellectual experience all work relationally as the *Appeal* mobilizes shock to strengthen his spiritual and logical case. If the pamphlet's anger does not define its significance, neither is it merely incidental to its argument. The text's theological concerns likewise do not contradict reason. The *Appeal*'s outrage at the state of the world instead grounds its radical liberatory project. God's inevitable justice in the face of white American atrocity is the sure foundation on which Walker builds the possibility of another world.

Walker emphasizes that racial slavery was categorically different from slavery that had existed elsewhere, at other times. Different—and worse. In no uncertain terms, he attributes that difference to "enlightened" Christianity: "They tell us of the Israelites in Egypt, the Helots in Sparta, and of the Roman Slaves, which last, were made up from almost every nation under heaven, whose sufferings under those ancient and heathen nations were, in comparison with ours, under this enlightened and Christian nation, no more than a cypher." Enslavement in the ancient world was slavery in name only; the condition of the enslaved in ancient times fundamentally differed from the modern predicament Walker saw threaded through both free and enslaved Black life. As he announces in the opening lines of the *Appeal*, "We, (coloured people of these United States,) are the most degraded, wretched, and abject set of beings that ever lived since the world began." This world-historical frame helps Walker deliver a stinging rebuke to "enlightened" and "Christian" white Americans. Pre-Enlightenment, Walker argues, Europeans were not capable of taking human beings by the millions and murdering them in every way imaginable. They quite simply did not have the necessary skills or tools: "While they were heathens, they were too ignorant for such barbarity. But being Christians, enlightened and sensible, they are completely prepared for such hellish cruelties." The idea that the heinousness of modern atrocity, from Atlantic enslavement to Nazi death camps, is not an aberration of Enlightenment but a direct result thereof has gained familiarity in academic circles and is often traced to the Frankfurt school. But it is already fully present in the *Appeal*, as it was in Haiti thirty years before.[37]

Thus, when Walker elsewhere espouses his own Christianity and his desire for the Enlightenment of Black people worldwide, it is a reconstructed Enlightenment, built back up from a base of faith in God's justice and speculative hope not for progress but for a radically new world. As Walker asserts, Enlightenment thinkers like Jefferson doubt Black humanity ("I advance it therefore as a suspicion only, that the blacks, whether originally a distinct race, or made distinct by time and circumstances, are inferior to the whites in the endowments both of body and mind"),[38] and deny Black genius ("Religion indeed has produced a Phyllis Whately [sic]; but it could not produce a poet"). Walker insists that the former is a type of absurdity and tackles the latter head on, stating that "unless we try to refute Mr. Jefferson's arguments respecting us, we will only establish them." To refute Jefferson, however, Walker must reconstruct Enlightenment humanism, and to do so he reshapes Descartes's formative doubt about humanity's relation to the external world to frame an alternate universalism that does not occlude racialization but exceeds it. Walker's engagement with Jeffersonian natural philosophy in the *Appeal* is well known and explicit. His recasting of Cartesian skepticism, though it has escaped the notice of prior commentators, is only just slightly further below the surface.

In arguing that racial enslavement's cruelty requires knowledge as its foundation, Walker engages Enlightenment tools and tropes directly. As Lewis R. Gordon writes, "A legacy of modern colonialism and racism is that to articulate the set of problems and concerns of Africana thought (a branch of philosophy centering the African diaspora) one must engage the tradition that accompanied its emergence in the modern world."[39] Walker, making "the most accurate observations of things as they exist," employs an empirical approach; he also makes teleological distinctions between "barbarian" or "heathen" peoples and civilized ones. Moreover, he prizes education: "ignorance" is the second of the four main sources of Black "wretchedness" that Walker's four articles identify. Yet, at the same time, his vision is speculative, imagining a just future world that although built from the compromised materials at hand, nevertheless fully rejects the impossibly vile present.

It is in article 2, "Our Wretchedness in Consequence of Ignorance," that Walker most fully formulates a philosophical vision capable of comprehending a future that breaks with the present status quo. In this stunning passage, Walker posits the potential nonexistence of the world. Set against a backdrop of threatened violence, Walker centers racial slavery and takes divine justice as his premise. This justice is thus not an abstract transcendent idea but rather an unshakeable material fact. "God is just," Walker writes in article 1, "and I know it—for he has convinced me to my satisfaction—I cannot doubt him." Indeed, it is Walker's certainty of God's justice that produces his radical doubt about the world's existence (fig 3.2):

> The whites want slaves, and want us for their slaves, but some of them will curse the day they ever saw us. As true as the sun ever shone in its meridian splendor, my colour will root some of them out of the very face of the earth. They shall have enough making slaves of, and butchering, and murdering us in the manner in which they have. No doubt some may say that I write with a bad spirit, and that I being a black, wish these things to occur. Whether I write with a bad or a good spirit, I say *if these things do not occur in their proper time, it is because the world in which we live does not exist, and we are deceived with regard to its existence.*—It is immaterial however to me, who believe, or who refuse—though I should like to see the whites repent peradventure God may have mercy on them, some however, have gone so far that their cup must be filled.[40]

If retribution proves untimely, Walker proclaims, it will not be a failure of divine justice. Rather, "it is because the world . . . does not exist." This is not unreasonable rage or rhetorical flourish; rather, Walker's skepticism about the continued existence of a world governed by the logic of racial slavery is a reasoned argument for his radical emancipatory project. Walker does begin by emphasizing an emotion: *desire*, specifically white desire for specifically Black slaves ("they want slaves . . . want us for their slaves"), which manifests Enlightenment dreams of classification and control. He describes this white desire as fatal greed that will necessarily overreach itself. Eventually, Walker posits, Black people will rise up and emerge victorious. White enslavers "shall have enough of" Black blood and degradation when "their cup [is] filled" on the day of redemption. Walker emphasizes the inevitability of that day of retributive encounter with a solar simile: "as true as the sun ever shone in its meridian splendor." This quotidian celestial fact, that sunshine at noon is bright, is indisputable, a perfect simile to describe the equally certain fact that "my colour" will "root . . . out of the very face of the earth" those overcome by the sin of greed. The clear light of reason and justice will prevail, sure as the sun will shine. Where David Hume famously argues that habit, rather than knowledge, underpins our belief that the sun will rise tomorrow, cut off so many thousands of the white Romans or murderers, and who carried his victorious arms, to the very gate of Rome, and I give it as my candid opinion, that had Carthage been well united and had given him good support, he would have carried that cruel and barbarous city by storm. But they were dis-united, as the coloured people are now, in the United States of America, the reason our natural enemies are enabled to keep their feet on our throats.

Beloved brethren—here let me tell you, and believe it, that the Lord our God, as true as he sits on his throne in heaven, and as true as our Saviour died to redeem the world, will give you a Hannibal, and when the Lord shall have raised him up, and given him to you for your possession, O my suffering brethren! remember the divisions and consequent sufferings of *Carthage* and of *Hayti*. Read the history particularly of Hayti, and see how they were butchered by the whites, and do you take warning. The person whom God shall give you, give him your support and let him go his length, and behold in him the salvation of your God. God will indeed, deliver you through him from your deplorable and wretched condition under the Christians of America. I charge you this day before my God to lay no obstacle in his way, but let him go.

The whites want slaves, and want us for their slaves, but some of them will curse the day they ever saw us. As true as the sun ever shone in its meridian splendor, my colour will root some of them out of the very face of the earth. They shall have enough of making slaves of, and butchering, and murdering us in the manner which they have. No doubt some may say that I write with a bad spirit, and that I being a black, wish these things to occur. Whether I write with a bad or a good spirit, I say if these things do not occur in their proper time, it is because the world in which we live does not exist, and we are deceived with regard to its existence.—

Page 23 from David Walker, *Walker's Appeal, in Four Articles* (Boston, 1829). Courtesy of the American Antiquarian Society

Walker sticks with a knowable fact: that the sun is bright at noon, even as he demonstrates that the habits of belief Hume viewed as inescapable are much easier to shake for those whose living circumstances are themselves the stuff of nightmares.

It would be impossible, and a mistake, to overlook the anger of this passage. Enslavers have gone too far; while some may still escape unharmed, Walker seems either blasé about or delighted by the fact that others' "cup must be filled." Yet the state of his own "spirit," whether good or bad, Walker rightly insists, is irrelevant. Walker's individual anger, his personal wish for retribution, is neither here nor there with regard to his claim, because his analysis goes much further than his own feelings. Indeed, he claims that the *world itself* is irrelevant, indeed *does not exist*, if the day he has been speaking of does not come *in its proper time*. Walker's purpose exceeds individual persuasion ("it is immaterial however to me, who believe, or who refuse"); he emphasizes instead the limitations of habitual belief that things must remain as they have been, over and against the weight of God's justice.

Walker's central claim is that if enslavers, whom the *Appeal* most often designates as "tyrants," do not soon curse the day they ever saw Black people, "it is because the world in which we live does not exist, and we are deceived with regard to its existence." Studies that focalize Walker's affective and political dimensions are stymied by this claim. For example, Finseth emphasizes what he sees as this passage's "ambiguity." He speculates that "Walker seems to aim for a stylized, studied ambiguity, perhaps to fray the nerves of his white readers, or perhaps, out of fear for his own life, to avoid the charge that he was advocating anything more radical than a faith in God's justice," but he concludes that "Walker really was not certain in his own mind what he envisioned."[41] For Finseth, this passage reveals the limitations of Walker's thinking about the relationship between national citizenship and racial belonging, which becomes clearest when Walker frames whites as the "natural" enemies of Blacks but also insists that it is the "whites" who have "made themselves" so, which implies that these enemies are not natural but constructed. Far from revealing holes or limitations in Walker's reasoning, I see this slippage as showing that Walker's phenomenological approach to the category of nature is fundamentally dynamic, capable of change and adaptation, as opposed to a static ontological approach to nature as given and therefore immutable.

In fact, Walker's claim about the world's possible nonexistence does not court ambiguity but instead clearly frames the nature of existence as a key issue for a Black thinker in 1820s America. For Walker, who has already told us that he is "in fact dead," existence is not the basis of reality, and justice, not life itself, is the supreme good. "I would suffer my life to be taken before I would submit" to the "hellish deeds" of enslavers, Walker states. "Yea, would I meet death with avidity far! far! ! in preference to such servile submission to the murderous hands of tyrants." The fact that God's justice grounds reality is not a limitation on the radicality of Walker's vision. Rather, for him, to accommodate oneself to enslavement's viscous degradation is to practice "treachery and deceit." To take God's justice as primary is to adopt a premise that is both speculative and foundational. This radical belief is speculative because of the stark "reality" of the institution of racial slavery and foundational because, without it, the world's atrocity is so extreme as to render that world itself impossible, its very existence the product of deceit.

A fascinating conception of deceit turns out to be central to the *Appeal*. The word itself, with its variants, appears fourteen times in the eighty-eight-page document, with "deceive" (and variants) appearing a further fourteen times. In Walker's usage, the word functionally denotes believing what is not true, with the origin of those false beliefs being less crucial than in more typical usage, where deceit generally assumes an identifiable deceiver. Thus, of white Americans, Walker writes, "They think because they hold us in their infernal chains of slavery, that we wish to be white, or of their color—but they are dreadfully deceived—we wish to be just as it pleased our Creator to have made us." This is not merely a syntactical anomaly; rather, Walker's usage highlights a key aspect of his theology. Because God's justice is uniquely knowable, deceit is what follows from resistance to that knowledge. To be deceived is thus to resist divine justice, to make inferences at odds with it, and therefore to become ensnared with evil or, as he puts it several times in the course of the *Appeal*, to be "dreadfully deceived." Thus, when Walker writes, "They [white Americans] think that we do not feel for our brethren, whom they are murdering by the inches, but they are dreadfully deceived," white Americans' misapprehension is only half the story. It is not simply that they are *mistaken*. The fact is that they are *deceived*: erring from the central truth of God's justice. Those who are "dreadfully deceived" may live in blissful ignorance day to day, but all the while they open themselves to retributive violence. This threatened violence always surrounds Walker's references to deception: "So did the Romans doubt, many of them were really so ignorant, that they thought the whole of mankind were made to be slaves to them; just as many of the Americans think now, of my colour. But they got dreadfully deceived. When men got their eyes opened, they made the murderers scamper." As we can see in this example, to be deceived is to resist the knowable truth of God's justice: while such resistance may produce gold and silver, it risks divine wrath. Dreadful, indeed. Walker's advice to white Americans, "for your good," is to shun deception or else "drag down the vengeance of God upon you. When God Almighty commences his battle on the continent of America, for the oppression of his people, tyrants will wish they never were born."[42] God's justice is the foundation of knowledge, and deception is willful ignorance of this clear fact. The importance of God's justice as the foundation of knowledge cannot be overstated, as Walker is directly responding to the intellectual cornerstone of modernity; namely, the questions of how we come to know and what can, with certainty, be known.

"Because the World Does Not Exist"

This question about the foundations of human knowledge is the quintessential modern question, framed by Descartes. As Gordon writes, "In most North American philosophical courses, modernity begins more with a whom than with a when, and that person is René Descartes."[43] Deceit also features centrally in Descartes's *Meditations on First Philosophy* (1641), which sets out to prove God's existence and the soul's immortality but instead establishes so-called radical doubt. Beginning with his first meditation, "Of the Things Which May Be Brought within the Sphere of the Doubtful," Descartes attempts to show, via six thought experiments or "meditations," that natural reason in fact proves that "God may be known more easily and with greater certainty than the things of the world."[44] Where Walker takes God's justice as his premise, unsusceptible to doubt, Descartes experiments with taking *nothing* as given, to show that God's existence and the human mind are knowable within the bounds of natural reason alone. Where Walker writes, "God is just, and I know it—for he has convinced me to my satisfaction—I cannot doubt him," Descartes by contrast says, "I have always thought that two issues—namely, God and the soul—are chief among those that ought to be demonstrated with the aid of philosophy rather than theology."[45] Walker admits of no ground on which God can be doubted, where Descartes opines that if the existence of God may be rationally deduced, *then* it would not be possible to doubt this knowledge. To deduce God's existence, Descartes maintains that he must first "raze everything to the ground and begin again from the original foundations."[46] Once he gets going, it turns out that the "things that can be called into doubt" are legion. They include anything gleaned from sense perception, because our senses are sometimes wrong.

Descartes's "dreaming argument," which proposes that there are no sure signs by which a person can tell whether they are awake, and not dreaming, is powerful enough to induce authorial vertigo: "As a result, I am becoming quite dizzy, and this dizziness nearly convinces me that I am asleep."⁴⁷ Just to be safe, Descartes decides to assume that in fact he is dreaming, not sitting by the fire in his dressing gown as he was just a few paragraphs ago so sure he was. Lest he allow himself to conclude that, even so, surely mathematical, geometric, and other such facts must "contain something certain and indubitable," despite the fallibility of sense perception and the ever-present threat of a dreamworld masquerading as reality, Descartes posits a potential "evil genius," or *genium malignum*, a divine power not supremely good but "supremely powerful and clever, who has directed his entire effort at deceiving me."⁴⁸ With this masterstroke, Descartes unleashes radical doubt: "Eventually I am forced to admit that there is nothing among the things I once believed to be true which it is not permissible to doubt." It is important to note, though, as it will be important shortly for understanding Walker's response to Descartes, that this achievement, of establishing the possibility of doubting literally everything in the world, relies on the possibility of a supremely powerful divine or supernatural being, albeit a deceptive one.

Having thus "raze[d] everything to the ground," Descartes finds an original foundation for knowledge and existence in his own thoughts. Emerging from his baptism by fire, that is, the dreaming argument and evil genius, he writes, "I judged that I could accept it [thinking] without scruple as the first principle of the philosophy I was seeking." Though his thinking may be the product of either a good or an evil divinity and though thinking may well not be housed in a body, he is forced to conclude that thinking's indubitable existence proves he is "at least something," as thinking exists, and thinking requires some sort of thinker, however abstract: "I am a true thing and am truly existing; but what kind of thing? I have said it already: a thinking thing."⁴⁹ Descartes moves from here to conclude that, because something with a lesser reality cannot produce something with a greater one, God must exist, because the thinking thing, which he has proven himself to be, has an idea of a supreme, perfect being. Because the thinker is himself demonstrably not perfect, that idea must have come from somewhere else, and it could not, logically, have come from anywhere other than such a supreme being itself. Thus, from violently cleared intellectual ground, Descartes gains certainty about his and God's existence, yet personal identity and the physical body maintain what he calls a "real distinction."⁵⁰

Indeed, it turns out to be not his rational proof of God's existence but the much more impactful sundering of mind and body Descartes formulated so memorably with his "cogito, ergo sum" that forms Western thought's ground zero.⁵¹ Enlightenment's core premises become "I think, therefore I am" and its corollary, "I am not my body." Rather than succeeding in making God's existence "evident to everybody" via his methodical approach to human knowledge, the Cartesian legacy is instead most often framed as an urgent, insoluble puzzle: What relation does our mental experience, our consciousness, bear to the external world, including the physical senses of our own bodies? In putting forward his dreaming argument and attendant *genium malignum*, Descartes unleashed radical doubt: "thinking" alone remains, everything else is uncertain. This Enlightenment prioritization of mind over body just as surely connects with colonialism and capitalist expropriation: it grounds the perspective that abstract reason indexes humanity and underwrites the drive to deny that such reason exists among enslaved, colonized, and other exploited peoples.

In a discussion of Atlantic slavery, Descartes's frisson of excitement at discovering himself to be a thing ("a true thing . . . a thinking thing") stands out. Descartes's connections to enslavement and its legacies are complex. In contrast to most of his philosophical contemporaries, he mentions slavery only twice in his writings (and obliquely even then). Yet he lived and wrote in Holland as the Dutch West India Company was establishing itself as the primary European trafficker of enslaved persons.[52] In Joan Dayan's view, it is Descartes's intellectual labor in *Discourse on Method* and *Meditations on First Philosophy* that clears the ground for the French Code noir, the system of laws governing enslaved labor in French colonies. "Descartes's methodical but metaphoric dispossession," Dayan writes, "becomes the basis for the literal expropriation and dehumanization necessary to turn a man into a thing."[53] On a material level, the commerce in human beings provided precisely the kind of leisured retreat needed for Descartes to conduct his thought experiment, withdrawn from the world, "sitting here next to the fire, wearing my winter dressing gown . . . holding this sheet of paper in my hands."[54] Descartes cites Amsterdam as an ideal place for his work precisely because it was a city full of "a very busy people more careful of its own business than curious of others'" providing "a solitary and retired" retreat, where a strong military presence ensured residents' ability to "enjoy the fruits of peace with the more security."[55] Writing a friend in 1631, he links this peace and security directly to enslaved labor, noting the satisfaction he felt seeing ships "come in, bringing us abundance of all that the Indies produce and every rare thing in Europe."[56] Material wealth, flowing from violently extracted labor to lavishly supply the metropole, literally furnished the material environment that yielded the human being as a "thinking thing."

Descartes's material benefit and positive view of the products of New World slavery would tend to confirm the idea that his philosophizing helped establish its emerging ideological bases. Yet others have argued that Cartesian universalism, whatever became of it in the hands of Enlightenment thinkers later on, ultimately inveighs against justifications for enslavement. As Timothy J. Reiss points out, the Cartesian thinker's disembodiment renders "everything except human mind as purely accidental, making all facets of body, including sex and skin color, insignificant."[57] More strongly, decolonial thinker Aimé Césaire, in his own *Discourse* (which bears a structural as well as titular relation to Descartes's own), calls later European classification of divergent categories of the human ("their insistence on the marginal, 'separate' character of non-whites" and their equally fervent insistence that their conclusions are "based on the firmest rationalism") a *betrayal* of the Cartesian legacy, a "barbaric repudiation, for the sake of the cause, of Descartes's statement, the charter of universalisms, that 'reason . . . is found whole and entire in each man,' and that 'where individuals of the same species are concerned, there may be degrees in respect of their accidental qualities, but not in respect of their forms, or natures.'"[58] In Césaire's view, the Cartesian cogito was an important marker of universal human being. At the same time, however, Césaire famously denounced colonization as "thingification,"[59] where the encounter between colonizer and colonized razed Indigenous societies, cultures, institutions, religions, lands, and art and replaced human contact with "relations of domination and submission."[60] Reason establishes universal human being, Césaire suggests, but not by limiting the human to a "thing."

Descartes was writing before enslavement was widely or explicitly racialized. Taking slavery as a permanent feature of human society, philosophers contemporary to Descartes debated its ethical basis: Was it natural law (e.g., some were made to serve others) or civil (e.g., capture in a just war or punishment for a crime)? Later thinkers tended to draw on those who saw it as part of natural law to establish racial difference as justifying enslavement, while insistence that enslavement could only be established in civil law, with no basis in natural, ultimately helped pave the way for antislavery jurisdiction like the Somerset case (1772), which held that slavery was illegal in England (though not its colonies), because it had never been established in civil (positive) English law and was, Chief Justice Lord Mansfield claimed, patently abhorrent to natural law.[61] Possibly Descartes intended his entire project to implicitly justify slavery and settler colonialism as part of natural law. In his opening letter, he emphasizes that knowing God does not require special revelation. Rather, this knowledge "is easier to achieve than the many things we know about creatures, and is so utterly easy that *those without this knowledge are blameworthy*."[62] Moreover, Descartes argues, the Bible itself supports this position that scripture is not necessary to know God: "in *Romans*

Chapter 1, it is said that they are 'without excuse' . . . [because] everything that can be known about God can be shown by reasons drawn exclusively from our own mind."[63] It is perhaps not too far a leap to imagine that "those without this knowledge" refers to Indigenous Americans and Africans. Their "blameworthiness," as non-Christians, would provide ethical grounds for their subjugation.

Yet regardless of what Descartes may have intended, Walker takes this Cartesian principle, that ultimately God may be more easily known than the things of this world, as promising freedom for subjugated peoples. Where Descartes takes radical doubt as his first principle, claiming everything else has been razed to the ground, Walker more robustly acknowledges that a prior step is a still more radical faith. Walker's distinctive ontology thus builds on this cornerstone to grasp a reality not separate from but intertwined with the speculative and the fantastical. Of course, the fact remains that even Descartes could not doubt the entire world without recourse to the supernatural intervention of an evil genius. Early on, Descartes anticipates resistance to his work, suggesting, "Perhaps there are some who would rather deny so powerful a God [for whom he a few paragraphs later substitutes an evil genius] than believe that everything else is uncertain."[64] From our own historical standpoint, after secularism's broad reach, is important to remember that modern philosophies do not jettison divinity in establishing humanism. Discussing Ethiopian philosopher Zara Yacob (1599–1692), whose 1667 *Hatata* inquires into faith's rationality, Gordon reminds us that for Africana as well as European thinkers of the seventeenth century, "critical self-examination of faith is not a threat to God but a presumption of the compatibility of faith with God. . . . [W]hereas medieval thought appealed to faith above reason, both men [Descartes and Yacob] ultimately saw reason and God as consistent. This is a feature of the rationalist dimension of Enlightenment thought."[65] In reconstructing Descartes's legacy, Walker likewise assumes belief in God as rational. Where Descartes plays with the idea that in the place of an omnibenevolent God there might exist an evil genius intent on deceiving humanity, Walker emphasizes several times in the *Appeal* that he is convinced that God is a God of justice: God is not a deceiver; rather, deception follows from failure to accept this universally knowable truth. God's justice is Walker's first principle: existence itself follows from it. Thinking is not primary, the world cannot be rebuilt on a foundation of thought alone, and humans are not things.

"A Peculiar Creature"

If Walker doubts the world but is convinced of God's justice, he is equally certain of Black humanity, though it was increasingly called into question in the centuries between Descartes and Walker. It can sometimes seem surprising, even paradoxical, that virulently dividing humans into biologically distinct races has roots in Enlightenment universalism. Yet as Immanuel Wallerstein has argued, *difference* too is an Enlightenment concept; "the other face of the inclusiveness of citizenship was exclusion."[66] Cedric Robinson emphasizes racialization's centrality to this history: "The tendency of European civilization through capitalism was . . . not to homogenize but to differentiate—to exaggerate regional, subcultural, and dialectical differences into 'racial' ones."[67] In modernity, then, "the human" has never been universal by default. Modern "scientific" classifications of the human created racialized, classed, and gendered "others." As Sylvia Wynter has shown, to allege these divisions as "biological" and "natural" is to conflate the human with capital-*M* "Man" (white, Western, male, heterosexual), while dividing the rest of us into sub- or even nonhumans. Twenty-first-century posthumanists, noting these many contradictions, have represented "the human" as a kind of reductio ad absurdum, a failed concept with which we ought to dispense as quickly as possible. Yet thinkers across the Black diaspora, from Fanon to Wynter and, more recently, Alexander Weheliye, have not been so eager to dispense with the human: they have instead sought its improvisatory, even speculative, renderings within the tradition of the oppressed. Walker stands as an early exemplar of this line of thought, though he rarely features in such scholarship. Thus, as we have seen, the *Appeal* powerfully exemplifies Sharpe's claims that Black life is human life overshadowing its own negation, persisting "in the wake" of slavery, of death, and even of consciousness. Walker's *Appeal* considers varieties of a universal humanity from the perspective of the oppressed and exploited. At the same time, Enlightenment ideas, not yet a century old, of genius as an unlikely lawbreaker, helped the *Appeal* circulate through circum-Atlantic print networks and establish his theory of outlaw humanism.

To make these points, Walker engages Thomas Jefferson's philosophical thought and political legacies still more directly than Descartes's skepticism. The historical vantage point is much closer, separated by just one generation and occupying proximate physical, if not socioeconomic, geographies. He names Jefferson as a key interlocutor, arguing that "unless we try to refute Mr. Jefferson's arguments respecting us, we will only establish them." Namely, Walker wants to dispel the belief, which Jefferson forwarded, that Black people constituted an inferior race, so far below the white race as to be effectively denied membership in what Walker terms "the human family." Where Jefferson regrets a perceived paucity of "evidence" regarding the particularities of the subspecies of *Homo sapiens* identified by Linnaeus: *Europaeus, Africanus, Asiaticus,* and *Americanus,*

Walker declares that the human's universal sameness is transparent and not in need of proof. "Man, in all ages and all nations of the earth, is the same. Man is a peculiar creature— . . . though he may be subjected to the most wretched condition upon earth, yet the spirit and feeling which constitute the creature, man, can never be entirely erased from his breast. . . . [H]e cannot get rid of it." Here Walker marshals a radical Black humanist universalism explicitly opposed to Jefferson's liberal biologist construction of the racialized human, divided by subgroups.

In *Notes on the State of Virginia* (1785), the only book he ever published, Jefferson famously enumerates multiple disparaging observations about Black people. Consistent with his faith in empirical method, he recognizes his evidence as limited and soundly critiques his fellow settler-colonists' ongoing failure to collect and collate the data needed to support his hypothesis that Black people comprise a "distinct race" that is intellectually and physically "inferior": "To our reproach it must be said, that though for a century and a half we have had under our eyes the races of black and of red men, they have never yet been viewed by us as subjects of natural history. I advance it therefore as a suspicion only, that the blacks, whether originally a distinct race, or made distinct by time and circumstances, are inferior to the whites in the endowments both of body and mind." In forwarding this as "suspicion," Jefferson builds on a tradition of Cartesian skepticism to draw the relationship between white and Black instantiations of the human into doubt. Jefferson slots directly into modern philosophy's trajectory when he queries Black and white humanity's parity and reproaches American natural history's "sluggishness" to establish racial distinctiveness as a fact rather than speculation. That is to say, after Descartes willed himself to imagine away his body and reconstructed himself as a "thinking thing," his intellectual heirs set out to determine the nature of that thing. As Gordon explains, "What is significant about the question of modernism is that it brought the human self as an object of study to center stage and along with it the problem of the human being that supports that self."[68] From this perspective, we can see that most glosses of modern humanism miss a key point. Humanism is commonly understood as taking the human, rather than the divine, as foundational to inquiry about the world and circumstances in which we find ourselves, yet Enlightenment humanism in actual practice precisely unmoors the human. Just as early theocentric models explored the nature and being of *divinity* (and set the stage, as we see in Descartes, for humanism), modern humanism relentlessly queries the nature and being of *humanity*.

Walker perceived that such thinking was dangerous: "This very verse, brethren, having emanated from Mr. Jefferson, a much greater philosopher the world never afforded, has in truth injured us more, and has been as great a barrier to our emancipation as any thing that has ever been advanced against us." Walker discerns that exposing the human to empirical science opens a troubling possibility that had not previously existed—namely, a finely regulated field of scientifically distinct humans. This is precisely how "Enlightened" Americans came to produce such unprecedented suffering among "the coloured citizens of the world." A hierarchical separation of biologically distinct human "races" replaced, or rather modified, the earlier great chain of being. Across the eighteenth century, Andrew S. Curran describes a "nefarious shift in the ontological status of 'black' and implicitly, 'white' anatomy," during which "the concept of blackness was increasingly dissected, handled, measured, weighed, and used as a demonstrable wedge between human categories. More than just a descriptor, blackness became a thing, defined . . . by its supposed materiality."[69] Although each race remained "human," or *Homo sapiens*, propertied white men stood atop the hierarchy, much as monarchs had in earlier theocentric models. Weheliye calls this economically motivated sociobiological process a "disciplining" of humanity "into full humans, not-quite-humans, and nonhumans." Blackness indexes "a changing system of unequal power structures that apportion and delimit which humans can lay claim to full human status and which cannot."[70] By the 1830s an influential race science emerged to disaggregate and discipline the human, just as Jefferson had wished. On a societal and economic level, the long-standing, entwined operation of criminalization produced and maintained these racialized gradations.

Recognizing these connections, Walker penned the *Appeal* in part to refute Jefferson. Ironically, in writing *Notes on the State of Virginia*, Jefferson himself was similarly concerned with refuting a science with which he disagreed and that operated against his interests. Specifically, the text refuted an influential European thesis of New World degeneration, which French naturalist Comte de Buffon most notably forwarded, along with Abbé Raynal and Abbé de Pauw. Buffon claimed that the "New World," because of its cold and humid climate, was a degeneration of the old, its animal life smaller and weaker (excepting reptiles and insects), its plant life less varied and vigorous. Raynal and de Pauw amplified this thesis to argue that even *European* plants, animals, and humans *also* became feeble and stunted when transplanted to the Americas. Jefferson feared for the new nation's future should such theories spread. Indeed, they were already widely held even beyond scholarly works such as Buffon's *Histoire naturelle*. Magazines, textbooks, and popular poetry espoused American degeneracy, and processes were afoot to stop European immigration owing to this growing scientific consensus.[71] In *Notes*, Jefferson presents extensive data to argue that American flora and fauna, from outsized mastodon fossils to Indigenous peoples, are not degenerate but actually bigger and better than their European counterparts.

Jefferson's anxieties for America's future should the degeneration theory spread still further were not limited to economic impact, European immigration, or public opinion. He also feared the incipient racialization of *all* American-born people that this theory encoded. In an era when environmentalism, or the view that human differences were ascribable to variations in climate and landscape, still predominated, Jefferson advocated for a science that would establish human difference as instead primarily innate: a modern science of race. While he certainly wanted to prove that the New World environment was superior, he also sought to demonstrate that human variation was linked not primarily to environment but rather to race: the subspecies Linnaeus forwarded, Jefferson opined, while tied to geography in their *origin*, held even when peoples from those subspecies moved to different climates. In sharp contrast to his aforementioned view of Black people, "inferior to the whites in the endowments both of body and mind," Indigenous Americans, Jefferson believed, would prove to be "formed in mind as well as in body, on the same module with the 'Homo sapiens Europæus.'" Thus, we can see Jefferson wanting to win on two counts: the New World climate is as good as, perhaps better than, the Old; and/but human subspecies or races do not change as a result of climate. Europæus remains Europæus; Africanus, Africanus.

White supremacy's staying power, of course, owes much to its lability, the way it shape-shifts, often in overtly self-contradictory fashion, to fit changing political and economic imperatives. The late eighteenth century represented a crisis point for white supremacy, and Jefferson threw his hat in the ring to protect white Americans from associations with degeneracy and more firmly position Black Americans as inferior.[72] Yet in any study of white supremacy, fidelity to the ultimate inconsistency that characterizes many sources remains crucial. This is certainly true of Jefferson's *Notes*, a text that is frequently at odds with itself. Like other white European, British, and American thinkers of his age, Jefferson remains only partially in thrall to his preexisting prejudices, and his natural history commitments do not always neatly align with his political and economic commitments.[73] As Curran shows vis-à-vis the primarily French context to which Jefferson was responding, this was also true of Voltaire, and even more notably Raynal. Raynal's *Historie* at once contains what Marlene Daut describes as some of the most pernicious descriptions of Black racial inferiority and, albeit with input from Jean de Pechméja, by far the era's most vociferous condemnation of slavery.[74] Via Pechméja, Raynal (whom Toussaint Louverture himself read in Haiti) even goes so far as to predict of the rise of a heroic Black liberator.[75] Likewise, Jefferson, in the very text that castigates Black intellectual capacity, also excoriates enslavement's fundamental immorality.

Take, for example, Jefferson's discussion of customs and manners in query 18, focalizing the danger enslavement poses to white people: "And can the liberties of a nation be thought secure when we have removed their only firm basis, a conviction in the minds of the people that these liberties are of the gift of God? That they are not to be violated but with his wrath? Indeed I tremble for my country when I reflect that God is just: that his justice cannot sleep forever." Though Jefferson, unlike Walker, is not noted for emotionality, such passages tell a different story. Figuring God's justice as a slumbering beast liable to waken at any moment and wreak havoc with the status quo, Jefferson is manifestly not "deceived," in Walker's sense. Rather, because Jefferson actually shares Walker's foundational conviction that God is a God of justice, he is therefore rightly afraid. Remarking that God's justice "cannot sleep forever," Jefferson conjures the Cartesian dreamer, as Walker will decades later:

> Considering numbers, nature and natural means only, a revolution of the wheel of fortune, an exchange of situation, is among possible events: that it may become probable by supernatural interference! The Almighty has no attribute which can take side with us in such a contest.—But it is impossible to be temperate and to pursue this subject through the various considerations of policy, of morals, of history natural and civil. We must be contented to hope they will force their way into every one's mind. I think a change already perceptible, since the origin of the present revolution. The spirit of the master is abating, that of the slave rising from the dust, his condition mollifying, the way I hope preparing, under the auspices of heaven, for a total emancipation, and that this is disposed, in the order of events, to be with the consent of the masters, rather than by their extirpation.

Where Jefferson despairs of enslavement's political, religious, or academic resolution, he fears that, unless "masters" like him "consent" to ending enslavement, apocalyptic race war may ultimately manifest as the "sure sign" that God (and his justice) is not sleeping.[76]

Jefferson's fears—that given a just God, enslavement's persistent atrocities can end only in bloody revolt—were realized in the Haitian Revolution. The revolution significantly impacted how white British, American, and European peoples developed and deployed the category of the human. On the heels of Haitian Black self-emancipation, white supremacist thought did not diminish but increased, with reinvigorated arguments for African intellectual inferiority, or what Curran describes as "cognitive blackness":[77]

> Much of what was ultimately written about the black African at this time can be tied to a belief in a new cognitive determinism that was increasingly projected on the nègre. In his 1797 *Etudes de l'homme physique et moral*, for example, J.-A. Perrequa portrayed black minds of an entirely "degraded nature" and "doomed sometimes to stupidity, sometimes to the most extravagant delirium of the imagination." ... In 1800, the influential philosopher Joseph-Marie de Gérando developed many of these ideas ... stating that the nègre's intellectual faculties were characterized by a type of mental "void."[78]

Such shifting debates about Black intellect in the late eighteenth and early nineteenth centuries interface directly with the ongoing efforts to discipline humans into racialized subgroups. Yet the question was not, as late twentieth- and twenty-first-century writers have presupposed, legislating whether those occupying these racialized subgroups were human. The question was how to establish human difference and make it politically, economically, and culturally meaningful.

Recently, literary scholars like Jeannine DeLombard and Stephen Best have argued that enslavers always recognized enslaved people as human. DeLombard points out that a transition in definitions of the human has perpetuated this misidentification: over the course of the twentieth century, the category of the human came to assume and imply dignity. Although this association of humanity and dignity existed during the era of New World enslavement, it had yet to become naturalized. DeLombard moves from this observation to stake a larger claim, that today's widespread belief that enslavers failed to see the enslaved as human relies on anachronistic misapplications of post–World War II understandings of the term. This larger claim, however, downplays the degree to which the category of the human was itself radically up for debate across the eighteenth and nineteenth centuries. Liberal white abolitionists, spurred on by Josiah Wedgwood, are clearly visible on this terrain. But Black radical thinkers like Walker and, as we have seen, Abraham Johnstone before him, also recognized that enslavers and white supremacists explicitly sought to restrict full humanity. In the eighteenth and nineteenth centuries, there was no singular definitive quality of the human, such as dignity. Thus, following the Haitian Revolution, it was precisely inasmuch as the resistant agency on display in Saint-Domingue obviously marked Black dignity that it occasioned a flurry of writing on Black intellectual inferiority. This dehumanizing discourse sought to establish full humanity as white people's exclusive property, even or especially in the face of Black assertion of universal humanity. Indeed, the dehumanizing racist ontologies this period generated, though overtly repudiated after the Holocaust, remain potent. Moreover, our present moment, a "genomic age" when belief in race as biology has troublingly begun to regain respectability, is perhaps not the time for scholars to disavow the relevance of the period's explicit and implicit attempts to dehumanize via racialization and criminalization.[79]

Nevertheless, the observation that the enslaved were in some real sense always recognized as human even as these dehumanizing discourses raged offers salutary reminders. As Walter Johnson has emphasized, it was precisely enslaved people's human capacities that made enslavement so profitable. Moreover, humans were, and are, perfectly capable of treating others whom they recognize as human abhorrently. Therefore, much as the tradition of liberal education might like to pretend otherwise, mere *recognition* of fellow humanity has never been sufficient to prevent atrocity. From this perspective, it becomes clear that racialization is not a problem of knowledge that needs to be solved by convincing humans to recognize others' humanity. It is not the job of education alone. As Walker demonstrates, it is a matter of justice, whether framed as political, economic, or divine. The question encircling Wedgwood's famous abolitionist medallion, "Am I not a Man and a Brother?" was indeed in this sense a rhetorical one. Nevertheless—as the medallion at the same time indexes—the category of the human was in this period explicitly, indeed hotly, contested. In abolitionists' hands, what was a problem of justice began to masquerade as a problem of knowledge.

Walker is clear in his position that Black people in America are "the most wretched, degraded and abject set of beings that ever lived since the world began." No matter how deplorable, how undignified their condition, Walker asserts that humans, universally, remain human. Taking a global, world-historical vantage point, Walker argues that it is precisely white *denial* of Black people's humanity that is so unprecedented: "Show me a page of history, either sacred or profane . . . which maintains, that the Egyptians heaped the *insupportable insult* upon the children of Israel, by telling them that they were not of the *human family*. Can the whites deny this charge?" Over nearly ninety pages, Walker repeats this kind of assertion many times. He frequently excoriates whites for treating Black men and women "even worse than they do the brutes that perish" and almost as often castigates Black people for what he perceives as their own brutish behavior ("I ask you, in the name of that God who made us, have we, in consequence of oppression, nearly lost the spirit of man, and, in no very trifling degree, adopted that of brutes?"). Yet nowhere does "brutalize" (to make animal) or "dehumanize" (to make nonhuman) appear, though both words have an Enlightenment provenance. And not only are all humans always and forever human, regardless of circumstance; all humans are imbued with a "spirit and feeling" they "cannot get rid of." Walker was deeply cognizant of the dangers that the white supremacist manufacture of a "scientific" regulation of distinct human types posed to Black life.

This is why, at the very moment when leading scientists sought to establish racial difference as *scientific*, Walker insists on the human's *peculiar* sameness: "Man, in all ages and all nations of the earth, is the same. Man is a peculiar creature—... though he may be subjected to the most wretched condition upon earth, yet the spirit and feeling which constitute the creature, man, can never be entirely erased from his breast.... [H]e cannot get rid of it." Black humanity, for Walker, is emphatically not a subject of knowledge. Like God's justice, Black humanity is ineluctable: it both mobilizes and exceeds doubt. The cornerstones of Walker's Black radical worldview, then, are universal humanity and divine justice. Moreover, pace DeLombard, it is precisely *dignity* that these dual premises confer: "If it were possible for the whites always to keep us ignorant and miserable, and make us work to enrich them and their children, and insult our feelings by representing us as talking Apes, what would they do? But glory, honour and praise to Heaven's King, that the sons and daughters of Africa, will, in spite of all the opposition of their enemies, stand forth in all the dignity and glory that is granted by the Lord to his creature man." We can see, then, that Walker responds to Thomas Jefferson's virulent questioning of Black humanity not so much by refuting his claims as by refusing them. For Walker, the human is a "peculiar creature" that always and in all cases knows itself to be human. In thus refusing to cede Black humanity as a subject of knowledge, Walker's denunciation of white supremacy far exceeds abolitionism's liberal framework.

"Endowments of Mind"

Given his universalism, it is not surprising that Walker's perspective throughout the *Appeal* is explicitly global. Indeed, he begins the pamphlet by stating his expectation that "all coloured men, women and children, of every nation, language and tongue under heaven, will try to procure a copy of this Appeal and read it, or get some one to read it to them.... Let them remember, that ... the day of our redemption from abject wretchedness draweth near, when we shall be enabled, in the most extended sense of the word, to stretch forth our hands to the LORD our GOD." Walker's is no small ambition: he quite literally wants to reach *all* "coloured" people on earth with his message that Black collectivity will precipitate oppression's inevitable, likely violent, end. The reach of this coalition Walker describes in almost superhuman terms: "enabled, in the most extended sense of the word." He predicts a supremely able worldwide coalition of Black people, endowed by their Creator with the capacity to change the world itself. Up to this point, I have discussed Walker's reconstruction of Cartesian skepticism: to draw the world into doubt, he shows that divinity must be assumed a priori. This allows him to refute the dominant Enlightenment genre of humanism, which purportedly establishes human being and equality but in fact throws both vertiginously into question. In this concluding section, I will demonstrate that Walker similarly excavates the modern category of genius. Where thinkers like Jefferson link genius with respectable individualism, Walker builds on Descartes and censures Jefferson to show that modern genius is in fact transgressive and collective.

Jefferson's proto-eugenicist conception of genius maps onto the racial hierarchies he theorizes in *Notes on the State of Virginia*. He holds that Indigenous Americans, unlike people of African origin, have many qualities in common with European people, including a capacity to produce works of lasting genius: "They astonish you with strokes of the most sublime oratory; such as prove their reason and sentiment strong, their imagination glowing and elevated." He frames this opinion in direct contrast to Black Americans, who, despite proximity to supposedly elevating European influences, do not in his view produce enduring art: "But never yet could I find that a black had uttered a thought above the level of plain narration; never see even an elementary trait of painting or sculpture." Jefferson was aware that any grounds for forming such conclusions were limited: his evidence was anecdotal and drawn from his own first-person experience. He was also, we will recall, quick to call out Buffon for theorizing American degeneracy on the basis of unreliable data. Perhaps to mitigate the hypocrisy of his own unsupported theorizing, he again critiques natural history's reticence in categorizing human differences: "The circumstance of superior beauty, is thought worthy attention in the propagation of our horses, dogs, and other domestic animals; why not in that of man?" Jefferson argues that, given the attention already paid to animal pedigree, cultivating superior human bloodlines must be equally worthwhile, despite European neglect in compiling the foundational research into human differences needed to support such a program.

These proto-eugenicist frameworks and the objectification they require reach horrifyingly through the twentieth century and indeed into the twenty-first, evincing a staying power surpassing institutional racism. Jefferson's embrace of humanity as an aesthetic-cum-scientific project (following Johann Friedrich

Blumenbach) reveals how the commodifying logics upholding North American institutional enslavement reach across, even as they establish, racial lines. This rhetorical question about eugenics' self-evident merit is of course not innocent or "merely" scientific: it encodes and predicts palpable violence. Jefferson's question shows that eugenicist objectification is all encompassing: superior "endowments of mind and body" ought to be a key consideration in propagating humankind writ large. This is not to say that such objectification does material harm to those atop this hierarchy: white people will benefit, and Black people will suffer, as what is determined to be "superior beauty"—whiteness—indeed comes increasingly to be "thought worthy of attention" in human reproduction. If the laws and logics of enslavement extend well past its historical era, and also entail a de facto animalization and objectification of all humans, Jefferson's extended ethnography typifies the anti-Black racism fueling these structures.

Jefferson views Black life as lacking the depth and imaginative qualities that undergird the humanist tradition. To argue that Black existence is primarily concrete and physical, rather than reflective and abstract, he claims that the experiences of love and grief alike are fleeting for Black people.

> They are more ardent after their female: but love seems with them to be more an eager desire, than a tender delicate mixture of sentiment and sensation. Their griefs are transient. Those numberless afflictions, which render it doubtful whether heaven has given life to us in mercy or in wrath, are less felt, and sooner forgotten with them. In general, their existence appears to participate more of sensation than reflection. To this must be ascribed their disposition to sleep when abstracted from their diversions, and unemployed in labour. An animal whose body is at rest, and who does not reflect, must be disposed to sleep of course. Comparing them by their faculties of memory, reason, and imagination, it appears to me, that in memory they are equal to the whites; in reason much inferior, as I think one could scarcely be found capable of tracing and comprehending the investigations of Euclid; and that in imagination they are dull, tasteless, and anomalous.

Jefferson makes these claims, that Black life is limited to rote memorization, lust, and passing feelings of disappointment or sadness, incapable of geometry, romance, and tragedy, in order to establish the greater value of white life. Black people have a strong "disposition to sleep" when not actively employed because their capacities for reflection and creativity are severely limited, like "an animal whose body is at rest, and who does not reflect," Jefferson opines. Of course, it is not surprising that limitations in Jefferson's thinking here are conceptual as well as ethical. In describing sleep as animal rather than human, Jefferson neglects the fact that for thinkers like Descartes, sleep is no impediment to reflection but instead a spur to dream, reason, and philosophize. Despite his own failure to reflect on the links between reflection, imagination, and sleep, Jefferson insists that Black life differs from white perhaps most saliently in the realm of imagination. Here again, he claims that "sensation" marks Black experience in contrast to the "reflective" complexities of the white experience he presents as normative.

In Jefferson's modern usage, "Genius" refers to the "particular talents" that spring from abstract, reflective capacities. His use aligns with ancient ideas of genius as a guiding spirit, imbued in all creation, but it combines this perspective with Enlightenment classificatory schemes in order to gauge the relative value of each group's individual artistic production. Thus the "genius and mental powers" of "Homo sapiens Europaeus" form the gold standard against which all other human "types" are to be measured. Jefferson's assessment African-descended people's genius is famously dim:

> Never yet could I find that a black had uttered a thought above the level of plain narration; never see even an elementary trait of painting or sculpture. In music they are more generally gifted than the whites with accurate ears for tune and time, and they have been found capable of imagining a small catch. Whether they will be equal to the composition of a more extensive run of melody, or of complicated harmony, is yet to be proved. Misery is often the parent of the most affecting touches in poetry.—Among the blacks is misery enough, God knows, but no poetry. Love is the peculiar oestrum of the poet. Their love is ardent, but it kindles the senses only, not the imagination. Religion indeed has produced a Phyllis Whately; but it could not produce a poet.

In this account, Black genius is marked by lack: apart from limited musical talent, which is sensual rather than harmonic, that is, rational, Jefferson claims that Black oratory, visual art, and poetry are nonexistent. His diminishment of Phillis Wheatly's achievement, as religious enthusiasm, not artistic skill or talent, extends even to what seems a willful mistaking of the celebrity poet's name, a thingification rendering her more "what" than "who." Given white supremacy's predilection for discarding opposing evidence, Walker is well aware that his own object lesson in the *Appeal*'s rhetorical tour de force will offer limited corrective. These and related passages disparaging Black genius are what Walker has in mind when he enjoins "each of my brethren, who has the spirit of a man, to buy a copy of Mr. Jefferson's 'Notes on Virginia,' and put it in the hand of his son. For let no one of us suppose that the refutations which have been written by our white friends are enough—they are whites—we are blacks." Where Jefferson refuses to credit Black genius, Walker does not make the same mistake about Jefferson.

Walker recognizes Jefferson's reach and his many key insights, and he knows that such an opponent requires direct confrontation. Castigating Jefferson's logic while praising his "great learning," he writes, "Has Mr. Jefferson declared to the world, that we are inferior to the whites, both in the endowments of our bodies and of minds? It is indeed surprising, that a man of such great learning, combined with such excellent natural parts, should speak so of a set of men in chains. I do not know what to compare it to." Describing Jefferson's "excellent natural parts," Walker likewise remains on Jefferson's natural history terrain, to underscore that by Jefferson's own terms, his conclusions are deeply flawed. Walker appropriates European associations of Blackness with darkness and violence to underscore Black capacity, agency, and humanity. He attacks Jefferson's description of God-given Blackness as "unfortunate," saying, "It pleased Him to make us black—which colour, Mr. Jefferson calls unfortunate ! ! ! ! ! !" Here again, Walker rejects Jefferson's move into subjective territory and away from either empirical or theological certainty: "But is Mr. Jefferson's assertions [sic] true? viz. 'that it is unfortunate for us that our Creator has been pleased to make us black.' We will not take his say so, for the fact." This "say so" is mere opinion. It is no substitute for either logic or material evidence, though, Walker claims, that evidence is forthcoming: "The world will have an opportunity to see whether it is unfortunate for us, that our Creator has made us darker than the whites." Precisely Black vengeance will provide the needed material evidence that Blackness *is* fortunate, for Black people, and unfortunate only from the perspective of the enslavers on whom that vengeance is released.

Frequently, Jefferson's "suspicions" about Black people's mental and physical inferiority silently morph into natural fact, "the real distinctions which nature has made." This presumed inferiority, alongside the historical circumstance of white injury and the speculation of future "provocations," form Jefferson's certainty that white and Black cannot peacefully coexist. Jefferson advocates Black colonization as a solution to the enmity that must naturally follow from centuries of racial exploitation:

> It will probably be asked, Why not retain and incorporate the blacks into the state, and thus save the expence of supplying, by importation of white settlers, the vacancies they will leave? Deep rooted prejudices entertained by the whites; ten thousand recollections, by the blacks, of the injuries they have sustained; new provocations; the real distinctions which nature has made; and many other circumstances, will

divide us into parties, and produce convulsions which will probably never end but in the extermination of the one or the other race.

Though Walker rejects Black inferiority, he follows Jefferson in vividly conjuring the specter of racial violence. Yet Walker is comparatively less dogmatic and more sanguine. As Kevin Pelletier notes, "Walker marshals the affects of love and terror and portends catastrophic consequences for America's slaveholders, even as he outlines a theory of sympathy that might save the nation from ruin."[80] Walker opposed Black colonization and devotes one of his four articles to railing against a particular deceit he dubbed "the colonizing trick," which aimed to further Black expropriation by enticing Black people to leave behind the wealth and prosperity their labor had engendered to start from nothing in new African settler colonies.

Whites must indeed eradicate their "deep rooted prejudices" for such a society to be possible, yet Walker, graciously, in the spirit of a universal humanity and true enlightenment, is willing to shoulder the burden of refuting Jefferson's speculations and answering his "physical and moral" objections to a just and shared future:

> Remember Americans, that we must and shall be free, and enlightened as you are, will you wait until we shall, under God, obtain our liberty by the Crushing arm of power? Will it not be dreadful for you? I speak Americans for your good. We must and shall be free I say, in spite of you. You may do your best to keep us in wretchedness and misery, to enrich you and your children but God will deliver us from under you. And wo, wo, will be to you if we have to obtain our freedom by fighting. Throw away your fears and prejudices then, and enlighten us and treat us like men, and we will like you more than we do now hate you, and tell us now no more about colonization, for America is as much our country, as it is yours.— Treat us like men, and there is no danger but we will all live in peace and happiness together.

Having already established universal humanity, Walker argues that history does not necessarily entail race war. Black people will happily live and work side by side with white people in any just future society. Walker's first principles of divine justice and universal humanity enable the possibility of peace that Jefferson's racial humanism disallows.

Where Jefferson states, "The Almighty has no attribute which can take side with us in such a contest," Walker asks, "Can the Americans escape God Almighty?" His answer is a resounding no. Yet peace is possible. Against Jefferson and related philosophical and political figures who exclude Black people from the aesthetic discourse of genius and then build on such exclusions to ultimately postulate the inevitability of racial violence, Walker's insistence of life from death entails a universal humanity and a collective genius that, albeit speculatively, allows for the possibility of another world. As we have seen, Walker embraces the Cartesian doubt about the world's existence. He thus claims both being and humanity, developing an alternate model for knowing that contravenes those styles of thought typically understood as Enlightenment. For Walker, to be convinced of its existence is first to see proof of justice. Where previous inheritors found in Descartes's legacy of radical doubt an unbearable loss of the world, Walker sees instead new ground from which freedom might spring.

Refusal to believe that the world is what it is may be painful for those living comfortable lives. For Walker, it is a beacon of possibility, as this refusal becomes a basis for global change. Walker's anger at the state of the world as he finds it is not simply volatile reactivity to white Americans' treatment of Black people. Instead, it indexes his recognition of reality's subjective aspects and his certainty that neither the reasoning mind nor the feeling body are reducible to "things." Walker's proactive doubt, his refusal to believe that the world is the way it is, is manifestly not despair. It is a radically hopeful first step toward changing that world via the imaginative construction of alternative realities. Walker's skepticism is unbelief in the unthinkable. This skepticism aims to transform what is unbelievable, unspeakable, and unbearable into the reasonable, comprehensible, and condonable, precisely by following the ethical imperatives that knowledge of divine justice and universal humanity require. His view comprehends a future that breaks radically with the present, because to be convinced of existence is first to see proof of justice. The possibility of the world's nonexistence is not terrifying but tantalizing, as it makes possible another world in which Black humanity can flourish.

In this speculative reworking of the Cartesian cogito, we might class Walker less as a founding father of Black nationalism and more as the first Afrofuturist, whose dreamworld of radical justice superseded the bloody, expropriative, avaricious 1820s United States that his senses revealed. In the 1994 essay "Black to the Future," in which he coined the term "Afrofuturism," Mark Dery questions why so few African Americans have written science fiction, an omission he finds "especially perplexing in light of the fact that African Americans, in a very real sense, are the descendants of alien abductees; they inhabit a sci-fi nightmare in which unseen but no less impassable force fields of intolerance frustrate their movements." While Dery is correct about science fiction's aptness for African

American concerns, it is a limited perspective on the genre indeed that fails to see the speculative "science fictional" aspects of Black cultural production across the centuries.[81] Cartesian contributions to "brain in a vat"–style science fiction are well known (*The Matrix* being a famous example). Where the Cartesian *genium malignum* threatened chaos in its dissolution of certainty about the world's existence, Walker's criminal genius persists in this same doubt and celebrates the potential nonexistence of this world: in so doing he awakens us to the fact that another world is indeed possible.

All accounts of genius concede its transgressive elements. But where most genealogies situate genius within Romanticism, Walker's outlaw humanism prompts us to revisit the category from the perspective of enslaved and free Black people. He occupies as well as theorizes the space of criminal genius, manifesting social existence not primarily as a writer or even as a living man but precisely in those spaces of death and transgression where liberal citizenship would most seem to exclude him. As we saw with Johnstone and Frost in the previous chapter and will see with Nat Turner in the next, this shift overturns a central aim of historically oriented scholarship: to return humanity to the dispossessed by belatedly establishing the humanity of those who had been excluded from the liberal project.[82] Calls to "give them back their agency" or "give voice" to the enslaved resound in such work even as multitudes did not seek or gain the kind of resistant agency that Walker scholarship typically emphasizes.[83]

Failure to recognize this aspect of Walker's project produces a liability to mistake him for an elitist guilty of diminishing Black culture and, indeed, genius. Sterling Stuckey, in his seminal study of Black culture during the era of enslavement, remains locked in this view:

> Walker helped establish a pattern repeated down to the close of the century and beyond—the almost total failure of most nationalists to recognize the artistic and spiritual genius of their people, a recognition essential to building on the positive and distinctive in black culture, to blacks estimating their cultural worth and that of the world around them. Failing even to acknowledge the existence of slave culture, though he had been exposed to it, he had little alternative to denouncing most of what he saw in Afro-American life as the tragic by-product of slavery and African backwardness.[84]

Stuckey emphasizes the cultural contributions of enslaved peoples in establishing the Black nationalist tradition, particularly the many direct links between what he termed "slave culture" and African cultures. He builds on Melville

Herskovits's rejection, in *The Myth of the Negro Past*, of the notion that enslaved and free African Americans retained nothing of their cultural heritage. Stuckey extends this work as a corrective to the argument, framed by E. Franklin Frazier in debate with Herskovits, that African American culture was distinct, retaining no direct African traces. His research guides readers through Walker's Wilmington and uncovers the numerous West African cultural practices to which Walker would have been exposed but does not directly mention. Yet while Stuckey's reading of Wilmington is itself useful and persuasive, his reading of Walker is thin.

Walker's vision was definitively community oriented. As he proclaimed in his speech at the founding of the Massachusetts General Coloured Association, "[There are t]wo and a half million coloured people in these United States. . . . Now, I ask, if . . . resolved to aid and assist each other to the utmost of their power, what mighty deeds could be done for the good of our cause?"[85] The *Appeal* was the culmination of this view. Describing Walker's foundational role in the later development of African American literary societies, McHenry states, "The importance of building coalitions, both to create a sense of national identity and collective spirit and to extend essential knowledge to the black community, would not have been lost on David Walker," who was centrally involved in developing "coalitions that would introduce new and specific ways to address the needs of the black community" and stood as forerunners to later literary societies that, likewise, would depend "on a sense of collective rather than individual effort."[86] *Pace* Stuckey, then, Walker's view of "Afro-American life" is not tragic but brimming with possibility, and, far from establishing "African backwardness," he champions Blackness as a harbinger of peace and justice. Stuckey misses all this because scholarly emphasis on the cultural contributions of enslaved peoples has too often gone hand in glove with critical privileging of Black self-determination as indexed by resistance and revolt. Across the board, this scholarship views Black cultural forms as an index of resistant humanity, resilient even in the face of the most horrific attacks. When scholars like Stuckey value Walker primarily for his militancy, they mistakenly view his *Appeal* as diminishing Black genius. Yet conceiving humanity as universal, in the face of enslavement's atrocities, Walker necessarily understands agency not as individualist but collective.

Exceeding abstract notions of the liberal, isolated subject, Walker's criminal genius does not demand recognition of the oppressed.[87] It does not clamor for admission to an Enlightenment universalism that somehow mistakenly excluded people like him. Neither does it reach for a past world that no longer exists. Rather, centering enslavement alongside racialization, Walker posits an outlaw humanism that, in straining the boundaries of legibility and law, may yet guide our unfinished projects of freedom. Assured of his existence, however degraded, Walker's reality incorporates justice not as some transcendent ideal but as a real force in the world-that-is (which, he suggests, we have reason to believe may indeed not be *this* world). His prophesy is that the collective, perhaps violent, enactment of these speculative realities will confirm the human not as possessive individual but as bearer of ineradicable justice for all people. Doubting the world itself *before* he doubts either divine justice or a universal human being, Walker meets the Enlightenment at its origin: the Cartesian cogito. When Walker writes in the *Appeal* that if apocalyptic race war does not shortly arrive, "it is because the world does not exist," he is not only making a theological argument about the primacy of divine justice. He is also placing Black humanity as ontologically prior to empirical reality and postulating criminal genius. Walker's proactive doubt, his refusal to countenance the world as it is, establishes the basis for world change. The Cartesian "evil genius" is a deceiver "of utmost power and cunning," whose potential to trick the senses threatens loss of the world: per Descartes, he "has employed all his energies to deceive me." But Walker's criminal genius is a liberator, whose selfsame potential for sense deception opens a speculative horizon of freedom.

CHAPTER FOUR

The Southampton Insurgency

In the context of the revolutionary Atlantic, 1793 was a pivotal year in the birth of criminal genius. Legal and cultural conceptions of crime blurred repeatedly: in the chaos of the yellow fever epidemic in Philadelphia, Toussaint Louverture's decision to join the Haitian Revolution, and Samuel Frost's retributive murder of Elisha Allen. The year also witnessed the legal trafficking of a woman later called Nancy from West Africa. She disembarked in 1793 in Southampton County, Virginia, to live and die legally enslaved. The historical record offers vanishingly little insight into her life or into how she would have experienced the Middle Passage's horrific dislocation. Though she was one of millions to board the floating tombs that metamorphosed free African women into enslaved, racialized American laborers, the written record fails to capture any firsthand account of their collective experience. While a handful of male-authored accounts exist, as Saidiya Hartman reminds us, "there is not one extant autobiographical narrative of a female captive who survived the Middle Passage."[1] If history has left Nancy's psychological, spiritual, and physical life opaque, it has nonetheless immortalized her son's name. After seven years away from her homeland, Nancy gave birth to Nat Turner. She quickly came to believe he was destined for greatness. But not before she attempted infanticide, an expression of her consuming hatred for life in Virginia's plantocracy. Acts like Nancy's formed part of what Lamonte Aidoo has described as part of a "genealogy of horror." For enslaved women, "the act of killing their children," or attempting to, was not a hideous crime but rather "an expression of black female agency, love, and insurgence against slavery."[2]

This chapter takes up this legacy of insurgence alongside the historical problems the archives of enslavement pose for understanding Nat Turner. *Partus sequitur ventrem*, following the condition of his enslaved mother, Virginia law classed Turner at his birth in 1800 as the property of one Benjamin Turner.[3] Just prior to his death by execution, the Southampton County Court convicted him of "conspiring to rebel and make insurrection," having "admitted he was one of the insurgents engaged in the late insurrection, and the Chief among them."[4] The date of this so-called crime, "conspiring to rebel and make insurrection," August 22, 1831, is one of the most-written-about dates in the annals of North American enslavement. But precisely what happened, and why, has been fiercely debated ever since Turner's enslaver Joseph Travis cried out to his wife in the middle of that night in shock and horror. This would be Travis's "last word" before "the work of a moment" sent husband, wife, and all their children to their deaths. Picking up where Travis left off, the popular press had much to say about that night. Newspapers, pamphlets, letters, and court records have left a historical archive brimming with (often conflicting) details, but ultimately these texts pose as many questions as they answer. Were the attacks on Southampton's enslaving families, beginning at the Travis house and encompassing more than fifteen households in all, motivated by passion: bloodlust, revenge, greed, or religious fanaticism? Or was the "work of death" that transpired that night political: Was it a revolt, a rebellion, an insurrection? This chapter argues that the framework of criminal genius addresses these enduring questions more productively than the empiricist historicist or the speculative literary approaches that have predominated in recent decades. I attend both to how the archive deploys the figure of the criminal genius and to how that figure develops in relation to Turner. This approach privileges the role of the aesthetic and decenters an authentic, historical Nat Turner. It acknowledges the limitations of the archive while also showing that any "choice"—between an outdated, racist interpretation of Turner as either a brigand or a fanatic, and a modern, retrospective figuration of Turner as a secular hero or freedom fighter—is a false one, as neither stands up to scrutiny.

Turner, thirty years old at the time of the insurgency, "had lived under the authority of as many as seven different adult slaveholders," most recently Travis. His legal owner was Travis's stepson, a twelve-year-old named Putman Moore. Moore would also die that night.[5] Though Turner seems to have played a secondary role in the murders themselves (with one exception, Margaret Whitehead), he led some sixty enslaved people the night of August 21 and into the morning of the 22nd.[6] They attacked sixteen houses, farms, and plantations and killed some fifty-seven members of Southampton's white enslaving families. The victims were disproportionately women, children, and infants.[7] It was the murder of infants that fueled, and sometimes still fuels, horror and outrage. Yet the Southampton Insurgency marked a grim chiasmus with Nancy's natal insurgency and with the legal doctrine of *partus sequitur ventrem*. The victims included a "little infant sleeping in his cradle" at the Travis house, who initially "was forgotten, until we had left the house and gone some distance, when Henry and Will returned and killed it."[8] In dying, this child followed the condition of its mother. Of those killed that night, ten were identified as mothers and thirty-one as children or grandchildren. As one newspaper reported five days after the attacks, "Their steps are everywhere marked with the blood of women and children."[9] The insurgents turned the enslavers' hereditary logic back on them. At the same time, the insurgents marked themselves for all but certain death. At his execution on November 11, 1831, Nat Turner made good on his mother's original attempt to save her son from enslaved existence.

Immediately after the events in Southampton in August 1831, there was an initial flurry of speculation that the "horrid massacre" was motivated by "banditry." After this theory died out, from the nineteenth century through the first half of the twentieth, the event was most often described in print as a "servile insurrection."[10] Yet this this characterization was contested from the beginning. Addressing Thomas R. Gray, his amanuensis and interlocutor, Turner calls the term "insurrection" directly into question: "You have asked me to give a history of the motives which induced me to undertake the late insurrection, as you call it."[11] This brief aside, "as *you* call it," indicates Turner's awareness that Gray's view of the event (as driven by what he calls Turner's "gloomy fanaticism")[12] explicitly differs from his own.[13] Herbert Aptheker likewise rejected "insurrection." His key early academic study favored "rebellion," which in his view acknowledged both the political dimensions and the scale of Turner's ambition: "An insurrection is not revolutionary; the aim of a rebellion is. A revolt is of less magnitude than a rebellion."[14] Henry Irving Tragle in turn revised Aptheker's designation. He agreed that "insurrection" failed to capture the political significance of the event, but in his introduction to his compilation of primary source material relating to the events in Southampton, he also rejects "rebellion," because of the event's relative numerical paucity (a force of a maximum of seventy persons and duration of less than seventy-two hours), along with the fact that Virginia law did not allow enslaved people to be tried for treason. Tragle's preferred term is thus "revolt."[15] Since Aptheker and Tragle's formative work, both "revolt" and "rebellion" have become the common descriptors, with Aptheker's preferred "rebellion" most often edging out "revolt," despite Tragle's later hesitations. Yet dissatisfaction with both has persisted. In his 2014 study, David F. Allmendinger highlights the fact that, a few days after Turner's capture, the *Norfolk Herald* reported that he was "very free in his confessions," including his belief that "he could succeed in conquoring [sic] *the county of Southampton* . . . as the white people did in the revolution."[16] Thus, while both "rebellion" and "insurrection" were common designations at the time, Allmendinger claims that "revolution" in fact "must have been the word [Turner] had in mind in the first sentence of his confession."[17] Notwithstanding this observation, Allmendinger himself most often uses the term "rising," which also appears in contemporary Black- and white-authored sources.[18]

Although this debate may seem stale and rhetorical, it has persisted because of its consequences for how we understand the event itself and what motivated it. I take on board many earlier scholars' viewpoints regarding specific designations' merits and weaknesses, and I generally agree with the historical arguments Aptheker, Tragle, and Allmendinger have variously put forward for the broad political motivations of Turner and his associates. Yet the lens of criminal genius suggests that another descriptor, lurking in the background of contemporary and historical accounts, may be the best of all: "insurgency." This term captures the many facets of the event as well as its deep political ambitions and the fact that it also, at the same time, stood in excess of these essentially legislative ends. "Insurgents" and "insurgency" are neither anachronistic, nor do they in any way minimize the event's significance. Both terms were used in 1831 yet, unlike Allmendinger's "rising," still today readily evoke the sense of radicalism that has rightly imbued interpretations of the event since the civil rights era. Perhaps most crucially, "insurgency," with its etymological connotations of *swelling toward* and *overflowing* aptly describes the liberatory horizon that shaped the event and its legacies of radical freedom, which exceeded strictly political or legislative aims such as legal emancipation.

The Southampton Insurgency, then, exemplifies criminal genius's creative, generative aspects by straining toward a radical freedom that exceeded established morality's frameworks. Although late nineteenth-century criminology is often credited as the first discourse to tie crime and genius together directly by associating the latter with ideas of degeneracy, the connection was actually forged decades earlier. *The Confessions of Nat Turner* and other documents representing the Southampton Insurgency offer a clear earlier linking of criminality and genius, and attention to this conjuncture helps us better understand both the insurgency and the early nineteenth-century category of criminal genius. It is neither the Romantic exceptional individual, nor the caricature archvillain that developed in the late nineteenth century. As with Walker's apocalyptic skepticism, we can see in the Southampton Insurgency Turner's reasoned argument for his own existence, rather than simply thwarted violence. The event's speculative horizon extends beyond legal reform and its politics of recognition. Bringing the lens of nineteenth-century criminal genius to bear on the Southampton Insurgency allows us to understand Turner as neither an individual hero nor an inscrutable madman but as a creative insurgent who, believing that another world was possible, moved beyond speculation to action. Turner and the other enslaved men and women who undertook this "work of death" rose against the legal statutes that upheld the slave system. But the fact of their resistance is not the event's most salient aspect: in violently challenging their legal status, the Southampton insurgents did much more than simply resist or seek to reform existing laws. Their "work of death" also conjured another world, beyond the grasp of law and rich with radical, transformative possibilities.

In the months following the insurgency, terror among white inhabitants of the Southern states seeded violent reprisals against enslaved and free Black populations, along with waves of repressive legislation further limiting enslaved peoples' access to literacy and ability to gather. By the late nineteenth century, the plantation myth and the rise of Jim Crow worked to bury the Southampton Insurgency's radicalism, although it persisted in African American vernacular traditions. Turner was represented in white historiography as a reprehensible individual who indiscriminately murdered innocent people for no conceivable reason other than his own fanaticism. By contrast, from the civil rights era to today, Turner is most often remembered as a revolutionary inspired by a deep sense of slavery's inherent injustice. To quote Malcolm X, "Nat Turner wasn't going around preaching pie-in-the-sky and 'non-violent' freedom for the black man."[19] For X and others, Turner has exemplified precisely the kind self-directed, willed, masculine resistance that remains the most familiar understanding of political agency. Given white supremacy's violent US history, it has naturally seemed imperative to restore such agency to the dispossessed. Yet, as I endeavor to show, when we read figures like Nat Turner as masculinist, self-determined exemplars of resistance, we wind up reinforcing the very history we seek to undermine. This chapter displaces the historical Turner from the center of the narrative, whether as presence or absence. Instead, I show how the problems of the historical record, in tandem with its certainties, in fact delineate the political specificity of the Southampton Insurgency: its illegibility generates its potency. In place of the masculinist hero, criminal genius offers a different story, with an insurgent, relational, and dynamic understanding of the human at its heart.[20]

"What Was Poetry . . . Is Now a Bloody Reality"

Recent decades have seen rigorous debate about the problems archival research poses to understanding Black experience. Recognizing that historical archives have been produced and maintained by those responsible for oppression, exploitation, violence, and other forms of harm, some have drawn the conclusion that these histories necessarily silence the voices of those thus harmed. Therefore, these scholars, writers, and artists argue, we must engage speculatively and creatively with the historical record and not allow it to dictate or limit what we can say. Hartman calls for a "critical fabulation" that remains faithful to what is known while also allowing scope to imagine what might have been.[21] By contrast, another set of scholars holds that archives themselves change based on what questions we ask. This perspective calls on academics to fill the silences of literary history not with speculative storytelling but rather with new lenses for further research. Eric Gardner thus enjoins scholars to rededicate ourselves to recovering those histories about which we say, too often and too quickly, "little is known."[22] And Derrick Spires notes, "Widening archives and accounts that decenter whiteness change the stories we can tell."[23] Criminal genius suggests one untapped vein to be mined between the poles of critical speculation and historical facticity. It weaves together insights from both lines of thought.

Among archives of enslavement, the Southampton Insurgency presents some unusual challenges. The events in Southampton constituted the deadliest armed insurgency to occur in North America since the thirteen colonies rebelled against Great Britain to achieve political sovereignty. As a result, and, unlike most archives of enslavement, the written and printed record relating to the Southampton Insurgency is characterized as much by abundance as lack. As Tragle writes, "The train of events which [Turner] set in motion can be ignored, but they cannot be erased; they are too deeply embedded in the written record of the time to allow that."[24] Although there has been more ink spilled over the Southampton Insurgency than perhaps any other discrete event in this history of North American enslavement, the result has not been greater clarity. This apparent richness has also been a source of confusion. The written and printed materials recording Turner's origin and life often do not hold up well under modern historiographic scrutiny. Moreover, we do not have straightforwardly reliable, Black-authored firsthand accounts of the insurgency itself. What we do have is the key account of the event, *The Confessions of Nat Turner, the Leader of the Late Insurrection in Southampton Virginia, as Fully and Voluntarily Made to Thomas R. Gray* (1831) (fig. 4.1). Gray was a local lawyer whose sympathies seem to have been with the

THE

CONFESSIONS

OF

NAT TURNER,

THE LEADER OF THE LATE

INSURRECTION IN SOUTHAMPTON, VA.

As fully and voluntarily made to

THOMAS R. GRAY,

In the prison where he was confined, and acknowledged by him to be such when read before the Court of Southampton; with the certificate, under seal of the Court convened at Jerusalem, Nov. 5, 1831, for his trial.

ALSO, AN AUTHENTIC

ACCOUNT OF THE WHOLE INSURRECTION,

WITH LISTS OF THE WHITES WHO WERE MURDERED,

AND OF THE NEGROES BROUGHT BEFORE THE COURT OF SOUTHAMPTON, AND THERE SENTENCED, &c.

Baltimore:
PUBLISHED BY THOMAS R. GRAY.
Lucas & Deaver, print.
1831.

Nat Turner and Thomas R. Gray, title page, *The Confessions of Nat Turner* [. . .] *as Fully and Voluntarily Made to Thomas R. Gray* (Baltimore: Lucas & Deaver, 1831). Courtesy of the Library Company of Philadelphia enslaving population.[25] The extent to which Turner's contributions to Gray's pamphlet were complete or voluntary has been extensively debated, but *The Confessions* is widely agreed to bear, at a minimum, significant relation Turner's own words. *The Confessions*, with its clear links to the gallows literary tradition examined in chapter 2, is nevertheless a unique document, with literary as well as biographical and historical value. It remains one of the most controversial texts from the period, as well as one of the most studied, with multiple monographs devoted primarily to interpreting it and myriad literary works, musical compositions, and works of visual culture relying on it as a factual basis or inspiration.

Alongside *The Confessions*, there exist numerous contemporary, explicitly white-authored accounts, including printed ephemera, periodical publications, and letters and diaries. Panic tinges most of these texts, which rehearse questions like "Who is this Nat Turner?" and what were "the real motives of the Blacks in this sudden and unlooked for revolt?"[26] There are also trial records for legal proceedings against forty-six of the insurgents, alongside local tax, census, and property records; several letters; and white- and Black-authored accounts of the violent reprisals visited upon enslaved and free Black people in the days and weeks following August 21–22. Allmendinger uncovered numerous local Southampton archives that allowed him to reconstruct the lives of other individuals associated with the events across multiple generations. He painstakingly combed "wills, deeds, inventories, court minutes, chancery records, marriage registers, free black registers, processioners' returns, tax lists, and poll books" to establish a much fuller context for the insurgency than anyone had before.[27] In a similar vein, just before Allmendinger, Alfred L. Brophy scrupulously analyzed court records to show how legal proceedings worked both with and against extrajudicial violence following the insurgency.[28] Brophy notes that such materials "tell a powerful story about the role of law in American history as a vehicle for establishing order," working, as it did, both "in conjunction with—and sometimes in opposition to—the extra-legal violence that accompanied the suppression of the rebellion."[29] Responses to the insurgency conjoined legal modalities (court detention, trial, and execution) and extralegal modalities (harassment, rape, theft, false incrimination, and violence against free and enslaved Black people). Firsthand Black- and white-authored accounts of the ensuing extralegal reprisals and further fears of violence from enslaved people also exist. This mixed bag of legal and extralegal responses in some ways reflects tensions within the insurgency itself. The insurgents attempted to shift Virginia's legal landscape in seeking emancipation, but they aimed ultimately at a much deeper transformation of racial, spiritual, and creative ways of being.

The existential threat that the insurgency posed to antebellum American society was not lost on contemporary Southerners. The tumultuous atmosphere of Philadelphia in 1793, discussed in chapter 1, seems to have paled in comparison with fear that infused much of the South following August 1831. Firsthand Black-authored accounts, such as the one included in Harriet Jacobs's 1861 account of her experiences while enslaved in nearby Edenton, North Carolina, reveal the extent of the terror gripping regions of the South following the Southampton Insurgency:[30]

> Those who never witnessed such scenes can hardly believe what I know was inflicted at this time on innocent men, women, and children, against whom there was not the slightest ground for suspicion. Colored people and slaves who lived in remote parts of the town suffered in an especial manner. In some cases the searchers scattered powder and shot among their clothes, and then sent other parties to find them, and bring them forward as proof that they were plotting insurrection. Every where men, women, and children were whipped till the blood stood in puddles at their feet. Some received five hundred lashes; others were tied hands and feet, and tortured with a bucking paddle, which blisters the skin terribly. The dwellings of the colored people, unless they happened to be protected by some influential white person, who was nigh at hand, were robbed of clothing and every thing else the marauders thought worth carrying away. All day long these unfeeling wretches went round, like a troop of demons, terrifying and tormenting the helpless. At night, they formed themselves into patrol bands, and went wherever they chose among the colored people, acting out their brutal will. Many women hid themselves in woods and swamps, to keep out of their way. If any of the husbands or fathers told of these outrages, they were tied up to the public whipping post, and cruelly scourged for telling lies about white men. The consternation was universal. No two people that had the slightest tinge of color in their faces dared to be seen talking together.[31]

Jacobs's description of the chaos this "troop of demons" visited upon enslaved populations and free Black people after the Southampton Insurgency stands as an important if chilling eyewitness account. Unnerved by enslaved people's violence, white people, both enslavers and unpropertied whites, retaliated, provoked in part by revenge and the desire to reinforce their power, in part by fear of new uprisings, and in part by the fact that Turner remained uncaptured. Their attacks, thefts, murders, rapes, and summary executions in the wake of the insurgency inflicted lasting intergenerational trauma. Fear likewise gripped white imaginations for some time across the South. One white Alabama resident interviewed later in life by Frederick Law Olmstead recalled, "When I was a boy [around the time of the Southampton revolt] folks was dreadful frightened.... I remember they built pens in the woods where they could hide, and Christmas time they went and got into the pens, 'fraid the n———s was risin'."[32] This nineteenth-century proto-survivalist white response stands in mirror opposition to widespread accounts of terror that reigned in Black communities in the aftermath of the insurgency.[33]

Turner disappeared immediately after the insurgency. He would not be captured until late October, and his execution came in November. In the interval between August and October, the first printed account of the insurgency appeared, Samuel Warner's *Authentic and Impartial Narrative of the Tragical Scene* (fig. 4.2). Warner drew explicit links between Southampton and Saint-Domingue (modern-day Haiti), identified Turner as an "artful" preacher and as the leader, and, as the woodcut illustrations vividly suggest, reveled in the bloodshed. Describing white corpses scattered across Southampton County, Warner writes, "Their mangled remains presented a spectacle of horror the like of which we hope our countrymen will never again be called upon to witness; a spectacle from which the mind must shrink with horror, when it contemplates whole families murdered, without regard to age or sex, and weltering in their gore."[34] As in gallows publications, like those relating to Frost examined in chapter 2, Warner leans into the descriptions of blood and violence. His description of Turner as an "artful black" with a "sly and artful manner" who "artfully represented himself" as a preacher to sway other enslaved people to his side also recalls the late eighteenth-century descriptions of Samuel Frost that most clearly frame him as a criminal genius. Likewise, much of the insurgency's early newspaper coverage addresses Turner's keen intelligence and ability to rally support from those around him. Both of these characteristics, intelligence and charisma, built his reputation as a prophet. In early September, for example, the *Richmond Compiler* explained, "This Nat seems to be a bold fellow, of the deepest cunning, who for years has been endeavouring to acquire an influence over the minds of these deluded wretches. He reads and writes with ease, it is said, and has long been a preacher."[35] This figure, of a bold, cunning, influential, and highly literate enslaved man, who was also widely seen as a religious figure, circulated across multiple newspapers. Also in early September, the *Constitutional Whig* remarked, "The universal opinion ... is that Nat, a slave, a preacher, and a pretended prophet was ... the actual leader, and the most remorseless of the executioners."[36]

Upon Turner's capture, a flurry of newspaper coverage ensued, all eager to

The Southampton Insurgency 141

Samuel Warner, "Horrid Massacre in Virginia," in *Authentic and Impartial Narrative of the Tragical Scene* (New York: Warner and West, 1831). Courtesy of the American Antiquarian Society

end speculation and at last secure a final answer to the question of motive. One example, in the *Richmond Inquirer*, teased future reports by promising "to obtain as accurate account as possible for this murderous Bandit. We shall place it upon record—in order, that if any future historian should hereafter paint him incorrectly, as the Albany *Fabulist* has the Insurgent Gabriel, the facts may be ready to refute his falsehoods."[37] Indicating that Turner "is said to be very free in his confessions," the *Norfolk Herald* both draws attention to and denies the revolutionary nature of the insurgency.[38] Headlined "NAT TURNER CERTAINLY TAKEN!" (fig. 4.3), the article continues Warner's representation of Turner as artful and continues to hinge on his reputation as a prophet. But its portrait is tinged with pathos: "He still pretends that he is a prophet, and relates a number of revelations which he said he had, from which he was induced to believe that he could succeed in conquering *the county of Southampton* (what miserable ignorance!) as the white people did in the revolution."[39] By including, even if only to disparage,

NAT TURNER CERTAINLY TAKEN!

We have been politely favored with the perusal of a letter from Southampton, to a gentleman in this place, from which we are enabled to give the following statement, corroborating the one published in our last, with some interesting additions:

Nat was shot at by Mr. Francis, (as stated in our last) on Thursday, (yesterday week,) near a fodder stack in his field, but happening to fall at the moment of the discharge, the contents of the pistol passed through the crown of his hat. He had the hat on his head when he was taken, with the shot holes in it, which he exhibited to show how narrowly he had escaped being shot.

Although he escaped from Mr. Francis, the rencontre caused a general turn out in the neighborhood, and on Sunday there were at least 50 men out in search of him, none of whom could have been two miles from the place where he was caught, at the time of his capture.

He was taken about a mile and a half from the house of Mr. Travis, the man he served, and whose family, including himself, were the first victims of this cruel fanatic and his besotted followers. He had made himself a sort of den in the lap of a fallen tree, which he had covered over with pine brush. His head was protruded through this covering, as if he was in the act of reconnoitering, when Mr. Phipps, (who had that morning, for the first time, turned out in pursuit of him) came suddenly upon him. Mr. Phipps not knowing him, demanded "Who are you?" and was answered, "*I am Nat Turner.*" Mr. Phipps then ordered him to hand on his arms, and he delivered up a sword, which was the only weapon he had.

Mr. Phipps then took him to Mr. Edward's, whence the news of his capture spread so rapidly, that in less than an hour a hundred persons had collected at the place, whose feelings on beholding the blood-stained monster, were so much excited, that it was with difficulty he could be conveyed alive to Jerusalem.

He is said to be very free in his confessions, which, however, are no further important than as shewing that he was instigated by the wildest superstition and fanaticism, and was not connected with any organized plan of conspiracy beyond the circle of the few ignorant wretches whom he had seduced by his artifices to join him. He still pretends that he is a prophet, and relates a number of revelations which he says he has had, from which he was induced to believe that he could succeed in conquering the *county of Southampton!* (what miserable ignorance!) as the white people did in the revolution.

He says the idea of an insurrection never crossed his mind until a few months before he started with it; and he considered the *dark appearance of the sun* as a signal for him to commence! His profanity in comparing his pretended prophecies with passages in the Holy Scriptures should not be mentioned, if it did not afford proof of his insanity. Yet it was by that means he obtained the complete control of his followers, which led them to the perpetration of the horrible deeds of the 22d August. [*Norfolk Herald.*

Turner's comparison of his bid for sovereignty with America's illustrious founding fathers, the *Norfolk Herald*, like the *Richmond Enquirer*, emphasizes the insurgency's political potency.

A few months before the insurgency, in January 1831, William Lloyd Garrison published the first edition of his important abolitionist paper, the *Liberator*, which aimed explicitly at ending legal enslavement. The *Liberator* diverged from other white-run abolitionist papers, like Benjamin Lundy's *Genius of Universal Emancipation*, in that it eschewed gradualism and demanded the "immediate and complete emancipation of all slaves." Although Garrison advocated passive and nonviolent resistance, the pages of the new paper frequently decried, in prose and verse that was at once fearful and jubilant, the imminence of bloody, apocalyptic divine retribution for the national sin of slavery. Thus, in a well-known response to the Southampton Insurgency printed in Boston on September 3, 1831, nine months after the *Liberator's* initial publication, Garrison exults:

> What we have long predicted—at the peril of being stigmatized as an alarmist and declaimer,—has commenced its fulfillment. The first step of the earthquake, which is ultimately to shake down the fabric of oppression, leaving not one stone upon the other, has been made. The first drops of blood, which are but the prelude to a deluge form the gathered clouds, have fallen. The first flash of lightning, which is to ignite and consume, has been felt. The first wailings of a bereavement, which is to clothe the earth in sackcloth, have broken upon our ears.
>
> In the first number of the *Liberator*, we alluded to the hour of vengeance in the following lines:
>
> Wo if it comes with storm, and blood, and fire,
>   When midnight darkness veils the earth and sky!
> *Wo to the innocent babe*—the guilty sire—
>   *Mother and daughter*—friends of kindred tie
> *Stranger and citizen alike shall die!* . . .
>
> Read the account of the insurrection in Virginia, and say whether our prophecy be not fulfilled. What was poetry—imagination—in January, is now a bloody reality.[40]

For Garrison, the images of strife that the *Liberator's* first issue conjured have now been made real by the recent event in Virginia, including its multiple infanticides. As a result, Garrison directs his readers to understand *his own* work (rather than Turner's) as prophecy: "Read the account . . . and say whether our prophecy be not fulfilled." At the same time, however, Garrison is keen to emphasize that his hands are clean. He defends against accusations that responsibility for the violence in Southampton rests with him and other "pacific friends of emancipation." Northern pacifist abolitionists do not incite violence. It is, Garrison argues, the very humanity of the enslaved, affronted by enslavement, that inevitably results in violence.

In bringing together his initial "prediction" of bloodshed with what he terms "insurrection in Virginia," Garrison strikes an apocalyptic note. Like Walker, Garrison suggests that it may well be easier to imagine the end of the world than the end of slavery. Evoking William Wordsworth's 1803 ode "To Toussaint L'Ouverture" (Thou hast left behind / Powers that will work for thee—air, earth, and skies— / There's not a breathing of the common wind / That will forget thee!), Garrison moves through all four elements. Stones tumble to earth, blood flows like water, lighting brings fire, and expressions of unspeakable grief pierce the air. Also recalling Walker's millenarian vision, Garrison views this violence as impersonal. Infants, mothers, daughters, friends, strangers, and citizens all are swept up in a divine, inevitable cycle of death and renewal. Yet "the crime of oppression is national," and the specific atrocities of enslavement, which Garrison frames as moral crime, show that "Humanity" itself is under siege. For Garrison, enslaved humans are not "black-brutes, pretending to be men." The enslaved are human and therefore naturally find "invitations to resistance above, below, around . . . in every field, in every valley, on every hilltop and mountain."[41] Like Wordsworth's response to Louverture, Garrison's commentary on Turner comes close to heroization. Yet he deflates the praise by using scare quotes: "Is it wonderful that they [the insurgents] should rise to contend—as other 'heroes' have contended—for their lost rights?" Garrison is keen to assert the humanity of the enslaved, but he nevertheless reserves any greater grandeur for himself and his own imaginative efforts. He quietly removes the mantle of the intelligent prophet from Turner and places it instead upon his own shoulders.[42] Turner the prophet and General Nat are brushed aside in the pages of the *Liberator* to elevate Prophet Garrison and his liberal, humanitarian visionaries. Garrison silences Turner and the other insurgents in order to marshal their (liberal) humanity to his cause. Evincing a similar failure of imagination, Thomas Wentworth Higginson asked during the Civil War, "Who shall now go back thirty years and read the heart of this extraordinary man?" And nearly 150 years later, twentieth-century historian Peter H. Wood insists on the historian's fundamental inability to understand Turner: "Ever since he was hanged and cut apart in 1831, this unknown black leader has been largely shrouded from view."[43] This tradition centers Turner precisely to disavow the radicalism of the insurgency.

The impulse to diminish, discredit, or even discard a Turner who cannot be definitively established as a resistant, heroic agent unites a further set of twentieth-century writers and scholars. Their position has rested on the fact that the extensive print archive, including *The Confessions*, newspaper articles, pamphlets, and legal records, arguably leaves gaps large enough to admit questions regarding such basic facts as whether Turner regarded the event as political and Turner's leadership role in it.[44] Novelist William Styron most famously called this into question in his own *The Confessions of Nat Turner* (1967). Yet he based his fictionalization on the false assertion that the print record was so meager that "any C+ history student" could digest it in a matter of days. Styron was roundly corrected by John Henrick Clarke, Tragle, and many others, who collectively showed that he (and Eugene D. Genovese, an influential historian who defended him) ignored a "living tradition of black America."[45] But Styron's well-documented ignorance notwithstanding, many well-informed writers and scholars have also expressed doubt about Turner's role in the insurgency and the nature of the event itself. For example, Scot French examined newspaper accounts and trial records that raise questions about the centrality of Turner's leadership, such as the testimony of an enslaved woman named Beck, who provided fifteen names and corroborating dates evidencing a year-long plot prior to the event but never discussed Turner. Both Genovese and Arna Bontemps ultimately found the Southampton Insurgency uninspiring, particularly because of a lack of sources that could reliably confirm Turner's role as an oppositional leader. Bontemps found Turner's "dreams" and "trance-like mumbo-jumbo" so off-putting as to encourage him to fictionalize Gabriel Prosser's unsuccessful revolt in *Black Thunder* (1936) rather than Turner's successful insurgency. Genovese likewise saw both Prosser and Denmark Vesey as better representatives of an international revolutionary movement.[46]

Henry Irving Tragle centers Turner in order to minimize the insurgency's liberatory horizon. In a lengthy digression in his 1971 commentary on the historical documents surrounding the Southampton revolt, Tragle rejects all possible explications of Turner's motive. He asserts instead that we ought to preserve "the mystery" intact out of respect for the gaps and fissures in the historical record. In his introductory remarks, Tragle emphasizes the question marks that immediately enfolded the revolt: "Why?, Why?, Why?, the papers asked in long and repetitious articles which habitually described those who had revolted as 'banditti.'"[47] The recurring "why?" signals a fascination with the question of motive, the very question that Tragle would prefer to set aside. In the beginning, possible answers were framed as enigmatic and contradictory. As we have seen, contemporary papers commonly described Turner and his associates as "banditti." Gray, in *The Confessions*, refers to Turner in quotation marks as "this 'great bandit.'"[48] But, at the same time, it was clear that the men involved in the revolt did not display key characteristics of bandits. They did not plunder but took only what they needed to continue their attack. Acquiring property was not their aim; their actions were not *against* so much as they were *outside of* the law. Moreover, at least four insurgents were free men, who could not have been fighting to remove the yoke of enslavement alone. Recognizing that Turner and his associates were neither looking for material gain nor all seeking legal freedom, Tragle frames two possible answers to the question of motive. The first is that the insurgency was, or rather (in Tragle's view) was believed by Turner and his associates to be, divinely inspired. The second is, as the editor of the Richmond *Constitutional Whig* maintained, that Turner and his associates "acted upon no higher principle than the impulse of revenge against the whites, as the enslavers of himself and his race."[49] Ultimately, Tragle rejects these and all other explanations of motive. In so doing he, like Garrison before him, undermines the idea Turner was a prophet, whether secular or divine. This liberal tradition, from Garrison to Higginson to Tragle, dictates we must leave the questions the Southampton Insurgency raises unanswered, because Turner himself did not (or, more precisely, could not) provide posterity direct access to his motivations.

Notably, and by contrast, Tragle assigns the white antislavery revolutionary John Brown the role of inspired and inspiring leader: "There can be no real analogy between John Brown and Nat Turner, beyond one based purely on the effect of their separate actions." Unlike Brown, Turner "wrote no letters and kept no records. Every record that remains was generated by those against whom he fought, and at whose hands he eventually died." For Tragle, Brown's verifiable paper trail renders him a true and prophetic revolutionary, whose ethical and religious principles drove his action. Tragle keeps Turner at the center of the event but silent. "Both were men of action, but Brown was in addition a tireless correspondent and a chronicler of himself. It is clear from his writings that he expected history to be his final judge." Tragle concedes that historical records relating to Turner "are not worthless," because they can "be used to achieve a historical view of both the man and the event." But this "historical view" is thin indeed: "We must accept at the outset that . . . when we seek to ask, why? We move immediately beyond the limits of the available evidence." For Tragle, only a "tireless chronicler" like Brown speaks power from beyond the grave.[50]

These examples evidence a long tradition that insists on silence as the only appropriate response to the insurgency. Garrison writes in the *Liberator* that, "for ourselves, we are horror-struck at the late tidings."[51] Genovese and Bontemps dismiss Turner because the historical record is insufficient to confer unshakeable hero status upon him. All have been eager to acknowledge enslaved people's humanity, yet this acknowledgment justifies eliding those aspects of enslaved experience that are not verifiable. Such a view holds that any attempt to imagine the subject position of the nineteenth-century Nat Turner is doomed, like William Styron's, to hideous failure. As the twentieth-century white grandson of Virginia enslavers, faced with an incomplete historical record, Styron can only go wrong in a novel like *The Confessions of Nat Turner*. And as the contributors to *William Styron's Nat Turner: Ten Black Writers Respond* robustly demonstrate, Styron most certainly did go very wrong. More recently, African American actor and filmmaker Nate Parker also fell short in his attempt to fictionalize Nat Turner and rectify past accounts. His 2016 film *The Birth of a Nation* depicts Turner as intensively masculinist and individualist, happy enough with enslavement until his wife's chastity is threatened. Western masculinity underwrites stories of the resistant Romantic hero and genius, whereas criminal genius strains against the limitations of these heavily gendered approaches to generate a more relational and collective imaginary.

The lens of criminal genius shows us that failures of imagination like those I have just outlined are not inevitable. An insistence on the discursive ineffability of enslaved experience has confused the inadequacy of the empirical record with the impossibility of reading what remains. This sensibility has too often validated an unwillingness to grapple with the Southampton Insurgency. In the days, weeks, months, and years following, Turner appeared in print at times as the embodiment of pure, indiscriminate evil, at others as a brave and brilliant leader. First at home, and then abroad after the revolt, Turner was hailed as a prophet as well as a general. Out of the Southampton Insurgency, we have a corpus that at once enables and requires a mode of reading that does not end in the recovery of Turner as a resistant liberal individual, however much he may also have been that. We in fact do not have access to his "voice" and cannot, by some historical feat of ethical determination, heroically "restore" it to him. Indeed, to do so in this case would be to miss the crucial collectivity that characterizes criminal genius and the alternative modes of being human to which it gestures. As Joseph Drexler-Dreis has argued, "The task of interpreting the meaning of Nat Turner and the Southampton slave rebellion . . . discloses the persistence of . . . the assimilationist pull of the destructive crystallization of the human person within Western modernity."[52] Like Jones and Allen, Rush, Johnstone, Frost, and Walker, Turner's agency was distributed: it operated not against but in concert with dehumanizing processes of objectification. This view decenters an authentic Nat Turner so that we might better train our sights on the liberatory potential of the Southampton Insurgency and its legacies.[53]

"I Surely Would Be a Prophet"

Unlike much of the periodical coverage that preceded his capture and execution, the single most influential document in the Nat Turner archive, *The Confessions of Nat Turner*, signally lacks any direct political or antislavery content. The pamphlet's omission of explicit politicism is often overlooked. Yet it is crucial because it both mirrors and refracts the limitations of the archives of enslavement broadly and those relating particularly to Turner's life. Moreover, I argue that it is this lack that has largely sparked the seemingly endless commentary and controversy about the events in Southampton as well as aesthetic interpretations of Turner. Gray published this pamphlet, with Turner's account ostensibly "as fully and voluntarily made to Thomas R. Gray," just days after Turner's November 11 execution. It was based largely on several days' worth of interviews immediately after his October 31 capture. *The Confessions of Nat Turner* has formed the basis of almost all of the myriad historical, fictional, and popular representations of Turner, from English historical novelist George Payne Rainsford James's *The Old Dominion; or, The Southampton Massacre* (1856), to Harriet Beecher Stowe's *Dred* (1856) and William Wells Brown's *The Negro in the American Rebellion* (1867), to William Styron's deeply problematic first-person novelization, which uses the same title as Gray's text (1967). Kyle Baker's 2008 graphic novel and Nate Parker's disastrous 2016 film likewise begin with Gray's pamphlet.

With fifty thousand copies at its first printing in Baltimore and an edition as recent as 2016, *The Confessions of Nat Turner* remains one of the most significant documents to have emerged from the history of racial enslavement in the United States. Christopher Tomlins has recently described it as "the best source, which is also almost the only source," for those interested in recovering Nat Turner.[54] Yet all recovery attempts must reckon with the fact that *The Confessions* may, or may not, represent Turner's own words. Scot French, citing Marxist historian Aptheker, who referred to the document as Turner's "so-called" confessions, is one of several major commentators who refute the work's veracity.[55] Contemporary historians Allmendinger and Patrick Breen take a more sanguine view, suggesting that there is much historical truth to be gleaned from the document. Still more positive is Thomas C. Parramore, the first to uncover an accurate picture of Thomas R. Gray as not an old man but as an indebted young lawyer. To Parramore, *The Confessions* represents a "collaboration" between Turner and Gray.[56] Caleb Smith enters such debates from a distance, noting a disconnect between historical and literary approaches to *The Confessions*: "Historians have tended to approach the text as a record . . . to be studied for its accuracy and detail," and "literary critics have been preoccupied with the question of authenticity, the presence or absence of Turner's original voice." Both Smith and Tomlins toe a line between the historical and the literary. Recognizing that *The Confessions* fails to deliver either reliable history or legitimate autobiography, Smith argues that it offers a "poetics of justice."[57] Tomlins's approach likewise emphasizes the formal and intellectual aspects of this key text. Arguing that the pamphlet is first and foremost "an exercise in ideation," Tomlins claims that previous inquiries have "read without sufficient care or curiosity," and he sets out to rectify this with a "speculative" approach to "recover the revenant Turner" by "treasur[ing] the scraps of empirical evidence" we have.[58]

What Smith and Tomlins astutely recognize is that the gaps, too, are susceptible to interpretation and therefore are an important part of the Southampton Insurgency's record.[59] Building on their approach, reading Turner as criminal genius places him in relation to collectivity and provides a counterpoint to well-rehearsed anxieties regarding the Southampton archive's limitations. As we have seen, these limitations in turn link directly to most prior scholarship's overt or covert emphasis on individuality, which Tomlins retains. By contrast, to read Turner in relation to a criminal genius prioritizes the insurgency's generativity; it is not an attempt to "recover" Nat Turner. An insurgent Turner constitutes a radical corpus that retains humanity, including but not limited to an oppositional stance. As criminal genius, Turner imagines and models other modes of being human, rather than claim individual agency or establish authenticity. These alternative modes encompass not only abstractions but also materiality, as with Johnstone and Frost. Such modes also account for religiosity, as we saw with Walker. When these aspects are taken together, the collectivity of the criminal genius stands in place of the individuality of the resistant hero.

Out of this multifarious and incomplete print beginning, Nat Turner was to become perhaps the most fiercely contested figure in the world of Black criminality and Black agency, and indeed he remains so to this day. To get past individualist approaches to Turner, we have to deal seriously with unlikely and deeply problematic sources. The first retrospective history of the Southampton Insurgency appeared in 1900, from the pen of William S. Drewry, a Southern historian who believed that enslaved people had constituted the happiest workforce in world history.[60] A direct descendent of the men who suppressed the revolt, his sources were white Southampton residents interviewed at the end of the century.[61] The fact that Drewry's allegiances and sources tie directly to his enslaving forbears has led scholars like Aptheker to state that "for the truth of the Turner event it would have been better if Drewry had never published."[62] Although twenty-first-century scholars cast allegiance with Turner and the other insurgents, they hew to modern secular empirical methods. Yet, as we have seen, despite apparent abundance, the insurgency's written traces nevertheless present deep lacunae, and, as a result, strict reliance on historical methods ultimately flattens Turner's characterization and silences the event's radicalism. Looking beyond resistance histories reveals that Drewry (despite himself, to be sure), though racist and operating outside the bounds of modern historiography, offers at times a clearer window onto potential genealogies of collective Black agency than some modern historians who look to Turner as a heroic individual.

For example, it is via Drewry that we learn that key detail with which I began and that Aptheker chose to omit: that Nancy sought an immediate end to her newborn child's enslavement. It was Drewry's account that showcased, even decades after abolition, how the enslaving Southern order saw Nancy's hatred of slavery as evidencing an unsound mind: "His mother, Nancy, is said to have been imported directly from Africa, and to have been so wild that at Nat's birth she had to be tied to prevent her from murdering him."[63] Drewry represented this moment as signifying Nancy's aberrance. But it also establishes the radical inheritance she bequeathed her son, and we can understand Aptheker's dismissal as a failure to see Nancy's own criminal genius. As Terri Snyder explains, "Africans and Europeans carried competing and changing ideas of good and bad deaths with them through the Middle Passage, and these concepts shaped their views of self-destruction."[64] Neither Drewry nor Aptheker was able to access this insight, but in keeping her story alive, Drewry helped preserve Nancy as locatable within a powerful African American legacy of impossible maternal struggle. In his graphic novel *Nat Turner*, Kyle Baker depicts precisely this moment to exemplify the insurgent power of genealogy. In turn, this history also places Turner's story alongside the best-documented attempt to liberate children through death, Margaret Garner's, immortalized as the inspiration for perhaps the most important novel of the twentieth century, Toni Morrison's *Beloved*.

Per Drewry, alongside additional Southern contemporary accounts, we also learn that Nancy's partner, Turner's father, showed the same spirit of insurgence when he later emancipated himself: "His father was also very high-spirited, and ran away when Nat was a boy, and was never recaptured."[65] Aptheker, seeking to frame Turner as an exceptional individual, marks this as a partial inheritance: "It is possible that he owed part of his revolutionary spirit to his father who, when Nat was a boy, ran away and was never recovered."[66] It has been suggested that Turner's father took up residence in the Great Dismal Swamp,[67] perhaps a living embodiment of the spectral "dark-throned king" of Poe's "Dream-land," which I examine in the final chapter.[68] The Great Dismal Swamp in Turner's time was known to have been home to the largest population of maroons, or self-liberated enslaved people, numbering well into the thousands.[69] It was a site of collective Black living that escaped the enslaving Southern power. Warner's *Authentic and Impartial Narrative of the Tragical Scene* includes an extended description of the Great Dismal Swamp in relation to the insurgency.[70]

The *Constitutional Whig* similarly dwells on how environment, as much as individual greatness, shaped the insurgency. This account, published almost two months before *The Confessions*, dwells much more explicitly on the racialized, politicized meanings that imbued Turner's reading of the natural and celestial world.

> To an imagination like Nat's, a mind satisfied of the possibility of freeing himself and his race from bondage; and this by supernatural means. To one thus situated, is it wonderful, that the singular appearance of the sun in August, should have tempted him to execute his purpose: particularly when its silvery surface was defaced by a black spot, which Nat interpreted into positive proof, that he would succeed in his undertaking. Nat encouraged his company on their route, by telling them, that as a black spot had passed over the sun, so would the blacks pass over the earth.[71]

Here, it is Nat's imagination, not alone but in concert with the natural world, that acts toward an enlarged conception of freedom. This excerpt echoes Walker's earlier outlaw prophecy: "As true as the sun ever shone in its meridian splendor, my colour will root some of them out of the very face of the earth." As Walker realized from Boston almost contemporaneously with Turner, the certainty of even the sun at noonday was not assured in the face of the profound injustice of racialized enslavement. Indeed, *The Confessions* confirms that the eclipse proved decisive for Turner: "I saw white spirits and black spirits engaged in battle, and the sun was darkened—the thunder rolled in the Heavens, and blood flowed in streams—and I heard a voice saying, 'Such is your luck, such you are called to see, and let it come rough or smooth, you must surely bare [sic] it.'"[72] Again, we have echoes of Walker, in particular the passage examined at length in the previous chapter: "No doubt some may say that I write with a bad spirit, and that I being a black, wish these things to occur. Whether I write with a bad or a good spirit, I say if these things do not occur in their proper time, it is because the world in which we live does not exist, and we are deceived with regard to its existence." As was the case for Walker, nature's message for Turner is that Spirit, the surety of a just God, and the equal certainty of unspeakable injustice render the continued existence of this world improbable. *The Confessions* likewise represents Turner operating in concert with nature, reading the signs of blood on tree leaves as well as celestial phenomena in a prophetic mode, as signaling the approach of divine justice.

The question of mode or genre becomes centrally important in seeking to understand Turner beyond questions of authenticity and individuality. The contrast between the archetypes of martyr and prophet offers one way of thinking about the historiographer's silencing of Turner. Such silencing may make Turner "human," but it also transforms him from the prophet he was widely held to be in the wake of the Southampton revolt—"Prophet Nat," who was described by the editor of the Richmond *Constitutional Whig* even before his capture as a "shrewd fellow, [who] reads, writes, and preaches,"—into a martyr sacrificed at the law's altar. Remembering him as a martyr rather than a prophet transforms Turner from an actor enmeshed in, yet responsive to, a particular cultural moment, a cocreator of history, to one whose agency must be identical with his death. For Garrison, the movement exemplified by the Southampton Insurgency was a transition "from poetry to bloody reality." Yet understanding Turner as a martyr leaves "the bloody reality," including indeed the poetry of the insurgency, unread, even as it enhances Garrison's own prophetic "poetry."

The Confessions' beginning highlights the Southampton Insurgency's prophetic temporality. Illustrating the capaciousness of prophecy as a literary mode, Ian Balfour dismisses the idea that prophecy might constitute a single, self-contained genre, arguing that it is "more appropriate to speak of 'the prophetic' than of prophecy, if the latter is a genre and the former a mode that can intersect with any number of genres from the ode to the epic, in either poetry or prose. There are even instances of drama that are as recognizably 'prophetic' as anything else."[73] Old Testament prophets, of course, not only predicted the future but chastised wayward communities and communicated their vision of a new future in a repaired world.[74] Turner states that to give "history of the motives which induced me to undertake the late insurrection," he must return to an event from his infancy, a moment when his parents discovered that he possessed knowledge of events that had transpired not in the future but in the past, before his birth. This uncanny knowledge, in conjunction with material emblems of his chosenness, "certain marks on my head and breast," convinced his family that he "surely would be a prophet . . . [and] was intended for some great purpose."[75] Born insurgent, straining toward a new horizon that links back to the past, Turner was charged on November 5, 1831, "with conspiring to rebel and make insurrection."[76] In *The Confessions* we have the story of a man who has been accused of committing a crime, who narrates his complicity in the deeds that constitute that crime, but who nevertheless pleads not guilty.

Thus, Turner's "confession" bridges the legal, literary, and religious aspects of confessional literature as a genre.[77] *The Confessions*, of course, also functions as an example of autobiography, aligning with autobiographies of escaped slaves. Yet it only briefly relates Turner's escape from enslavement: "After remaining in the woods thirty days, I returned, to the astonishment of the negroes on the plantation, who thought I had made my escape to some other part of the country, as my father had done before." This detail serves ultimately to underscore Turner's dedication to following his spiritual commitments, which at that moment appear as returning "to the service of my earthly master" but of course ultimately culminate in armed insurgency. At the same time, Turner's flight from fugitivity marks his return from outlaw status. Turner thus metamorphoses across *The Confessions*: he moves from boy wonder, to enslaved worker, to fugitive outlaw, to spiritual leader, to convicted criminal. *The Confessions* registers these shifts in part by its generic instability, merging poetry, "true crime" writing, confession, autobiography, and bildungsroman, all the while employing a prophetic mode. The criminal genius of the Southampton Insurgency, in contrast to Romantic genius's distance, abstraction, and detachment, reveals a "transcendence" that is active, material, and distributed. It aims not at escape but at insurgency. The pages of *The Confessions* present the insurgency in a prophetic mode and show Turner drawing on multiple agencies, his own and those of others, to cocreate a powerful example of antebellum criminal genius.

"The Type and Genius of Deep Crime"

Understanding *The Confessions* in prophetic literary mode, generically unstable, castigating the present and pointing toward an alternative path, offers a fruitful way to read the insurgency not for authenticity but instead for its opacity. What do the gaps and silences themselves say? Especially considered alongside a contemporary pamphlet like Walker's *Appeal* or a publication such as Garrison's the *Liberator*, *The Confessions*' lack of explicit politicism can be jarring. Many have reasonably suggested that this silence should be attributed to Gray's role as amanuensis. However, records suggest that Turner had at least two additional opportunities to speak in political, public venues: first at his trial and then again at his execution.[78] In both cases he refused to add or to clarify what he had already communicated. This silence is itself meaningful. With it, Turner places himself in a literary genealogy that includes Milton's Satan, who promises his fellow fallen angels "full bliss" in a newly created world before being metamorphosed into a snake, and Shakespeare's Iago, who once condemned, proclaims, "From this time forth I never will speak word." He also anticipates the fictional enslaved insurgent, Melville's Babo: "Seeing all was over, he uttered no sound, and could not be forced to. His aspect seemed to say: since I cannot do deeds, I will not speak words." At the moment of *The Confessions* when we might expect his explicit political condemnation of enslavement, Turner instead relates a vision, also Miltonic, of Black spirits battling white spirits. This vision reveals to him that "the time was fast approaching when the first should be last and the last should be first."[79] This replacement of political speech with oblique reference to Matthew 20:16, the parable of the vineyard workers, does not index Turner's passivity or a failure of the historical record. Rather, it clears space for richly imagined possible worlds.

Interpretive difficulties do not disappear when we view the Southampton Insurgency through the lens of criminal genius. But we gain something crucial: key perspective on the significance of Turner's opacity. A literary, imaginative mind-set reveals the insurgency's potentiality, rather than the meaningless silence of the oppressed when records have been kept by the oppressors. *The Confessions* suggests that Turner's refusal to speak after his indictment is an extension of a lifelong practice of keeping himself aloof and apart.[80] Echoing Benjamin Franklin's famous description of the equal importance of being and seeming industrious, Turner explains that he attempted to maintain the appearance as much as the reality of his greatness: "I studiously avoided mixing in society, and wrapped myself in mystery, devoting my time to fasting and prayer." In this telling, Turner seeks illegibility and enters society not for sociability but rather to assume the role of genius, breaking old laws to shape new paradigms. Criminal genius is not transcendent and timeless but local and situated, with an agency that unites voluntarism with collectivity. Therefore, its narratives, representations, and performances are not static and transparent but dynamic and ambiguous. Turner cultivates opacity.

The period's most famous linking of criminality and creative genius appeared just around the time of the insurgency, in a series of essays by English writer Thomas De Quincey on murder in relation to art: "On the Knocking at the Gate in Macbeth" (1823), "On Murder Considered as One of the Fine Arts" (1827), and "Second Paper on Murder Considered as One of the Fine Arts" (1839). Notably, "On Murder" contains the first recorded use of the word "aesthetic" in the English language. In the United States, Edgar Allan Poe picks up this thread in his writing. While I will explore this connection in Poe's poetry in the next chapter, I want to underline here its presence in his short fiction. Famously, Detective C. August Dupin designates the would-be blackmailer of "The Purloined Letter" (1844) as "the *monstrum horrendum*, an unprincipled man of genius." Earlier and more directly than the Dupin tales, "The Man of the Crowd" (1840) specifically thematizes criminal genius's inscrutability: at the beginning and end the narrator dwells on the hearts of those "burdened" with "the hideousness of mysteries which will not *suffer themselves* to be revealed." He likens the consciences thus burdened to a "certain German book" that "does not permit itself to be read" (*"er lasst sich nicht lesen"*). Although an obsession drives the narrator to classify human types, the tale ultimately performs neither the sanitized codification of later criminology nor the reverent silencing of later historians but instead a mode of reading opacity itself.

"The Man of the Crowd" opens with the narrator convalescing after an illness, seated by a window in a London coffeehouse. He looks out at the crowd on the street and notes "the innumerable varieties of detail, dress, air, gait, visage, and expression of countenance" among all the passersby. He delights in categorizing them—noblemen, merchants, attorneys, tradesmen, stock-jobbers, clerks, gamblers, and so on—and makes increasingly fine distinctions within these groups. Pressing his face against the glass as night falls, the narrator finds himself caught short by a countenance marked by "the absolute idiosyncrasy of its expression." With the hundreds he had already examined, he found that "I could frequently read, even in that brief interval of a glance, the history of long years." But by contrast *this* face is inscrutable and as a result fascinates him utterly. He cries out, "How wild a history . . . is written within that bosom!" Though perplexed, the narrator nevertheless discerns that particular volume contains criminal genius, and it transfixes him: "There arose confusedly and paradoxically within my mind, the ideas of vast mental power, of caution, of penuriousness, of avarice, of coolness, of malice, of blood-thirstiness, of triumph, of merriment, of excessive terror, of intense—of extreme despair." This idiosyncratic merger of intelligence, transgression, and joy challenges the narrator and makes him all the more determined to read this book. Despite his physically weakened condition, he gets up and follows the man around London on foot, all night long. Finally, he gives up and circles back to his initial conclusion. Resignedly, or perhaps even joyfully, the narrator embraces impossibility and pronounces that the man he has been following embodies "the type and the genius of deep crime . . . the worst heart of the world" and asserts, "It will be in vain to follow; for I shall learn no more of him, nor of his deeds." This individual "singularly aroused, startled, fascinated" him, and yet our narrator concludes as he began, with the suggestion that "perhaps it is but one of the great mercies of God that *es lasst sich nicht lesen.*"

In Poe's story, crime takes shape as an unclassifiable social remainder: it does not permit itself to be read. What the narrator cannot categorize he finds himself compelled to criminalize.[81] Yet, however unreadable, the criminal is nevertheless still a book, still invites reading. The narrator's assertion that this "worst heart of the world" is the "type and genius of deep crime" plays on this dynamic. Evoking both the malleability of "typeface," or print, "type" is a word that, of course, also designates classification or "typing," with which the narrator began while sitting at the coffeehouse. The narrator remarks in the first paragraph that "the essence of all crime is undivulged." And the story is recursive, ending where it began: with the narrator "absorbed in contemplation" of crime's opacity. Starting and ending with the paradox of a book that does not permit itself to be read, "The Man of the Crowd" refuses to conflate illegibility with taciturnity. The insight this tale offers is that illegibility does not equal silence but rather generates narrative.

This understanding that opacity drives narrative rather than foreclosing it remains crucial to any study of criminal genius, and it shows a way out of the literary-historical bind that has framed a false choice between reading and silencing Turner. As we have seen, from the 1830s to the present day, many who have sought to understand Nat Turner have concluded that, to respect his authentic, historical, "actual" self, we must recognize Turner's ultimate silence. On the other side, those wishing to read Turner in an individualist vein, as a hero, insist on his transparency, against the evidence. Both conclusions result from well-meaning but misguided attempts to acknowledge Turner's humanity (and by extension enslaved people's humanity writ large). We see this as early as Garrison's 1831 assessment. But it would be a mistake to discount the volubility of those, like Turner, convicted of a crime, even when their authentic individual personhood seems out of reach. As we have seen, to be convicted of a crime was to attract enormous attention from the popular press. This legal-print cycle affirmed the inclusion of African Americans, even those who were enslaved, in judicial processes, albeit generally only insofar as they could be held criminally liable.[82] As Jeannine DeLombard has shown, African Americans gained the public presence and civic authority needed to fight for liberal citizenship through criminalization, however paradoxical.

By contrast, what the Southampton Insurgency highlights is the more radical agency that this juridical-print circuit helped enable. Racialized criminalization also produced criminal genius, with its distinctive merger of voluntarist and materialist agencies. In the body of print surrounding the Southampton Insurgency, we find an aestheticization of Turner's life and deeds. Turner *himself* may, or may not, have cultivated opacity as described in *The Confessions* and suggested in his reported refusal to speak publicly when the opportunities arose (for my part, I believe the evidence suggest he did, but we cannot know for sure). Regardless, the imaginative possibilities that emerge from this nexus point to how, rather than recuperating Turner the subject of law, we might instead attend to the radical potential that aesthetic objectification enables.[83] Histories of capitalism and slavery underscore the commodity status of the enslaved: enslaved men and women were money, transferrable property, "hands" that, as Edward Baptist stresses, could be "put in the pocket" of their enslavers at a moment's notice.[84] And at the same time, white writers frequently aestheticized enslaved and other Black people to uncover white interiority, as Toni Morrison established more than twenty years ago in *Playing in the Dark*. Thus, as US capitalism transformed people of African origin into racialized commodities, it also produced what Morrison calls "Africanist" art objects, aestheticized representations of Black people that populated antebellum US literary production. There are key similarities between the these intimately related forms of racialized objecthood: the laboring commodity and the art object shore up white well-being, both material and psychological. However, as the Southampton Insurgency clearly reveals from all sides, sometimes the effects were deadly, claiming enslavers' lives and threatening their reigning ideologies. Attending to this insurgency as "fine art" suggests that aesthetic objecthood can sometimes generate the possibility of a more capacious humanism.

Beginning with recollections from childhood, Turner notes that all the adults in his world frequently remarked on his mental acuity. "My grand mother, who was very religious, and to whom I was much attached—my master, who belonged to the church, and other religious persons who visited the house, and whom I often saw at prayers, noticing the singularity of my manners, I suppose, and my uncommon intelligence for a child, remarked that I had too much sense to be raised, and if I was, I would never be of any service to any one as a slave."[85] The superficial oddness of this syntax speaks volumes. Turner's description identifies the racialized death sentence accompanying "uncommon intelligence." What this indicated to Turner's elders, some years after Nancy's initial attempt on his life, was that the child "had too much sense to be raised." Such an intelligent enslaved child was more likely to meet with an untimely demise than to reach adulthood. If he did make it to adulthood, his usefulness "as a slave" would be sharply limited. The path before him was, like Walker's, the path of the outlaw. As Snyder explains, "The terms of Virginia's statute declared slaves to be outlaws for a variety of offenses, but particularly for 'unlawfully absent[ing] themselves from their masters and mistresses service' and by lying, hiding, and lurking in 'obscure places,'" all of which Turner did. "All whites could, at their own discretion and by whatever means they chose, apprehend and kill outlawed slaves."[86] Turner's intelligence, and actions springing therefrom, would serve only to increase his liability to premature death.

Turner describes his deep powers of mental attention to Gray in some detail: "To a mind like mine, restless, inquisitive, and observant of everything that was passing, it is easy to suppose that religion was the subject to which it would be directed, and although this subject principally occupied my thoughts—there was nothing that I saw or heard of to which my attention was not directed."[87] With this description, Turner pushes against Gray's characterization of him as a religious fanatic. It was natural, he states, for one so mentally attuned, to be drawn to religion; yet while religion "principally" preoccupied him, Turner emphasizes that it was far from his sole focus. Moreover, as Drexler-Dreis has argued, "Turner's religious orientation is not an abandonment of material reality but a way of connecting life on the material level with divinity."[88] Turner's acquisition of literacy is particularly striking. It shows his sharp intellect while underlining that his gifts are not only intellectual but also preternatural: "The manner in which I learned to read and write, not only had great influence on my own mind, as I acquired it with the most perfect ease, so much so, that I have no recollection whatever of learning the alphabet—but to the astonishment of the family, one day, when a book was shewn me to keep me from crying, I began spelling the names of different objects. . . . [T]his learning was constantly improved at all opportunities."[89] Turner amazes others with his uncanny ability to master language. Acquiring literacy came so naturally that he formed no recollection of it. In lieu of an account of *how* he learned to read, Turner instead describes further instances of knowledge that should have been obtained by experience but for him were somehow innate. "Whenever an opportunity occurred of looking at a book, when the school children were getting their lessons, I would find many things that the fertility of my own imagination had depicted to me before."[90] In his encounters with books, Turner does not *learn* so much as he rediscovers what he is astonished to find he had already imagined beforehand.

This prophetic foreknowledge recalls the incident that Turner represents as foundational to all that followed. He begins his account of his life by describing how, at three or four years old, he stunned his family by displaying knowledge of events that had transpired before his birth:

> It is here necessary to relate this circumstance—trifling as it may seem, it was the commencement of that belief which has grown with time, and even now, sir, in this dungeon, helpless and forsaken as I am, I cannot divest myself of it. Being at play with other children, when three or four years old, I was telling them something which my mother, overhearing, said it had happened before I was born—I stuck to my story, however, and related some thing which went, in her opinion, to confirm it—others being called on were greatly astonished, knowing that these things had happened, and caused them to say in my hearing, I surely would be a prophet, as the Lord had shown me things that had happened before my birth.

The sense that Turner was blessed with the gift of prophecy owing to this innate knowledge introduces an insurgent temporality to *The Confessions*. Baker's powerful graphic novel juxtaposes precisely this bit of text from the *Confessions* to an illustration of a group of children rapturously listening to Turner, who stands beneath a thought bubble showing a silhouetted Black baby thrown headfirst from a ship into the gaping jaws of a hungry shark.[91] The suggestion, of course, is that what the young Turner had knowledge of—what he knew yet could not, should not have known—was an insurgent matrilineal legacy. He knew that his mother, along with other insurgent mothers before Nancy, had cast their infant children to death rather than allow them to live and die enslaved. Baker's juxtaposition makes sense, because it is this prophetic foreknowledge that sets in place the unshakeable belief that, even as he sits "forsaken," Turner "cannot divest" himself of; namely, that he was uniquely attuned to divine knowledge.

Turner goes on to depict himself not only as devoted to prayer but also as a young inventor and scientist, spending all the time he could find "making experiments in casting things in moulds made of earth, in attempting to make paper." For the skeptical reader, Gray supplies a note indicating that, "when questioned as to the manner of manufacturing those different articles, he was found well informed on the subject."[92] Turner was not successful in everything he attempted but was convinced that even the failures mattered: "Many other experiments, that although I could not perfect, yet convinced me of its practicability if I had the means." There is a particular poignancy to this in the context of the forsaken position from which he narrates it, as he awaits execution for his role in an insurgency whose importance was not measurable by the immediate achievement of its aim but would continue to unfold for centuries.

Turner's account of childhood precocity and experimentation evokes familiar accounts of the early years of the "great minds" of Enlightenment science, philosophy, and literature. Like Locke and Newton, Mary Shelley's Victor Frankenstein, and Brockden Brown's Carwin, Turner began as a sharply attentive child, distinguished from early age for exceptional powers of mind. All spare time was devoted to acquiring additional learning, to performing experiments, and to prayer, in order that he might attain a greater understanding of both the natural and spiritual world. This representation of Turner's early life connects his *Confessions* to ideas delineated roughly fifty years prior, in the *Critique of Judgment*. Immanuel Kant famously defines genius as the ability to "apprehend the imagination ... and to intuit it in a concept that can be communicated without the constraint of rules ... while at the same time it reveals a new rule that could not have been inferred from any earlier principles or examples."[93] Turner's mental capabilities combine the enthusiasm of prophetic and religious experience, the exultation of imaginative practice, and the rationalism of scientific experiment. Throughout *The Confessions*, Turner underscores his morality, but, as in Kant's description, he is not bound by the same rules as others but instead generates new ones for those "good minds" that might follow his exceptional example.

Thus, *The Confessions* recounts one important early recollection of criminal activity as follows: "I was not addicted to stealing in my youth, nor have ever been—Yet such was the confidence of the negroes ... in my superior judgment, that they would often carry me with them when they were going on any roguery, to plan for them."[94] The young Turner's superior judgment brings him naturally into the role of leader, outside or beyond the strictures of law. Playing the role of criminal genius even as a child, he plots collective transgressions (fig. 4.4). Yet at no point does *The Confessions* ever precisely outline Turner's motives. Instead, it describes his communication with the Spirit that spoke to the biblical prophets, explains the signs sent to him, and catalogs the bloody events themselves.

From the stage of history, channeled in crucial ways through the pages of Gray's pamphlet, Turner emerges as an intellectually gifted, exceptional individual, a man apart who not only defied the status quo but believed that he did so in direct communication with God.[95] Gray's overarching description of Turner raises many more questions than it answers:

> He is a complete fanatic, or plays his part most admirably.... Possesses an uncommon share of intelligence, with a mind capable of attaining any thing; but warped and perverted.... He is below the ordinary stature, though strong and active, having the true negro face, every feature of which is strongly marked.... The calm,

Orville Victor, "Nat Turner & His Confederates in Conference," in *History of American Conspiracies: A Record of Treason, Insurrection, & Rebellion in the United States of America* (New York: James D. Torrey, 1863). Courtesy of the American Antiquarian Society

deliberate composure with which he spoke of his late deeds and intentions, the expression of his fiend-like face ... clothed with rags and covered with chains; yet daring to raise his manacled hands to heaven, with a spirit soaring above the attributes of man; I looked on him and my blood curdled in my veins.[96]

Gray leaves readers with more paradoxes than simple formulas. What should we make of his coolness and composure? Is he a fanatic or an artificer? How might we make sense of his degraded physicality (clothed in rags, manacled, short), taken together with a seemingly transcendent spirit and superior mind, "capable of anything"? The difficulties of deciphering Gray's intentions and effects are pronounced and striking.[97] This is a pamphlet that was published with an audience of enslavers in mind yet was seen by the *Liberator* as potentially fomenting sympathy and admiration for Turner.[98] Gray's suggestion that Turner's mind was in some sense deficient, "bewildered and confounded ... endeavoring to grapple with things beyond its reach," stands in stark contradiction to his concluding assessment, that Turner, "for natural intelligence and quickness of apprehension, is surpassed by few men I have ever seen." Moreover, the body of *The Confessions* forcefully and immediately undermines the preface's assertion that Turner's mind was "confounded."

Gray's claim that Turner possessed a spirit "soaring above the attributes of man," that he surpassed almost anyone, Black or white, he had ever met in "natural intelligence" seems remarkable and stands as evidence of how malleable biological racism and attendant notions of genius still were in the antebellum period. In the nineteenth century, Gus Stadler explains, "genius became less explicitly tied to rhetorics of publicity and nation. Instead, it took on greater significance as a symbolic medium for representing a troubled model of the individual."[99] That is to say that the term becomes closely associated with the meaning it has today. Rather than evoking a unity, or collective spirit (the genius of the French, for example, or as in the title of Benjamin Lundy's abolitionist paper, *Genius of Universal Emancipation*), "genius" came to denote exceptional, extraordinary capacities and abilities, or the man or woman who has these capacities. At the same time, however, in the nineteenth century, the category of the individual genius retained a gravitas that it has lost today, when it is often used hyperbolically or in jest. *The Confessions*' representation of Turner as genius has all the gravitas of the nineteenth century and none of the later caricature. More importantly, it retains the aspect of collectivity associated with an earlier conception of genius as defining spirit. Gray's central gambit, to constrain Turner's radicalism by positing him as an exceptional individual, although influential, proves limited. Turner himself traces his sense of personal power to his family, his grandmother ("to whom I was much attached"), his parents ("my father and mother strengthened me in this my first impression, saying in my presence, I was intended for some great purpose"), and other members of his community.[100] And his inspiration, as we have seen, came from his reading of celestial and natural phenomena, channeled through the lens of his African American Christianity (as he said to Gray, when asked whether he had any knowledge of other rebellions occurring around the same time, "Can you not think the same ideas, and strange appearances about this time in the heavens might prompt others, as well as myself, to this undertaking?").[101]

Because genius is directly tied to his insurgent criminality, it remains situated and collective, weaving together voluntarist, cultural, and material forces. Attending to the aesthetic figuration of Turner as a criminal genius, we return to the idea of an inscrutable Nat Turner—but with a difference. His taciturnity is the reserve of genius, refracting a radical world that almost came to be. Reading Turner's actions in planning and perpetrating the attack, his ostensible communications with Gray, whatever form their interaction actually took, and the material technologies that made the print dissemination and consumption of these stories available, we can understand the Southampton Insurgency as more than the story of one heroic individual. The insurgency enlisted and developed relatively new formulations of the criminal as a genius whose agency is common and widely distributed across a network of people, places, and objects.

The Atlantic world in which the Southampton Insurgency unfolded is typically seen as consolidating liberal individualism as foundational to both national identity and citizenship.[102] This familiar story is often told in relation to "self-made men" like Benjamin Franklin, though it also plays a key role for some Black writers, like Frederick Douglass, who delivered his address "Self-Made Men," more frequently than any other.[103] Seeing figures like Nat Turner as self-determined exemplars of resistance reinforces this story. Reading Turner as criminal genius points in a different direction. As we have seen in previous chapters, criminal genius's racialized, distributed agency expands the liberal view of agency as individual and autonomous. Rather than being enacted by a universal abstract self, it is shared across human and nonhuman lines. The cloaking of liberalism in republican virtue in early America in part enabled the perpetuation of an alternative, collective structure of power and belonging: criminal genius.[104] The aesthetic legacies of the Southampton Insurgency allow us to consider the condition of enslaved humanity differently. The choice is not between autonomous, resistant agent and passive victim.

Placing the aesthetic aspects of the Southampton Insurgency on an analytic par with the event's historical veracity, we find a model of material distributed agency that pushes against the abstractions of liberal capital. *The Confessions of Nat Turner* explicitly characterizes Turner as a criminal genius. Why? Is this characterization a result of Turner's own words? Did something about Turner, such as his personal charisma, inspire Gray to represent him in this way? Was it a result of Turner's own cultivation of the cloak of genius both during his life and at the time of his capture and execution? Or was the choice to figure Turner as a criminal genius a product purely of Gray's imagination? These questions all center motivation, intent, and authenticity. They are all immensely interesting and, like Poe's "man of the crowd," worthy of pursuit. Yet we should not let them distract us from exploring the figuration itself, because the very fact that *The Confessions* and related documents portray Turner as a criminal genius, even apart from the question of *why*? is highly significant for our thinking about so-called nonhuman agencies.[105]

As we have seen, the Southampton Insurgency is not easily read, and it remains in key respects illegible. Yet criminal genius helped reimagine a world that, as of 1831, lacked concepts adequate to the needs of a powerful, independent, intelligent, and ethical individual who was also enslaved and therefore limited in his choices: "daring to raise his manacled hands to heaven." As De Quincey explains, "The blaze of his genius absolutely dazzled the eye of criminal justice."[106] As much an imaginative, aesthetic creation as a social, scientific, or historical reality, the criminal genius illustrates Black insurgency in the face of the state's monopoly of violence, all the while highlighting what Uri McMillan describes as "the personal and artistic risks incumbent in becoming and/or performing as an object."[107] Although the printed and archival record remains incomplete, the Southampton Insurgency made and continues to make demands on us. Born from a radical genealogy of insurgent mothering, more poet than victim, more tactician than soldier, more prophet than martyr, Nat Turner figures antebellum criminal genius uncaricatured and uncontained, bridging voluntarist and materialist agencies and capable of expanding the forms of life available to those who have been called socially dead.[108]

As with Frost in the 1790s, criminal genius emerges in relation to the Southampton Insurgency in the 1830s not solely as an assertion of individual agency or as a way of accessing the insurgents as a subjects rather than as objects of history. Instead, criminal genius maps out an alternative to liberal humanism and forensic personhood. Unlike Frederick Douglass, who would articulate his entrée from enslaved existence into the realm of individual rights and his assertion of agency within a hostile society largely through education and self-discipline, we can read the Southampton Insurgency within the nexus of criminality and genius that had taken shape in the popular imagination by the 1830s. When we focus our energies on somehow returning liberal agency to the enslaved, we undercut the existence of other genres of humanity. The radical aesthetic, imaginative legacies of Southampton Insurgency show that we can consider the condition of humanity differently. A better account of the lives and legacies of those classed and treated as nonhuman must attend to material agencies, such as the insurgency's unsettled print legacy, as well as voluntarist agencies like that of Turner himself.

CHAPTER FIVE

Fugitive Aesthetics

> I have reached these lands but newly
> From an ultimate dim Thule—
> From a wild weird clime that lieth, sublime,
> > Out of SPACE—Out of TIME.
>
> > —*Edgar Allan Poe, "Dream-Land" (1844)*

Stéphane Mallarmé long ago singled out "Dream-Land" as one of Edgar Allan Poe's most characteristic poems, and its refrain "Out of SPACE—Out of TIME" remains one of Poe's most frequently quoted lines.[1] Yet the poem itself has been virtually unstudied throughout the twentieth and twenty-first centuries. Formalist critics dismissively described "Dream-Land" as a transcendent "no place of no reference" that succeeds in "block[ing] the process of signification altogether" or as "just what the title promises: a description of the topsy-turvy world of dreams."[2] Although later historicist studies of Poe's work ubiquitously reference the poem's refrain to denounce the "genius" that falsely claims to transcend everyday life, they regard the poem itself as an essentially uninteresting example of the evasive work of the aesthetic.[3]

The fact that "Dream-Land" has seemed an unremarkable paean to the genius that we must resist in order to historicize testifies to a long-standing, but misguided, fissure in US literary studies. A false dichotomy between aesthetic autonomy and historical engagement has pervaded the field. As Paul Gilmore notes, critics over the past several decades have tended to equate "New Critical formalism with aesthetics in toto."[4] Although "a historicized, politically sensitive, even progressive idea of aesthetics" developed in studies of British literature in the 1990s, a similar aesthetic turn was much slower in coming to Americanist literary criticism.[5] Perhaps more surprising is the fact that very little of this newer work has addressed Poe.[6] Poe has in many ways defined the category of the aesthetic in nineteenth-century US literary studies, and so his relative absence from this scholarship is striking.[7]

As discussed in the introduction, it was during the eighteenth and nineteenth centuries that "genius" came to denote a producer of highly original aesthetic works. From his own time through to the twenty-first century, Poe has often been taken to exemplify just this figure. One early review of Poe's work stated that the young writer was "evidently a fine genius," and one character in the 2012 James McTeigue film, *The Raven*, proclaims, "God gave him a spark of genius and quenched it in misery!"[8] Yet this interest in anything like Poe's "genius" has all but disappeared. Most influential scholarship of the past several decades has focused on Poe's centrality to broader historical and political contexts, rather than to aesthetics. Following Toni Morrison's 1993 assessment that "no early American author is more important to the concept of American Africanism than Poe," critics have produced nuanced studies of American literature in general, and of Poe in particular, in relation to race and history.[9] This is right and warranted but limited by the fact that this scholarship has aimed almost exclusively at "demystifying" the aesthetic, by focusing instead on history as the occluded cause of artistic works.[10] Yet, as the lens of criminal genius has shown, aesthetic and historical forces are inextricably bound up with one another.

This chapter examines genius and racialized criminality in Poe's fugitive poetics, his theory and practice of aesthetic escape. Because Poe's work has remained a cornerstone of both formalist and historicist approaches to US literature and because, like the purloined letter, "Dream-Land" has all along been hiding in plain sight, it offers an ideal locus to understand criminal genius in US culture. T. S. Eliot described Poe's work as "the most interesting development of poetic consciousness" of the century,[11] and this chapter traces how Poe, over the course of his career, refracts a conception of aesthetic genius very different from those anachronistic histories centering white genius. The hallmarks of the understanding of genius that most influenced Poe were *not* originality, autonomy, and freedom but rather convertibility, enmeshment, and circumscription. "Dream-Land" is suffused with the relentless apposition of the material and the spiritual that characterizes the most memorable moments in Poe's oeuvre, as when the monomaniacal narrator of "Berenice" identifies the idealized eponymous character with her hard, white teeth or when a black raven croaking "Nevermore" comes to emblematize the purity of lost love. Colin Dayan has argued that in such works Poe creates "pulsing border-grounds where things and thoughts, clods of earth and disembodied spirits alternate, poised in their rites of conversion."[12] But unlike many of these poems and tales, which have been successfully read symbolically, psychologically, or through philosophical or historicist lenses, "Dream-Land" stubbornly resists reading practices that prioritize either formal or historical features. Its endless entanglements require instead an interpretive practice that reads text, human action, and indeed the natural world itself alongside one another.[13]

"Dream-Land" is the product of a series of revisions that spanned most of Poe's career. Across these revisions, we can see Poe's aesthetic theory developing, his practice coming to relate equally to the formal, the historical, and the political, with emphasis on the material and natural world. Poe's commitment to constructing and theorizing aesthetic experiences in which readers might fully immerse themselves is well known. As he states in "The Philosophy of Composition," "If any literary work is too long to be read at one sitting, we must be content to dispense with the immensely important effect derivable from unity of impression—for, if two sittings be required, the affairs of the world interfere, and everything like totality is at once destroyed." The author must, Poe stresses, use every tool available to create an immersive experience for the reader. Describing Poe's production of aesthetic experience, Dayan speaks of Poe's "preference for surfaces over depths."[14] Rachel Polonsky notes that Poe's discussions of aesthetics, though sometimes drawing on Romanticism's "conceptual vocabulary, its rhetoric and its metaphors redirect critical attention onto technique, to art as a clever illusion which the artist controls like a mathematical or mechanical problem."[15] Yet Poe's aesthetic surfaces are by no means uncomplicated.[16] They are not hard, refractive productions but rather immersive, containing contradictory impulses.

Numerous scholars have established that the broader history of aesthetics is intimately bound up with the history of race and enslavement. As Simon Gikandi has recently pointed out, this connection "is sometimes so obvious that it does not demand any deep hermeneutics."[17] Yet the link between race and the aesthetic is often evanescent or phantasmagorical. Citing the ubiquity of tropes of invisibility in Black radical aesthetics, Fred Moten has argued that these alternative forms of presence offer ways "to be seen, instantly and fascinatingly recognized as the unrecognizable," and Saidiya V. Hartman has explicated the link between "hypervisibility" of enslaved Black bodies and the necessary "obscurity" and "opacity" of Black cultural production.[18] Both Moten and Hartman are discussing African American aesthetic production, while Poe has rightly been linked to a white supremacist ideology.[19] His aesthetics is, of course, also tied to race and grounded in the interconnection and convertibility of what is visible on the surface and what remains, to use one of his favored terms, "indefinitive." As Dayan points out, Poe undoes any simple opposition between "scientific reason" and "poetic intuition" or "material fact" and "visionary knowledge."[20] Connecting surface and depth more dramatically than any of his other poems or tales, "Dream-Land" does not aim to obscure social realities like race but rather works through the myriad material entanglements of life, art, and environment.

The aesthetic that underpins "Dream-Land" is not isolated, abstract, and individualist but part of an embedded, embodied collective. "Dream-Land" offers *neither* a representation of transcendent Genius (often associated with Poe himself) *nor* an instance of the aesthetic functioning as deceptive veneer (as historicist readings of Poe often argue).[21] It limns instead a different form of genius, exemplified, however unexpectedly, by maroons in the Great Dismal Swamp of Virginia and North Carolina. The escape "Dream-Land" evokes is—at one and the same time—the escape of genius into a world of "fugitive poems" (a widely used nineteenth-century term describing poetry that transports readers out of the here and now) and the escape of previously enslaved people into the Great Dismal Swamp.

"The Consciousness of Locality"

The publication history of "Dream-Land" and related poems indicates the poem's centrality to Poe's aesthetic project across a span of two decades. Poe published some iteration of this poem multiple times between 1827 and 1845. The full version of "Dream-Land" first appeared in *Graham's Magazine* in 1844, and several times Poe republished a shorter version, which excised two repetitions of the refrain.[22] *Tamerlane and Other Poems* (1827) includes the related "Dreams," "Visits of the Dead," and "The Lake," which, as I will show, describes a landscape akin to the one we find in "Dream-Land."[23] Significant portions of these three poems find their way into Poe's second volume, *Al Aaraaf, Tamerlane, and Minor Poems* (1829), where they are reworked in "Spirits of the Dead," "A Dream," and "Fairy-land." "Fairyland," which also appeared in his 1831 collection, included lines virtually identical to those used in "Dream-Land." John Neal singled them out for special praise in the earliest published review of Poe's poetry:

> If E. A. P. of Baltimore—whose lines about "Heaven" . . . are, though nonsense, rather exquisite nonsense—would but do himself justice, he might make a beautiful and perhaps magnificent poem. There is a good deal to justify such a hope.
>
> > Dim vales—and shadowy floods,
> > And cloudy-looking woods,

Whose forms we can't discover,
For the tears that—drip all over.²⁴

Neal's hopes for E.A.P.'s poetry likely were not realized when this quatrain, nearly verbatim, found its final home in "Dream-Land." The later poem intensifies the illogic with which Neal found fault. Despite its ubiquitous citation and anthologization, we can number "Dream-Land" among those Poe works that Dayan has described as "really bizarre, apparently nonsensical, and most stylistically jarring."²⁵ Yet it is the poem's very nonsensical qualities, its jarring, discordant effects, that make it so crucial for understanding Poe's aesthetics.

Being kidnapped, thrown into an unknown environment, forcibly transported from one place to another, with one's self-identity and ties of kinship under constant attack: these are hallmarks of the experience of enslavement. The opening of "Dream-Land" performs these operations in reverse. Here, normatively white readers are transported to the recesses of what will prove to be a metaphorical and literal swamp, well known as a haven of safety for the self-emancipated. The opening lines of "Dream-Land" unfold as a tangle of syntax, meter, rhyme, and narrative content that calls into question even the basic categories of time and space. It would be difficult to overstate the sense of dislocation that characterizes the first octave. All lines, except one, begin by pairing a preposition with an indefinite article: "By a" "Where an" "On a" "From an" and "From a." Yet this string of locational phrases does little to help orient even the most careful readers, who are inexorably drawn "Out of SPACE—Out of TIME."

> BY a route obscure and lonely,
> Haunted by ill angels only,
> Where an Eidolon, named NIGHT,
> On a black throne reigns upright,
> I have reached these lands but newly
> From an ultimate dim Thule—
> From a wild weird clime, that lieth, sublime,
>   Out of SPACE—Out of TIME. (1–8)

The indefinite article "an," along with the descriptive adjectives "ultimate" and "dim," at once grant and deny specificity to "Thule," the mythical land at the northernmost ends of the earth.²⁶ Clearly, the speaker has traveled by a little-known, isolated route. Yet do the "ill angels" of the second line haunt the route, "these lands," or dim Thule itself (if these latter two are indeed distinct)? It is impossible to tell. Likewise, it is unclear just where it is that the Eidolon reigns.

Poe is mixing Romantic and classical imagery here. An eidolon is a ghost, phantom, or image, and in this use of the word Poe is referring to the Greek theosophical concept of a shadow or astral double of a departed physical being. Ultima Thule refers to a mythical island on the northernmost borders of the world. Thus, answers to the larger questions of precisely who the speaker is, where he has traveled, or even where he has "newly" arrived become increasingly opaque as the poem proceeds.

In this first stanza, it seems apparent that "dim Thule" is an alien place, and "these lands" are home to the speaker as well as his audience. Yet by the third stanza it starts to seem as if "this ultimately dim Thule" may be where the poem's *readers* reside. The speaker's home ("my home") may in fact be the otherworldly region he has begun to describe. The final couplet of the fourth stanza, "And thus the sad Soul that here passes / Beholds it but through darkened glasses," further aligns the reader, as opposed to the speaker, with the "traveler, traveling through [Dream-Land]." Bespectacled and perusing a firsthand account of someone who has perhaps inhabited, rather than merely traveled through "Dream-Land," the reader is distinguished from the speaker. Although this "wild weird clime" is foreign to us, it seems that it may well be familiar to the speaker.

Faced with the poem's unanswerable questions, one might conclude, as Poe's "Mr. B." did of the *Confessions of an Opium Eater* in the satiric "How to Write a Blackwood Article" (1845), that what we find here is "glorious imagination— . . . and a good spicing of the decidedly unintelligible."[27] Yet the poem's onslaught of indecipherable indexicals, along with its seeming separation of the speaker from the reader, do not figure ethereal transcendence, absence, or placelessness. The directional markers that the poem insistently assembles point somewhere. The problem is not a lack of a place; it is rather an excess of location—we get too much direction, not too little—along with the darkness or "dim"-ness that characterizes the place in question. Poe elsewhere identifies such pregnant obscurity as a hallmark of successful poetry, which in his view offers a "suggestive indefinitiveness of meaning, with the view of bringing about a definitiveness of vague and therefore of spiritual *effects*."[28]

Following Poe's logic, I propose that the "vague and therefore spiritual . . . effect[]" of this poem's "indefinitiveness" is the interweaving of place and person. This interrelation between locality and identity is also in play in "The Colloquy of Monos and Una" (1841). In the year following his death, Monos relates, "The consciousness of *being* had grown hourly more indistinct, and that of mere *locality* had, in great measure, usurped its position. The idea of entity was becoming merged in that of *place*. The narrow space immediately surrounding what had been the body, was now growing to be the body itself."²⁹ Here "being" and "locality" merge, as body comes to occupy the space from which it once perceived itself as being distinct. We see this as well in a later tale, "The Domain of Arnheim" (1846), which exemplifies Poe's inclination to elide person and place when the fictional "voyager" of the second half of the tale finds himself, in body and mind, in thrall to the sensuousness of the landscape that surrounds him.³⁰

This breakdown of the distinction between interior and exterior, place and person is quintessentially gothic. As Benjamin F. Fisher notes, Poe admirers often wrongly assume that he invented gothic fiction. In point of fact, Poe was a relative latecomer to the genre, and some contemporary critics "deplored his wasting talents on what they deemed had become an outmoded type of fiction."³¹ Although some scholars, including James M. Hutchinson, have proclaimed that Poe scholarship needs to move "beyond Gothicism,"³² the recent reconception of the gothic in relation to US literature that we find in the work of Nancy Armstrong, Leonard Tennenhouse, and Siân Silvyn Roberts suggests otherwise. Tennenhouse has demonstrated the centrality of the gothic in the work of creating an English diasporic culture in the Americas that would both reproduce and fundamentally change English culture. Gothic was crucial to nineteenth-century Anglophone literary history and developed in close relation to the sensationalized gallows tradition.³³ As Leslie Fiedler noted long ago, American literature "is almost essentially a gothic one," and the expansive subjectivities of the gothic that newer scholarship particularly highlights are important to my delineation of criminal genius.³⁴ Although most critical discussion of the gothic has focused on prose fiction, poetry is particularly important in tracing alternate subjectivities. "The Raven," "The Conqueror Worm" (1843), "The Haunted Palace" (1839), and, of course, "Dream-Land," with its evocation of nightmarish landscapes, ghouls, and a ruler named "NIGHT" seated atop a "black throne," are key gothic poems.

Natural and built environments, from the craggy castle to lone wood or the "dead waters" of "Dream-Land," have long been recognized as a defining element of the gothic. Charles Brockden Brown, one of the earliest American gothic writers and an important influence on Poe, famously strove to rework the gothic as American by igniting "the passions and engag[ing] the sympathy of the reader" not with "castles and chimeras" but instead with uncanny or sublime landscapes.³⁵ Calling into question the importance of locale to the gothic, however, recent critics have argued that attention to setting is ultimately not a meaningful way to distinguish the American gothic from its Old World counterparts. For example, Siân Silvyn Roberts proposes that the American gothic does not differ significantly from British or continental traditions in its use of "autochthonous themes, settings, characters or authorial biography" but rather in its production of "a complex and wholly distinct" diasporic political subject.[36] Where the British gothic ultimately underwrites a stable, self-determining individual, the American gothic imagines "a constellation of different narrative personas whose mutability and adaptability make them ideally suited to a fluctuating Atlantic world," or the "gothic subjects" her book's title announces.[37]

Roberts assesses the gothic as productive of "porous, fluid singularities that circulate through wider networks of information and feeling," rather than some "originary, ordered, proprietary self."[38] Yet it nevertheless remains the case that to recognize those entities "that exist only in and through their relation to others rather than as ontologically ordered beings that exist prior to social relations," we must attend carefully to particularities in environment as well, to relations among persons and places that are not exclusively social but also material.[39] Noting that Poe's "sense of environment . . . did not necessarily separate interior and exterior, rural and urban," Hutchinson rightly asserts the need "to think more about Poe's relationship to the environment." Yet given the fact that the gothic is the genre that most insistently collapses such separations, I disagree that it is limiting "to define 'environment'" in relation to "gothic setting."[40] Place matters, especially in relation to personhood.

Brockden Brown imagined that the "western wilderness" would become the de facto setting for an American gothic. Yet in "Dream-Land," with its "Titan woods . . . / [and] Lakes that endlessly outspread," we begin to see that the American gothic setting par excellence will not primarily be the vast, distant open stretches of "unoccupied" land, which were in actuality populated by relocated tribal peoples, Indigenous Native Americans, and white settler-colonists. Although the American gothic is sometimes set in the West (to great effect), the South is where it most fully takes root: notably in and around the cramped, close, and strangling swampland that confounded would-be investors and offered refuge to what Daniel O. Sayers has termed "diasporan exiles" (fig. 5.1).[41] These included Native Americans; African American fugitives and some fugitive European American laborers, including Irish indentured servants; and, at least in legend, song, and poetry, the lonely hearts who sought solace for their losses in its shadows.[42]

"Gone to the Dismal Swamp"

The swamp is not simply another, newer gothic setting. Instead, the melding of place and person, human and nonhuman, land and water that we find in the swamp is broadly constitutive of aesthetic theory and practice across Poe's fiction,

Photograph of Lake Drummond. Courtesy of the United States Fish and Wildlife Service

poetry, and criticism. We see the attraction to dark and unbearably close settings, whether the cells of the Inquisition in "The Pit and the Pendulum" (1842), the catacombs in "The Cask of Amontillado" (1846), or the tarns and living tombs of "The Fall of the House of Usher" (1839) and "Berenice" (1835). Such locales are perfectly suited to the strain of disidentification that underlies Poe's ubiquitous questioning of the distinctiveness of human and animal, waking and sleeping, even life and death.[43] As David Miller has argued, the swamp dissolved clear categories for nineteenth-century Americans, who endowed it with "an animism that is both spiritual and material and yet neither."[44] Neither land nor water but both, the swamp is a terraqueous "wetland" in which, as Monique Allewaert has emphasized, "land becomes sea" and "the fantasy of the bounded body" dissolves.[45] The surface terrain of the swamp is viscous, fecund, and ungovernable, and the deeper social history of the swamp is equally generative. Thus, it is in the swamp that "Dream-Land" aligns the bereaved lover and the maroon as two figures for creative genius. This wetland geography generates the connections, mediations, and repetitions across time and space, "the transported presence of places into other ones."[46]

More powerfully than any other swampland, the Great Dismal Swamp captured the popular imagination in the middle decades of the nineteenth century.[47]

Long infamous in local tales and legends, the Great Dismal was a "very substantial tract of extremely remote land" stretching across Virginia and North Carolina, with the 3,100-acre Lake Drummond at its center (fig. 5.2).[48] During the period in which Poe first wrote, revised, and published "Dream-Land" and related poems, the Great Dismal Swamp came into national prominence in Samuel Warner's 1831 description, *Authentic and Impartial Narrative of the Tragical Scene Which Was Witnessed in Southampton County*, which, as I have discussed, enjoyed a wide distribution in the wake of the Southampton Insurgency. Warner included a lengthy description of the Great Dismal, in which Turner took refuge before his capture. The proximity of the swamp to the site of the insurgency, as Daphne Brooks remarks, "canonized antebellum perceptions of the Great Dismal as an environmental obstacle course" and cemented, for a time at least, the "cultural infamy" of swamps in general and Great Dismal in particular as "haunting and treacherous territory."[49] By the time "Dream-Land" was published, the Great Dismal Swamp was firmly entrenched in US culture.

The short story "A Day in a Railway Car" (*Godey's*, 1842), evidences the Great Dismal's imaginative reach. In this tale, an elderly woman living alone in a boarding house, when questioned about her well-being, replies that although she has little left to live for, she has "not yet got into the Dismal Swamp."[50] The Great Dismal Swamp carried a broad cultural resonance. Raised in Virginia, Poe is known to have visited the Great Dismal and to have been influenced by poets and artists who represented this place.[51] In "The Philosophy of Furniture" (1840), Poe lists John Gadsby Chapman's painting *The Lake of the Dismal Swamp* as being particularly well suited to the walls of a "well-furnished" room (fig. 5.3), one of those "landscapes of an imaginative cast—such as the fairy grottoes of Stanfield, or the lake of the Dismal Swamp, of Chapman."[52]

Just as travelers to Great Dismal Swamp encounter Lake Drummond at the center of the swamp, when readers come to the middle of "Dream-Land," they find lakes that "outspread / Their lone waters, lone and dead." In one of Poe's earliest published poems, "The Lake" (1827), the speaker describes a similar "wild lake with black rock bound / And the tall trees that tower'd around." Commentators have asserted that "The Lake" (which was included, provocatively for our purposes, as one of the "Fugitive Pieces" in *Tamerlane and Other Poems*) was inspired Poe's visits to the swamp's Lake Drummond, a "strange body of water ... believed to be poisonous" (83, 536).

Thomas Moore, an Irish poet, also visited the swamp and penned "A Ballad: The Lake of the Dismal Swamp" (1803). The ballad's foreword indicates Moore's reliance on a local legend: "They tell of a young man who lost his mind upon the

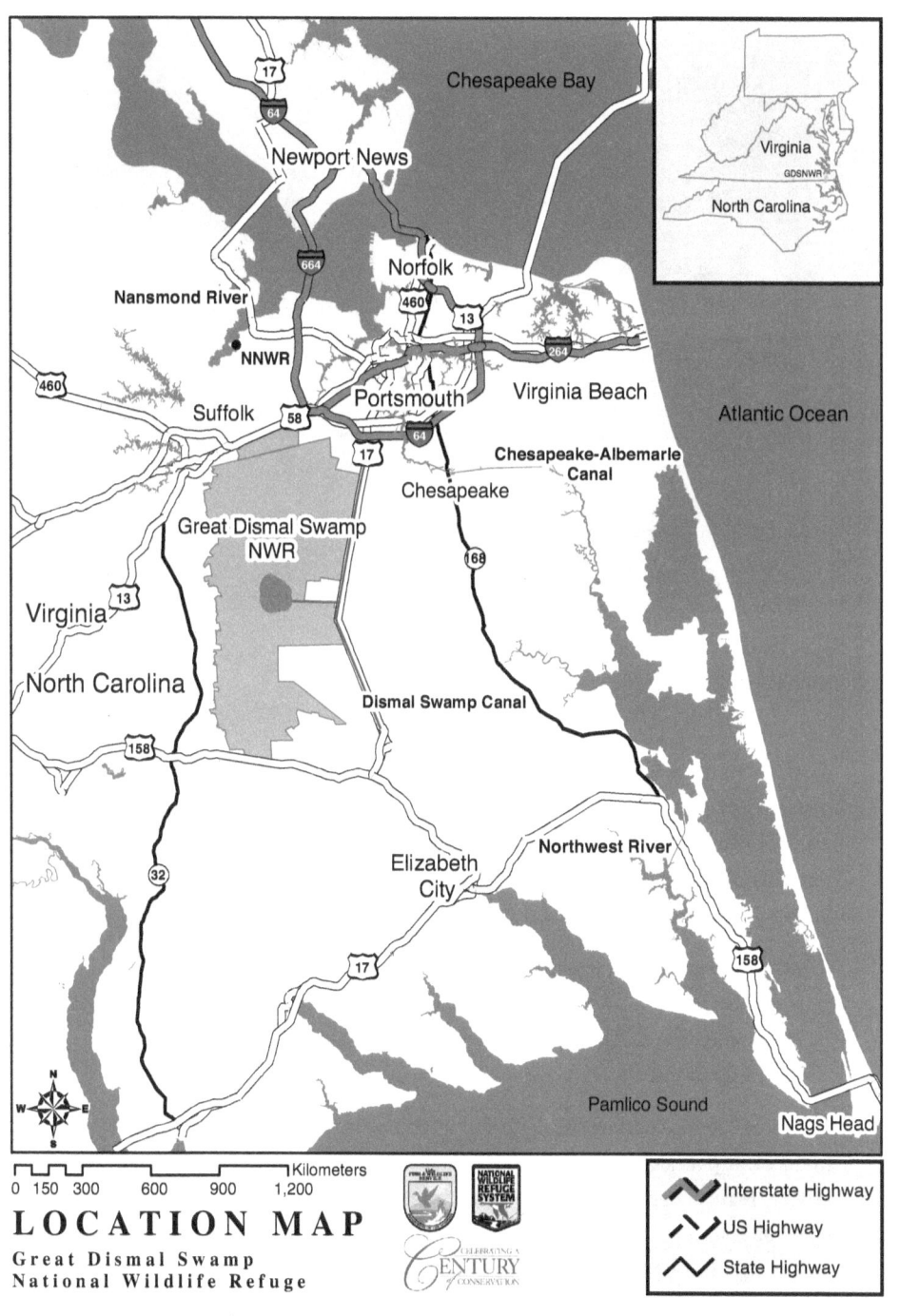

LOCATION MAP
Great Dismal Swamp
National Wildlife Refuge

Courtesy of the United States Fish and Wildlife Service

John Gadsby, *The Lake of the Dismal Swamp*, c. 1825. Courtesy of the American Antiquarian Society

death of a girl he loved, and who, suddenly disappearing from his friends, was never afterwards heard of. As he had frequently said, in his ravings, that the girl was not dead, but gone to the Dismal Swamp, it is supposed he had wandered into that dreary wilderness, and . . . been lost." Moore suggests that this heartbroken lover was a dreamer and melancholic:

> when, on earth, he sunk to sleep
> If slumber his eyelids knew
> He lay where the deadly vine doth weep
> Its venomous tear.[53]

In Moore's bereaved lover, able to fall asleep only amid the deadly swamp, we find a clear poetic source for Poe's speaker in "Dream-Land." Poe, who admired Moore, reanimates this this lost young man, familiar both from local legends Poe would have heard in his youth and from the poetry he later read.

Though the poem is foreboding in much of its imagery, the penultimate stanza proclaims that Dream-Land is a peaceful place for the soul burdened by experience: "for the heart whose woes are legion / 'T is a peaceful, soothing region—" (51–52). The poem reaches an emotional high point when the speaker proclaims, "For the spirit that walks in shadow / 'T is—oh 'tis an Eldorado!" (53–54). The rapture of his tone suggests the speaker's spiritual affinity with "Dream-Land," a sense that is solidified in the following line, which sets up a contrast between the speaker and "the traveler, traveling through it" (55). Here in "dim Thule," we find another evocation of Poe's early poem "The Lake," which speaks of "the solitary soul that could make / An Eden of that dim lake."[54] Both "Dream-Land" and "The Lake" take inspiration from Moore's "I Wish I Was by That Dim Lake," a poem Poe praised as "more profoundly—more wierdly [sic] *imaginative*, in the best sense" than any other in the English language. The speaker of "Dream-Land" is himself "A spirit who walks in shadow" (53), lost to the world at large but at home in this dusky "Eldorado." He appears, in other words, like nothing so much as another one of Poe's bereaved lovers.

By extension, the speaker also represents the poet par excellence. Like the speakers of "The Raven" (1845) and "Annabel Lee" (1849), the pain of lost love has separated him from the society:

> And so, all the night-tide, I lie down by the side
> Of my darling—my darling—my life and my bride,
> . . . In her tomb by the sounding sea.

Such a mourner, of course, occupies the most privileged place in Poe's aesthetics. In "The Philosophy of Composition" (1846), Poe famously proclaims that the death "of a beautiful woman is, unquestionably, the most poetical topic in the world"; therefore, it is "beyond doubt that the lips best suited for such a topic are those of a bereaved lover."[55] To retain the height of poetic power, one must surrender to the *"Mournful and Never-ending Remembrance"* that Poe in that essay suggests the raven ultimately emblematizes: "And my soul *from out that shadow* that lies floating on the floor / Shall be lifted—nevermore."[56] Unable to make his psyche whole in the face of deep loss, the melancholic poet in Poe's aesthetics is a figure of broken personhood positioned "out of SPACE—out of TIME." In Freudian terms, he is not a mourner who visits "Dream-Land" in order to return to everyday life; he is the melancholic who fully inhabits his loss.[57]

But bereaved lovers were not the only spirits casting shadows "Out of SPACE—Out of TIME." The Great Dismal Swamp was best known as the home of maroons and their descendants: it contained "the largest population of maroons in North America in the eighteenth and nineteenth centuries with thousands of individuals taking part over that span."[58] Herbert Aptheker notes that maroons "carried on a regular, if illegal, trade with white people living on the borders of the swamp,"

"Now I had long nurtured a wish to see one of those sable outlaws who dwell in the fastness of the swamp." Porte Crayon, *Harper's New Monthly Magazine*, September 1856. Courtesy of the American Antiquarian Society

which suggests that those familiar with the area, like Poe in his boyhood, would have been well aware of their presence.[59] The print record tells a similar story: "From the last quarter of the eighteenth century, discussions of maroons in the Dismal Swamp appeared regularly in various types of documents, including newspapers" (fig. 5.4).[60] Two years before "Dream-Land," Longfellow published a vastly different, idyllic representation in "The Slave in the Dismal Swamp" (1842). As Dayan notes, Poe condemned the poem as "a shameless medley of the grossest misrepresentation."[61] In Longfellow's depiction, the swamp is a welcoming, place "bright and fair."

All things were glad and free;
Blithe squirrels darted here and there
And wild birds filled the echoing air
With songs of Liberty! (21–25)[62]

Longfellow writes in support of the abolitionist movement, to excoriate and correct the problem of enslavement. Yet in his representation of the Great Dismal Swamp, the only thing troubling in the landscape is the "hunted," long-suffering enslaved man, "infirm and lame."[63] By contrast, "Dream-Land" dwells with the disaggregation of self that the swamp brings into view.

In the popular imagination, the swamp and its terrors were in fact much more often associated with Black strength than weakness. Among the more famous examples of Great Dismal Swamp maroons were Nat Turner's father, who, as we have seen, was reported in print and oral accounts to be a resident there. The Southampton Insurgency was also linked to the swamp, as in an early report from Richmond Dragoon, dated two days after the event, on August 23, 1831: "I have been diligent in my inquires to obtain information that can be relied on. The result is, about two hundred and fifty negroes from a Camp meeting about the Dismal Swamp set out on a marauding excursion, and have for the sake of plunder, murdered about sixty persons, none of them families much known."[64] Drawing on the myriad associations between Turner and the swamp, Harriet Beecher Stowe later answered those who criticized the passivity of Uncle Tom with *Dred: A Tale of the Dismal Swamp* (1856). The eponymous Dred was a maroon who prophesied a violent end to enslavers and fostered a welcoming community in the nethermost reaches of the swamp for those who had escaped enslavement. Notably, Harriet Jacobs's birthplace was just south of the Great Dismal, surrounded by smaller swamps and maroon communities. She features these swamps at key moments in *Incidents in the Life of a Slave Girl* (1861), including Jacobs's harrowing account of her own *petit marronage*, or temporary escape, to the snaky swamp.

Although the Great Dismal sheltered any number of runaways in the short term, its unique geography sustained *grand marronage*, or the establishment of permanent maroon communities. Aptheker has posited that up to fifty maroon communities existed across the slaveholding states; nevertheless, Tommy Lee Bogger points to the Great Dismal as "one of the few places in the United States where geographic conditions made it possible for a large colony of runaways to establish a permanent refuge."[65] The white abolitionist journalist James Redpath documented the account of a former Dismal Swamp maroon who later settled in

Canada: "Dar is families growed up in dat dar Dismal Swamp dat never seed a white man, an' would be skeered most to def to see one. Some runaways went dere wid dar wives, an' dar childers ar raised dar."⁶⁶ Currently, historical archeologists led by Sayers are engaged in the first-ever exploration of the communities that existed in the Great Dismal Swamp from 1607 through the Civil War. Though the material evidence is still being compiled, it corroborates the documentary record: "Inhabitation of the swamp by maroons . . . continued until at least the end of the Civil War."⁶⁷

In "Dream-Land," maroons first appear as ghouls, in a line that is visually and metrically offset from the rest of the poem:

By the dismal tarns and pools
    Where dwell the Ghouls,— (35–36)

Other than "Out of SPACE—Out of TIME" this is the only line indented to the right and the only line that presents a sharp break with the metrical pattern. "Out of SPACE—Out of TIME" has grabbed all the attention. But without a doubt "Where dwell the Ghouls" is—visually, metrically, and in relation to signification—the most important line in the poem. "Where dwell the Ghouls" is hidden in plain sight nearly dead center in the poem, just after the description of the lake that recalls Lake Drummond. The stanza begins by echoing the image of dead white purity in "the snows of the lolling lily." With the phrase "murmuring lowly, murmuring ever," this stanza gently reincorporates the movement from the beginning of the previous stanza. Space and time are doubled here, as this reincorporation gives the whole not only an echoing effect of sound carried across time but also a mirroring effect of place replicated elsewhere, much like the reflective surface of those lone and dead waters.

As we approach these Ghouls, the description of the place, though still hauntingly "indefinitive," gains a measure of palpability:

By the grey woods,—by the swamp
Where the toad and the newt encamp,—
By the dismal tarns and pools
    Where dwell the Ghouls,— (33–36)

Here we have "grey woods" and "dismal tarns" surrounding "the" (definitive) "swamp." In his extended description of the swamp at the center of his account of the Southampton Insurgency, Warner writes, "It is within the deep recesses of this gloomy Swamp, 'dismal' indeed, beyond the power of human conception, that the runaway Slaves of the South have been known to secret themselves for weeks, months and years, subsisting on frogs, tarripins, and even snakes! And when these have failed them, would prefer becoming the victims of starvation to returning again to bondage!" The poem's "dismal tarns and pools," like Warner's swamp, "dismal indeed," nevertheless stand as home to reptiles and refugees alike, "ghouls" who have traded enslavement's living death for a home in the swamp, "beyond the powers of human conception."

"Out of SPACE—Out of TIME"

Frogs, fugitives, and poets are not opposed in Poe's poetics: they are, rather, apposed. But genius/enslaved and aesthetic/swamp are not mere metaphors or stand-ins for one other. Instead, the poem reconfigures what art means by aligning its imaginative "escape" with the escape of the fugitives into the swamp. Maroons find freedom in the swamp even as they remain fugitive from the law of the state. Their freedom is the "fugitive liberty" that Barnor Hesse has located in the Black radical tradition. Not wholly bound by either the metaphors or the materiality of enslavement, this liberty is bound up with the "colonial aporias, liberal antinomies and racial atrocities in the formative constitutions of Western polities and concepts of liberty," even as it seeks to escape them.[68] By apposing poet and maroon, "Dream-Land" invites consideration of how the figure of the genius merges with the "escapologist," committed to "eluding, revealing and interrogating the liberal-colonial suturing of Western liberty as whiteness."[69]

This notion of the genius as an enmeshed escapologist rather than an abstracted subject turns out to be surprisingly ubiquitous in the Romantic era. Kant's formulation of genius is often cited as the source the consummate, self-determined individual that critiques of the ideology of the aesthetic impugn. Yet even in *Critique of Judgment*, the figure of the genius emerges as the producer of aesthetic objects, governed by nature and characterized not by independence but by entanglement: "[Genius] cannot itself describe or indicate scientifically how it brings its product into being, but rather . . . gives the rule as nature, and hence the author of a product that he owes to his genius does not know himself how the ideas for it come to him, and also does not have it in his power to think up such things at will or according to plan, and to communicate to others precepts that would put them in a position to produce similar products."[70] As in "Dream-Land," Kant's genius is subject to the natural world, does not know the source of that which he produces, and does not control it. Likewise, the impetus for aesthetic creation comes not from the ultimate sovereignty of the individual genius but from the involvement of genius with a larger environment. This is not to suggest that Poe's conception of genius and the aesthetic is identical to Kant's.

Critique of Judgment was not translated in its entirety into English until 1892, and the question of Kant's influence on Poe has been much debated. While many assert that Kant reached Poe solely via Coleridge, Glen A. Omans has argued that Poe read German well enough to have read Kant in the original.[71]

Although Poe has long stood as a model of troubled, Romantic Genius, when we look at places in Poe's writing where he discusses genius directly, we can see more clearly the multiple and racialized ways that the category operated in his lifetime. Geoffrey Hartman has described a tension in Romantic poetics between the capital-G Genius and the genius loci: "The artist's struggle with his vocation—with past masters and the 'pastness' of art in modern society" evokes a larger struggle "of genius with Genius, and of genius with the genius loci (spirit of a place)."[72] The ghouls of Poe's poem stand in contrast to the Genius or transcendent spirit of Romantic poetics. Unlike ghosts or spirits—supernatural creatures that travel with ease through time and space—ghouls are tied to a specific locality. Where the Genius represents a spirit that is deep, profound, unbound, and expansive, the genius loci is a ghoul closely tied to local environment. Occasionally, we do find Poe making Romantic statements about genius such as "The higher genius is a rare gift and divine."[73] Moreover, Poe, prone to fictionalizing his own life story, often represented himself as precisely this kind of exceptional genius. In the words of biographer Kenneth Silverman, by late adolescence Poe, like Turner, "had cultivated an image of himself as a precocious genius, cursed from birth and recklessly adventurous."[74] But despite his effort to increase his social standing by romanticizing his past and exaggerating his abilities, Poe neither articulated nor espoused a systematic formulation of the artist as an exceptional individual who boldly asserted a singular path to liberation, heedless of social consequences or moral considerations. Poe's aesthetic theory and practice remains fundamentally incoherent; as often as Poe was seemingly guided by Romantic ideals of consummate artistry, he was equally invested in the mechanical aspects of literary production. As Polonsky argues, Poe's "works of taste and criticism" form the "coordinates of a fundamentally uncoordinated body of aesthetic theory which ultimately turns away from the possibility of theorizing about art."[75] It is important to remember that Poe's relation to Romanticism predates the transcendentalists', whom Poe harshly critiqued.[76]

Although the conception of the alienated artist-genius, the poète maudit, has predominated in Poe's subsequent cultural canonization, it was only just beginning to take vague form during his lifetime. In fact, Poe did not emphasize freedom, as a reading of Poe as a Romantic or as an early proponent of *l'art pour l'art* might anticipate, as a necessary condition for creation. Instead, he valued constraint. Poe argued that a writer must keep his aim of originality "always in view," but not out of a desire for transcendence. The reason is entirely mundane: "He is false to himself who ventures to dispense with so obvious and so easily attainable a source of interest."[77] Originality for Poe, as Jonathan Elmer notes, "is not, as it were, a simple given but is rather purely relational, the mark of difference."[78] Poe highlights the necessity of material external to the genius himself in the process of creation: "So long as the universe of thought shall furnish matter for novel combinations, so long will the spirit of genius be original, be exhaustless—be itself."[79] For genius to be "original," then, it must remain interwoven with a material environment.[80] The "universe of thought" is not pure ideality; rather, it "furnishes matter" for the poet. In "Dream-Land" that matter is the Great Dismal Swamp.

However unlikely, the maroon thus emerges as a type of genius, a figuration that Poe resisted and yet was drawn toward in his ongoing critique of Enlightenment humanism. Though bound up with environment and place, Poe's genius is definitively "out of" those conceptions of space and time that, as Johannes Fabian has argued, are needed for Western cultural and political imperialism "to accommodate the schemes of a one-way historical progress, development, modernity (and their negative mirror images: stagnation, underdevelopment, tradition)."[81] For enslaved peoples, development and modernity often meant sale away from friends and loved ones. Finding stability and a longed-for stasis on the mucky surfaces of the swamp rather than smoothly navigating the open expanses of the western frontier, the maroon/ghoul emerges as the genius loci of Poe's poem. As Daylanne K. English demonstrates, "differential temporalities and differential justices in the United States" characterize African American experience and culture: "time and justice are not established realities," but are "actually contingent and unevenly available . . . political fictions."[82] Evoking widely held beliefs (including Poe's own) that apocalyptic racial violence was imminent, Poe further figures the place and (non)persons of "Dream-Land" outside regnant conceptions of time and space by reference to the apocalyptic book of Revelation.[83] Like martyrs awaiting final judgment, in "Dream-Land" one finds "white robed forms of friends long given, / In agony, to the worms, and Heaven."[84]

If the description "Out of SPACE—Out of TIME" in Poe's most aestheticized poem refers to a differential temporality and spatiality, rather than the transcendence of time and space, then the essentially allegorical approach that often guides historicist readings falls far short of its mark. And Poe himself was famously hostile to allegory, as we see in his late review of Hawthorne: "In defence of allegory, (however, or for whatever object, employed,) there is scarcely one respectable word to be said."[85]

To understand the workings of genius in the nineteenth-century United States, we do not need to unveil the ground beneath the figure via the depth hermeneutic that undergirds historicist criticism. Instead, we need to understand artistic practice as mediation and limitation, even theft: a fugitive genius. The swamp of "Dream-Land" suggests that the contours of aesthetic philosophy and concepts of genius were shaped not only by those at the center of Anglo-European culture who authored key works on these subjects, white Anglo-European philosophers and poets such as Kant and Samuel Taylor Coleridge, but also by those at the periphery: enslaved people and criminals, especially the fugitive or maroon, who was at once formerly enslaved and criminal.[86] All of these figures come together in the specter of the "Eidolon, named NIGHT" who reigns in "Dream-Land," seated atop a "black throne." This Black king is invoked in each of the four repetitions of the refrain. In the penultimate stanza, the reader learns that he has forbidden clear sight in this aesthetic space:

> Never its mysteries are exposed
> To the weak human eye unclosed;
> So wills the king, who hath forbid
> The uplifting of the fringed lid; (57–60)

When in the surround of "Dream-Land," the abstract and abstracting eye or "I" of the Enlightenment subject must be closed: its regnant modes of being are not primarily visual and rational. The "unclosed" eye, when associated with an idea of mind separated from the body, cannot see anything at all. Yet Poe anticipates Bruno Latour, for whom to have a body "is to learn to be affected, meaning 'effectuated,' moved, put into motion by other entities. If you are not engaged in this learning you become insensitive, dumb, you drop dead."[87] Dream-Land is not the sanitized, incorporeal plane of existence reached only by the sleeping or the dead. Instead, it is a space of embodiment and embeddedness in a material environment. Poe's genius, more genius loci than Genius, engages an aesthetic that is not pure, isolated, hard surface but instead murky, connected, soft, like the swamp itself.

"To Be Shady / to Be White"

In my reading of "Dream-Land," experiments with form, relation to poetic antecedents, processes of revision, and Poe's own writings on poetics join with knowledge of local legends, economic motivations, and intimacy with the Virginia landscape. None of these become the context that unlock the poem's meaning. Rather, these are several of the "many connecting elements" that come together in a swamp aesthetic that engulfs the distinction between the literal and the figurative, text and context. "Dream-Land" thus emerges as one of the "ecological accounts" that Allewaert has identified across the eighteenth and nineteenth centuries. Such accounts, inspired by the swamp, represent human and nonhuman forces working together to undermine "the fantasy that subjects remained distinct from an object world that was simply acted on."[88]

In its exploration of conditions of existence that are simultaneously within, alongside, and outside the material and temporal, "Dream-Land" points to a way past some limitations in historicist approaches to the subject of race in Americanist scholarship. Such studies take race and enslavement as the unconscious yet literal ground from which figurative language like Poe's springs: the cause is race or enslavement, and the effect is Poe's gothic macabre horrors, as well as his pure, otherworldly realms. As we see in volumes such as J. Gerald Kennedy and Liliane Weissberg's *Romancing the Shadow: Poe and Race*, many important readings of Poe have operated on this suggestion that a disavowed historical "reality" is buried beneath the "aesthetic" surface of Poe's tales and poems.[89] By contrast, Maurice Lee holds Poe staunchly to account for his "absolute" and entirely conscious racism.[90] As Lee demonstrates, "Unconscious production is a consciously theorized aspect of Poe's thought—both in his metaphysics of race and in his thinking on art."[91] Although I am persuaded that Poe's racism was conscious, his fugitive aesthetic exceeds this "context."

Against the cause-and-effect logic that often drives literary scholarship, "Dream-Land" confounds any operative distinction between the literal and the figurative, the "real world" and an "aesthetic realm."[92] Angus Fletcher's identification of "environment-poems" as those poems that "surround us in exactly the way an actual environment surrounds us" is helpful in conceptualizing this interweaving of history and aesthetics in "Dream-Land" and in Poe's work more broadly.[93] The environment that "Dream-Land" enacts swallows up "the old distinction between the world within the poem and the world 'out there' outside the poem."[94] The world "within" the poem is not a place of refuge to be read solely on its own terms; neither is the "outside" of the poem a place of pure historical fact untouched by the world of imagination and fantasy.

While I have been emphasizing the geography of the swamp in the poem, we can also see an integration of discrete locales in the poem's simultaneous invocation of geographies that are polar ("ultimate dim Thule") as well as tropical. This enmeshment of polar and tropical geographies helps solidify the fugitive

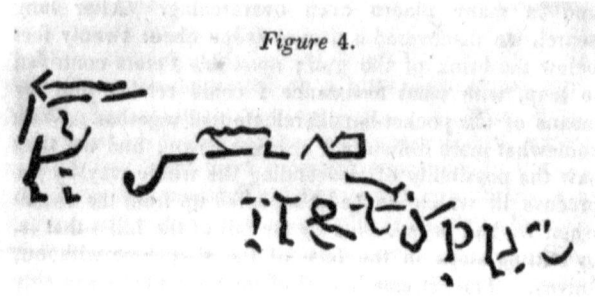

Illustration of hieroglyphic formation of chasms in *The Narrative of Arthur Gordon Pym* (1838). Courtesy of the American Antiquarian Society

presence of raced embodiment in "Dream-Land," since this pairing also appears in *The Narrative of Arthur Gordon Pym* (1838). The suggestive figuration of raced embodiment in the ghouls as well as the black-throned king of "Dream-Land" resonate with the novel's more direct treatment of race on the fictional Antarctic island of Tsalal, with its Indigenous Black inhabitants and their deathly fear of whiteness. Tsalal is an "island of chasms," and just as the "chasms and caves" of "Dream-Land" tantalize with "forms that no man can discover," the mysterious hieroglyphic chasms of Tsalal form what appear to be hieroglyphs or alphabetic configurations, which Poe's fictional editor reads as racially inflected messages from the land itself: "to be shady" and "to be white" (fig. 5.5).[95] Literally and figuratively, Blackness is inscribed in both environments.

By tracing multiple lines of connection from a poem whose significance has seemed obvious even to readers inclined to disagree about everything else, we open a window onto a much more expansive view of nineteenth-century conceptions of the distributed, racialized agency of a fugitive aesthetic. "Dream-Land" is not an ahistorical allegory: neither the maroon nor the swamp function as the original social reality behind the poem's surface. Rather, the poem moves readers between depth and surface, context and text, literal and figurative.[96] The powerful insight that attention to this short poem offers, then, is that history is not the bedrock that grounds aesthetic effects. Instead, neither maroons nor poets are wholly circumscribed by histories like the history of enslavement. Especially where a construct as complex as Blackness is involved, history is not ontologically secure but rather the product of common efforts, including aesthetic practice. "Dream-Land" demonstrates the necessity of broadening our critical gaze to see how history and the material world come together as part (but not the whole) of the stories we tell about those living beyond regnant modalities for reckoning space and time.

Rather than standing in for one another, genius/maroon and aesthetic/swamp cohabit in "Dream-Land." This happens not on the hard surface of the poem but in the soft quagmire of the swamp that gives it its form and the "indefinitiveness" that generates a multiplicity of connections. As in "The Purloined Letter," published the same year as "Dream-Land," that which we seek is directly in our line of sight. The criminal genius, more ghoul than ghost, pursues an aesthetic that is not hard, isolated, and pure—but instead distributive, connected, and dynamic. Poe creates a living, chaotic environment in which poet, maroon, reader, and critic all must struggle for footing. In so doing, he draws, perhaps despite himself, on the criminal genius's distributed agency and finds that it is racialized, situated, collective, and expansive—like the damp, dark, and fertile ecology of the swamplands that still comprised much of the nineteenth-century Southern United States.

CONCLUSION

New Forms of Crime

Discussing the imbrication of law in African American literature from the eighteenth to the twenty-first centuries, Karla F. C. Holloway asks, "When the ethic of use and abuse attached to persons who were property became constitutive, how, then, did blacks reconstitute their own bodies within the same law that had dismembered them?"[1] Across these pages, I have shown that criminal genius, with its collective agency comprising resistant individualism alongside material and distributed forms, was, for a time, one answer to this question. Whether taking the form of the zombie, outlaw, convict, insurgent, or fugitive, each iteration of criminal genius throughout this study is assimilable into a narrative of masculinist, heroic, individual agency. Yet the lens of criminal genius reveals a different narrative: the actors I study here—Jones and Allen, Rush, Johnstone, Frost, Walker, Nancy and Nat Turner, and the Great Dismal Swamp maroons—are notable not only insofar as they asserted individual agency in a society hostile to their existence, though they each did that. They also map out an alternative to the classical liberal subject who articulated individual rights and established agency via education and self-discipline. A figure like Frederick Douglass of the 1845 *Narrative*, who shows "how a slave was made a man" through education, determination, and valor (the famous fight with Covey), stands as a useful counterpoint to the criminal genius.

By contrast, each of these chapters reveals a racialized collective agency, which traverses phenotypical differences and even, in Poe's case, exceeds (though it certainly does not erase) his overt individual racism. Jones's, Allen's, and Rush's thwarted virtue, Johnstone's communitarian vision, Frost's idiosyncratic ethics, Walker's enraged skepticism, Turner's violent legend, and Poe's fugitive poetics all rely on a racialized nexus of criminality and genius to imagine and create new, more capacious worlds, rather than simply avow individual agency in this one.

Several of the figures I looked at here were criminalized despite not having broken any laws. Jones, Allen, Rush, and Johnstone all exemplify Lisa Cacho's argument that law breaking does not produce criminalization; criminalization is instead a racialized sociogenic process. Once we see criminality and "differential inclusion" as "as *effects* of the law,"[2] rather than divergences from it, we can begin to see the limitations of projects that set out to redeem individuals misrecognized as criminal, for example, by showing their principled resistance or self-determination. Thus, rather than exposing racialized criminality as a misplaced descriptor of actually heroic historical individuals, across these pages I have instead explored how creative genius develops in tandem with the criminalization of Blackness in the first half of the long nineteenth century. In so doing I have sought to reveal a distributed agency that unsettled attempts to consolidate white supremacy in the era before Jim Crow and the rise of explicitly racialized incarceration.

Yet categorization as criminal has more often produced harm. In the late nineteenth century, statistical linking of Blackness and criminality, for example, in Frederick L. Hoffman's *Race Traits*, which appeared in 1896, promoted claims like "the colored race shows of all races the most decided tendency towards crime."[3] Countering the well-worn objection to prison abolitionism, that imprisonment helps to curb and reduce social harms, Ruth Wilson Gilmore has explained that a modern abolitionist framework looks to limit harm writ large. She emphasizes the harm that those categorized as criminal experience because of that categorization. Gilmore's framing is both clear and persuasive. It helps us understand how, in a US context, classing someone as criminal racializes them and renders them vulnerable to harms despite phenotype. As with Samuel Frost in chapter 2, such racialization is not limited to the postbellum period. On the flip side, Abraham Johnstone experienced racialized criminality's danger firsthand when his freedom precipitated his criminal status. His "Address" was in many ways an attempt to mitigate his concerns that his own conviction, however wrongful, might nevertheless "be made a handle of in order to throw a shade over . . . all those of our color," despite the fact that "a vast majority of whites have died on the gallows when population is accurately considered."[4] Early African American print culture often set out to counter the linking of crime and Blackness. As Brian Baaki has demonstrated, *Freedom's Journal*, founded in 1827 as the first African American newspaper, set out explicitly to "dismantle associations of black people with crime." Editors Samuel Cornish and John B. Russwurm did this by collecting and reprinting "reports of murders, suicides, thefts, rapes, and accidental deaths previously printed in papers throughout the nation . . . to create a firm impression of the depravity of white people."[5]

These important efforts from early African American print culture did not stop the late nineteenth-century rise of criminology, a social science that shored up racialized criminality in the wake of the Thirteenth Amendment. Building this base, the German American statistician Hoffman gathered supposedly "valuable statistics of crime" that, he claimed, "show without exception an excess of criminality on the part of the negro as compared with the white race."[6] Hoffman, along with Italian criminologist Cesare Lombroso and others, was part of a circum-Atlantic effort to link crime and race via statistical analyses and narratives of degeneracy. The United States played a key role in this late nineteenth-century move spanning sociology, biology, and literature to rein in the radical potential of criminal genius.

In the United States, Arthur MacDonald, Lombroso's protégé, asserts, "Criminals are endowed with a particular kind of genius."[7] MacDonald's criminal genius intensifies genius's passionate and creative facets: "Now and then there are criminals with genius, who invent new forms of crime. . . . With poets and artists crime is more frequent; they are dominated more by passion than those engaged in severe inductions or deductions."[8] Descending from Kant's understanding of the genius as an individual who appears infrequently and acts or creates with the highest degree of originality, MacDonald theorizes criminal genius as marked by a passion for writing.

Criminologists seeking to delineate criminal genius as a liminal state between sanity and insanity countered the racialized revolutionary potential that a merger of genius and criminality generated via print toward the end of the nineteenth century. They opined that with the criminal genius, markers of genius manifest themselves via acts that are either artistic or criminal (or both) but lack the substance of rational genius. MacDonald further qualified the genius of the criminal genius in ways that track with racialization: "Criminals of genius lack either the foresight or the necessary cunning to carry their projects through to the end; at the root of their character there is a lightness that is sure to show itself. In general their genius is more of a knavish and clever nature; they lack coherence and continuity in mental work; what they have of this is powerful but it is intermittent."[9] We can hear echoes of Thomas Jefferson's racial theories ("their existence appears to participate more of sensation than reflection") in this diagnosis of the criminal genius's "lightness" and "powerful but . . . intermittent" ingenuity.

The linking of genius and criminality is to this day often understood as beginning with criminology. But Lombroso and MacDonald did not invent or discover criminal genius, nor did any of their contemporaries. Instead, these criminologists took over an existing formation, if one that has been submerged, hidden, fugitive, and in so doing contained the revolutionary potential inhering in racialized concepts of genius and criminality in the late eighteenth and early nineteenth centuries. As I have shown throughout this book, clear framings of criminal genius are already visible in popular crime writing by end of the eighteenth century, and this formation become fully solidified by the 1830s, when publications describing the Southampton Insurgency highlight both Turner's rare intelligence and its relation to criminal activity. It is precisely this "subtype" of criminal genius that Lombroso describes as "mattoid," whose "crimes are nearly always committed in public under the pretext of contributing to the general good."[10]

The late nineteenth-century rise of criminology was in some ways a natural outgrowth of the century's earlier penal reform movement, which had largely realized its aim of abolishing public punishment but had by no means "cured" the "disease" of crime in the way reformers like Benjamin Rush had envisioned. As a result, white and Black criminals were increasingly liable to be sentenced to confinement in the penitentiary, rather than to undergo public punishment. In arguing for the advantages of private punishment at the end of the eighteenth century, Rush had conceived of a universal benevolence that gestures, however bizarrely, beyond liberal humanism's tenets:

> Everybody acknowledges our obligations to *universal* benevolence. But these cannot be fulfilled, unless we love the whole human race, however diversified they may be by weakness or crimes. The indignation or contempt which is felt for this unhappy part of the great family of mankind, must necessarily extinguish a large portion of this universal love. Nor is this all—the men, or perhaps the women, whose persons we detest, possess souls and bodies composed of the same materials as those of our friends and relations. They are bone of their bone, and were originally fashioned with the same spirits. What then must be the consequence of a familiarity with such objects of horror, upon our attachments and duties to our friends and connections, or to the rest of mankind? If a spectator should give himself time to reflect upon such a sign of human depravity, he would naturally recoil from the embraces of friendship, and the endearments of domestic life, and perhaps say, with an unfortunate great man, after having experienced an instance of treachery in a friend, "Oh! That I were a dog, that I might not call man my brother."

... It is the prerogative of God alone, to contemplate the vices of bad men, without withdrawing from them the support of his benevolence.

Exposure to humans plagued by "weakness or crimes" does great harm to those humans not so afflicted, Rush argues, because the "indignation or contempt which is felt" is inevitable. This sense of indignation or contempt, like the disgust Aaron Bancroft praised in his auditors at Samuel Frost's execution, weakens human fellow feeling. Employing the passive voice, Rush highlights the inescapability of this revulsion, which in turn requires that criminals be segregated, shut off from society in horrific "abodes of misery." Situated on society's literal and figurative margins, penitentiaries could refashion these fellow humans, who are nevertheless also "objects of horror," into productive fellow citizens. It is not vengefulness but rather a universal obligation of benevolence dictating that criminals must be so isolated.

Both Rush and Bancroft underscore the fact that the very question of who counts as human was at stake in society's response to criminality. Rush's example of the man who, witnessing a friend's depravity, wishes himself a dog recalls Bancroft's execution sermon for Frost ("Were you thought capable of his crime, you would exclaim, 'Are we dogs, that we should do this thing?'"). For Rush, unlike Bancroft, a move toward private punishments is necessary to realize "universal love" and protection from the "disease" of criminality. If humankind constitutes a single "great family . . . bone of their bone . . . originally fashioned with the same spirits," then those who become "objects of horror," precisely because they remain also human, need to be carefully guarded, lest they transmit the full (and horrific) range of human potentiality to others. Rush's universal is clearly structured on a logic of the exception, or inclusion by exclusion. But, by recognizing (again, in contrast to Bancroft) the shared humanity of the convict, it gestures, albeit obliquely, toward alternative universalisms that are not so structured. The criminal genius embraces a full range of being human beyond a politics of recognition, a humanism that works with and alongside material and imaginative realities to create the conditions of possibility for a liberated future.

As the excerpt from Rush indicates, prison reformers wanted rehabilitated felons to rejoin society upon their release. Later sociologists and criminologists focused on the recidivism that in point of fact often resulted. Yet the pens of former convicts revealed another angle altogether. Many early nineteenth-century ex-convicts, like white memoirist W. A. Coffey, experienced extreme social isolation upon their release: "In the very home of his father, he is an alien."[11] Coffey here echoes Rush's profound sense of alienation in the wake of the yellow fever epidemic. His words also evoke Orlando Patterson's argument that "social death" is the essential feature of enslaved experience. Patterson's view of enslavement, as primarily a social rather than a property relation, holds that the key aspect of what one loses under enslavement is not freedom per se, nor humanity. It is social life, the ability to make and maintain various and multiple points of connection to a wider community. Coffey's view extends this sense of social death toward the condition of the penitentiary prisoner. Scholars have critiqued Patterson's theory of social death for reinforcing a view from above and ensuring that those deemed "dead" remain passive and silent.

The criminal genius points to the fact that the concept of social death is best understood as more than a mere metaphor. Unlike Coffey, an educated white man who had to experience incarceration to understand what it meant to live as one who is dead, Walker, as a free Black contemporary of his, had a lifetime's worth of such understanding without ever setting foot in a prison. Before he entered the penitentiary, Coffey writes, "it was always to my mind a horrid place, and I naturally expected to find every visage sad, every eye sunk, every cheek pale, and every heart among the convicts, uncommonly depressed. The severity of punishment—the solitude of adversity—the bleakness of their prospects—the agony of their destitution—the horrid result of their crimes—I assuredly thought, were fully calculated to produce such appearances."[12] Before imprisonment, Coffey had imagined that convicts were creatures apart and alone, shadows of humanity. Wanting to change this perception of the criminal, his memoir was in part an attempt to assert the possibility of sympathy with the socially dead. It was therefore a project with repercussions beyond the framework of penitentiary punishment. Six years later, Walker, addressing "the colored citizens of the world" from an outlaw position of death-in-life, likewise creates a sense of community among those who have shared the experiences of violence, natal alienation, and dishonor. As we saw in chapter 3, death could not impede Walker's political work; it was in fact foundational to it. The dead, as Philadelphia's yellow fever corpses show, even at their most gruesome, are neither passive nor silent.

Thus, the theory and praxis of criminal genius did not so much anticipate but was *grounded in* that space that Fanon called the "zone of non-being" and that more recent criticism has identified variously as "flesh" (Hortense Spillers), "the reaper's garden" (Vincent Brown), "habeas viscus" (Alexander Weheliye), or "the wake" (Christina Sharpe). These perspectives take Black life's precarity not as a condition but rather as the unrelenting threat under and through which another future becomes possible. Brown's work on enslaved culture resignifies Patterson's social death: "To see social death as a productive peril entails a subtle but significant shift in perspective, from seeing slavery as a condition to viewing enslavement as a predicament, within which enslaved Africans and their descendants never ceased to pursue a politics of belonging, mourning, accounting, and regeneration."[13] Social death is not an end but a beginning. For Brown, "the stuff of death and dissolution" has nourished robust Black cultures; in Fanon's foundational assessment, the "arid" and "extraordinarily sterile" zone of nonbeing marks the site where an "authentic upheaval can be born."[14] Weheliye takes up Spillers's call to "make a place for this different social subject," the degendered Black body not as monstrous but as a reconstructed human. Likewise, Sharpe's "wake work" reads "something else, some other knowledge, into that space" of dispossession, the "ace down my wrist" that Black motherhood bequeaths in excess of structural poverty.[15]

Each of these thinkers takes imbrication in such spaces (the wake, the zone of nonbeing, the reaper's garden, the flesh) as the condition of possibility for another world. On this view, Black politics and art are not lacking but luminous, shot through with possibility. This body of scholarship also complicates an important, yet now-familiar, story of resistant agency and Black self-determination. As crucial as recognition of Black resistance has been, an exclusive focus on voluntarist self-determination eclipses the myriad other—often more collective and material—ways Black life has constellated and signified. Such stories of resistant Black agency all too easily subsume figures like Turner and Walker. As a result, work interested in thinking agency differently rarely discusses such individuals, let alone white figures like Frost or Poe. Marginalized white criminals like Frost disappear into popularized caricatures with no political efficacy; Walker the Black firebrand winds up obscuring Walker the theorist of universal Black humanity; Poe's entanglement with a liberatory Black imaginary seems like a puzzle that needs solving rather than an obvious, indeed historically necessary, intertext for his fugitive aesthetic; Turner the revolutionary hides the insurgent role of print and narrative in shaping a Black collectivity.

By expanding our view of genius beyond individualist constructions, and seeking its material connections to criminality, we can locate, within a US and African American literary tradition, alternative understandings of human being and doing, especially for the dispossessed. As Curran writes, "If, during the era before 'Enlightenment,' blackness came into relief against a synthesis of biblical exegeses and vague physical explanations dating from antiquity, during the eighteenth century, the concept of blackness was increasingly dissected, handled, measured, weighed, and used as a demonstrable wedge between human categories. More than just a descriptor, blackness became a thing, defined . . . by its supposed materiality."[16] Exploring what this alignment of Blackness and materiality might have inadvertently made possible, I have sought more expansive understandings of humanity than the Enlightenment, traditionally understood, has produced. I have followed Frantz Fanon's query "In reality, who [and what] am I?"[17] and Sylvia Wynter's critique of white supremacist ontologies of "Man" as the Western world's "referent-we," a false universal figuring the human as a cisgendered, heterosexual, white man. And I have brought historicist and literary critical methods to the ethical project of opening up, or perhaps even abandoning, models of subjectivity as isolated and sovereign associated with colonialism and slavery.

The criminal genius is suffused with social death's radical potentiality. Figures like Jones, Allen, Johnstone, Walker, and Turner astutely castigated the white supremacy that placed Black life under permanent threat. Yet across the long nineteenth century, Black death-in-life was not blithely or blandly metaphorical, opposed by a still more abstract freedom. As free Black people in a nation that sanctioned enslavement, Walker and Johnstone both occupied an impossible space. Yet from within that outlaw space, Johnstone created a theory and praxis of a beloved community, and Walker creatively asserts existence: "Know the world, that I am one of the oppressed, degraded and wretched sons of Africa, rendered so by the avaricious and unmerciful, among the whites.— . . . I count my life not dear unto me, but I am ready to be offered at any moment. For what is the use of living, when in fact I am dead." Existence, for Black and other criminalized people, is coextensive with death's ongoing reality. Walker here literalizes a question underlying much nineteenth-century literature, from gothic fictions to the autobiographical writings of previously enslaved people, who endured social death yet lived to tell the tale: Can the dead speak? Walker's crucial legacy of outraged resistance to white supremacy has long been established, while Johnstone has at times been all but forgotten. Yet as I have shown, their construction of a distinctive theory of the human, grounded in recognition of Black people's unequal liability to premature death (per Gilmore), has gone virtually unremarked. Gayatri Spivak posed the question of the possibility of speech most famously regarding postcolonial theory's subaltern subjects.[18] Her answer was an emphatic no: an important rebuke to Western intellectuals' problematic construction of "self-knowing, politically canny subalterns" who, in the end, represent none other than "the intellectuals . . . themselves."[19] Yet for the criminal genius, subaltern status, which Frost calls enslavement and which Walker calls death, is no barrier to speech. This is because Spivak's "speaking" is the provenance of capital-*M* Man: the authentic, self-willed, individual expression of one who, in Spivak's terms, "speak(s), act(s) and know(s)" directly "for himself." Criminal genius speaks otherwise: the bodies of work the figures in this book have left behind are not necessarily "authentic" self-expression but rather communication within and across social and civil death.

If most present-day readers readily acknowledge claims to justice expressed by criminalized and racialized figures like those I have studied here, valuing their intellectual and creative contributions has proved more difficult. In fact, they have always been entwined. Centering justice's material force, sometimes through words and sometimes by deeds, criminal genius forged speculative, liberatory connections, improvisations, and collectivities that majoritarian histories have largely erased. We find modes of "unbounded sociality . . . existing without space and time" and "beyond the doctrine of Man":[20] in Jones and Allen's neighborliness and in Johnstone's mutual obligation; toward Walker's horizon of justice and Turner's insurgent genealogies, and deep within the Great Dismal Swamp maroon's fugitive poetics. Displacing the resistant hero, criminal genius, whether figured as zombie, outlaw, convict, insurgent, or fugitive, offers powerful historical examples of world breaking and world making.

> There in one view we grasp the mighty whole,
> Or with new worlds amaze th' unbounded soul
>
> —*Phillis Wheatley, "On Imagination"*

NOTES

Introduction • *"Nourished in Vice"*

1. John Brown, quoted in Sharon M. Harris, *Letters and Cultural Transformations in the United States, 1760–1860* (Farnham, UK: Ashgate, 2013), 206.
2. Sydney Smith, "Rev. of *Statistical Annals of the United States*, by Adam Seybert," *Edinburgh Review* 33 (1820): 69–80.
3. Sydney Smith, quoted in Robert E. Spiller, "The Verdict of Sydney Smith," *American Literature* 1, no. 1 (1929): 7.
4. Smith and his well-heeled English contemporaries accrued wealth not only through capital inhering in enslaved people themselves (a perfectly legal intercolonial trade in enslaved persons continued in the British colonies long after the international trade was outlawed in 1807); they also profited from trade in goods that enslaved people produced. These monies continued to be a major source of British wealth for more than half a century after the 1833 Slavery Abolition Act ended legal enslavement across the British colonies. Gregory E. O'Malley, *Final Passages: The Intercolonial Slave Trade of British America, 1619–1807* (Chapel Hill: University of North Carolina Press, 2014), 334.
5. Maria W. Stewart, "Address to the African Masonic Hall," in *Maria W. Stewart, America's First Black Woman Political Writer*, ed. Marilyn Robinson (Bloomington: Indiana University Press, 1987) 64–65.
6. Herman L. Bennett, "'Sons of Adam': Text, Context, and the Early Modern African Subject," *Representations* (2005): 18.
7. Bryan Wagner, *Disturbing the Peace: Black Culture and the Police Power after Slavery* (Cambridge, MA: Harvard University Press, 2009), 15.
8. James Hardie, *The History of the Tread-Mill: Containing an Account of Its Origin, Construction, Operation, Effects as It Respects the Health and Morals of the Convicts, with Their Treatment and Diet; Also, a General View of the Penitentiary System, with Alterations Necessary to Be Introduced into Our Criminal Code, for Its Improvement* (New York: printed by Samuel Marks, 1824), 13.
9. H. Bruce Franklin, *Prison Writing in 20th-Century America* (New York: Penguin, 1998), 4.
10. Douglas A. Blackmon, *Slavery by Another Name: The Re-enslavement of Black Americans from the Civil War to Word War II* (New York: Icon Books, 2008).

11. Angela Naimou, *Salvage Work: US and Caribbean Literatures amid the Debris of Personhood* (New York: Fordham University Press, 2015), 41.

12. Wagner, *Disturbing the Peace*, 7.

13. James C. Oleson, *Criminal Genius: A Portrait of High-IQ Offenders* (Berkeley: University of California Press, 2017), 35.

14. Oleson, *Criminal Genius*, 58–59.

15. Oleson, *Criminal Genius*, 58.

16. Oleson, *Criminal Genius*, 35.

17. Lisa Marie Cacho, *Social Death: Racialized Rightlessness and the Criminalization of the Unprotected* (New York: New York University Press, 2012), 4–5.

18. Cacho, *Social Death*, 4.

19. Cacho, *Social Death*, 29.

20. Frantz Fanon, *Black Skin, White Masks*, trans. Charles Lam Markmann (New York: Grove Press, 1967), 179.

21. Karen Halttunen, *Murder Most Foul: The Killer and the American Gothic Imagination* (Cambridge, MA: Harvard University Press, 1998), 4.

22. I am indebted to a conversation with Lindsey Grubbs for this insight.

23. Cacho, *Social Death*, 6.

24. Sylvia Wynter, "Unsettling the Coloniality of Being/Power/Truth/Freedom: Toward the Human, after Man, Its Overrepresentation—an Argument," *CR: New Centennial Review* 3, no. 3 (2003): 257, 263, 260.

25. Sylvia Wynter and Katherine McKittrick, "Unparalleled Catastrophe for Our Species?," in *Sylvia Wynter: On Being Human as Praxis*, ed. Katherine McKittrick (Durham, NC: Duke University Press, 2015) 9, 31, 39.

26. Giorgio Agamben, *The Open: Man and Animal*, trans. Kevin Attell (Stanford, CA: Stanford University Press, 2004), 25.

27. Agamben, *The Open*, 25–26.

28. John Locke, *An Essay Concerning Human Understanding*, ed. R. S. Woolhouse (1689; New York: Penguin, 1997), 312.

29. Dylan Rodriguez, "Criminal," in *Keywords for African American Studies*, ed. Erica R. Edwards, Roderick A. Ferguson, and Jeffrey Ogbonna Green Ogbar (New York: New York University Press, 2018), 58.

30. There were exceptions to this, notably the Missouri freedom suits in which more than three hundred enslaved people, before Dred Scott, sought liberty through the courts. See especially Lea VanderVelde, *Redemption Songs: Suing for Freedom before Dred Scott* (New York: Oxford University Press, 2014); Kelly M. Killington, *In the Shadow of Dred Scott: St. Louis Freedom Suits and the Legal Culture of Slavery in Antebellum America* (Athens: University of Georgia Press, 2017); and Ann Twitty, *Before Dred Scott: Slavery and Legal Culture in the American Confluence, 1787–1857* (New York: Cambridge University Press, 2018).

31. Percy Bysshe Shelley, "A Defence of Poetry," in *The Norton Anthology of Theory and Criticism*, ed. Vincent B. Leitch (New York: W. W. Norton, 2001), 715.

32. J. Hector St. John de Crèvecoeur, *Letters from an American Farmer* (New York: Oxford University Press, 1998/1782), 215.

33. Hugh Blair, *Lectures on Rhetoric and Belles Lettres* (London: Bayes and Son, 1823), 21.

34. Ralph Waldo Emerson, "The American Scholar," in *Emerson: Essays and Lectures*, ed. Joel Porte (New York: Library of America, 1983), 58.
35. Nathaniel D. Mitron Hirsch, *Genius and Creative Intelligence* (Cambridge, MA: Sci-Art, 1931).
36. Simon Gikandi, *Slavery and the Culture of Taste* (Princeton, NJ: Princeton University Press, 2011).
37. Gikandi, *Slavery*, xii.
38. Breny Mendoza offers a lucid précis of these key insights from María Lugones. See Breny Mendoza, "Coloniality of Gender and Power: From Postcoloniality to Decoloniality," in *The Oxford Handbook of Feminist Theory*, ed. Lisa Disch and Mary Hawkesworth (New York: Oxford University Press, 2016), 117.
39. This includes but is by no means limited to works by Sylvia Wynter, Katherine McKittrick, Susan Buck-Morss, Nikhil Pal Singh, Nick Nesbitt, and Alexander Weheliye. Susan Buck-Morss, *Hegel, Haiti and Universal History* (Pittsburg, PA: University of Pittsburg Press, 2009); Nikhil Pal Singh, *Black Is a Country: Race and the Unfinished Struggle for Democracy* (Cambridge, MA: Harvard University Press, 2005); Nick Nesbitt, *Universal Emancipation: The Haitian Revolution and the Radical Enlightenment* (Charlottesville: University of Virginia Press, 2008); Alexander Weheliye, *Habeas Viscus: Racializing Assemblages, Biopolitics, and Black Feminist Theories of the Human* (Durham, NC: Duke University Press, 2014).
40. William Wells Brown, *The Black Man, His Antecedents, His Genius and His Achievements* (New York: Thomas Hamilton, 48 Beekman Street, 1863), 215–16.
41. Brown, *The Black Man*, 234–35.
42. Brown, *The Black Man*, 280.
43. Brown, *The Black Man*, 6.
44. Edward Young, "Conjectures on Original Composition," in *Critical Theory since Plato*, ed. Hazard Adams (New York: Harcourt Brace, 1971), 338–47, 341.
45. Young, "Conjectures," 342.
46. Young, "Conjectures," 341.
47. Thomas De Quincey, "Sketches Life & Manners," *Tait's Edinburgh Magazine*, March 1838.
48. Emerson and other thinkers, both Romantic and Enlightenment, frequently use the term genius to describe the "permanent" qualities of people, as in the title of his 1835 lecture, "Permanent Traits of the English National Genius." This collectivist understanding of genius, as describing the particular, supposedly innate, characteristics of human groups or places, was as widespread among Romantics and transcendentalists as the more individualist sense for which they are remembered. Yet even in the case of the Saxon people when Emerson notes their "genius" for activity, virility, and violence, this genius is itself a passive quality, "permanent," "natural," and inherent, attaching itself to Saxon people without any effort on their part. Nell Irvin Painter, *The History of White People* (New York: Norton, 2010), 166–67.
49. Thomas Jefferson, *Notes on the State of Virginia* (London: printed for John Stockdale, 1787).
50. Immanuel Kant, quoted in Pauline Kleingeld, "Kant's Second Thoughts on Race," *Philosophical Quarterly* 57, no. 229 (2007): 573.

51. Hortense J. Spillers, "Mama's Baby, Papa's Maybe: An American Grammar Book," *Diacritics* 17, no. 9 (1987): 80.

52. Arthur Schomburg, quoted in Arna Bontemps, "Special Collections of Negroana," *Library Quarterly* 14, no. 3 (1944): 190.

53. Britt Rusert, *Fugitive Science: Empiricism and Freedom in Early African American Literature* (New York: New York University Press, 2017), 62–63.

54. Gregory Pierrot, *The Black Avenger in Atlantic Culture* (Athens: University of Georgia Press, 2019), 10.

55. In this work I join Leonard Keith, who has paid careful attention to Black formalist poets to show that they can adapt Euro-American frameworks of genius to achieve existential, anti-racist self-definition. Leonard Keith, *Fettered Genius: The African American Bardic Poet from Slavery to Civil Rights* (Charlottesville: University of Virginia Press, 2005).

56. Ivy G. Wilson, *Specters of Democracy, Blackness and the Aesthetics of Politics in the Antebellum U.S.* (New York, Oxford University Press, 2011).

57. Wilson, *Specters of Democracy*, 8.

58. See also Fred Moten, *In the Break: The Aesthetics of the Black Radical Tradition* (Minneapolis: University of Minnesota Press, 2003).

59. Moten, *In the Break*, 1.

60. Mel Y. Chen, *Animacies: Biopolitics, Racial Mattering, and Queer Affect* (Durham, NC: Duke University Press, 2012); and Urmila Seshagiri, *Race and the Modernist Imagination* (Ithaca, NY: Cornell University Press, 2010).

61. Jane Bennett, *Vibrant Matter: A Political Ecology of Things* (Durham, NC: Duke University Press, 2009), ix.

62. Bennett, *Vibrant Matter*, 3, 107.

63. Wynter, "Unsettling," 257–337; Aimé Césaire, *Discourse on Colonialism*, trans. Joan Pinkham (New York: Monthly Review Press, 1972, 2001); Frantz Fanon, *The Wretched of the Earth*, trans. Richard Philcox (New York: Grove Press, 1963, 2004).

64. Zakiyyah Iman Jackson, *Becoming Human: Matter and Meaning in an Antiblack World* (New York: New York University Press, 2021), 17.

65. Weheliye, *Habeas Viscus*, 8, 9–10.

66. Barnor Hesse and Juliet Hooker, "Introduction: On Black Political Thought inside Global Black Protest," *South Atlantic Quarterly* 116, no. 3 (2017): 443.

67. Because the protocols of New Historicism have often invisibly relied on a liberal view of agency (despite an ostensible stance against Cold War liberalism), these studies often implicitly or explicitly aim to recover and restore liberal agency to these excluded individuals. See Alan Liu's nuanced and sensitive reflection on the methods and meanings of New Historicism (*Local Transcendence: Essays on Postmodern Historicism and the Database* [Chicago: University of Chicago Press, 2008]); and Jennifer Fleissner's discussion of historicism in relation to American literary studies ("Historicism's Blues," *American Literary History* 25, no. 4 [2013]: 699–717).

68. Walter Johnson, "Agency: A Ghost Story," in *Slavery's Ghost: The Problem of Freedom in the Age of Emancipation* (Baltimore: Johns Hopkins University Press, 2011), 8.

69. Excellent examples of such work are numerous. They include Joanna Brooks's incisive analysis of Black counterpublics ("The Early American Sphere and the Emer-

gence of a Black Print Counterpublic," *William and Mary Quarterly* 62, no. 1 [2005]: 67–92); Jeannine DeLombard's provocative recovery of the unlikely origins of African Americans' civic personhood in crime publications (*In the Shadow of the Gallows: Race, Crime and American Civic Identity* [Philadelphia: University of Pennsylvania Press, 2012]); and Simon Gikandi's powerful description of the ways in which slavery shaped the culture of taste, which African slaves and their descendants in turn cultivated in order to assert their own selfhood, in *Slavery and the Culture of Taste*.

70. Walter Johnson, "Slavery, Reparations and the Mythic March of Freedom," *Raritan* 27, no. 2 (2007): 52.

71. Edward Larkin, "Exceptionalism, Agency, and the Misunderstood Origins of American Culture," *Early American Literature* 52, no. 1 (2017): 193.

72. Immanuel Kant, *The Critique of Judgement* in *The Norton Anthology of Theory and Criticism*, ed. Vincent B. Leitch (New York: W. W. Norton, 2001), 533.

73. For a powerful rethinking of the nature, role and place of social death in African American cultural expression, see Vincent Brown, "Social Death and Political Life in the Study of Slavery," *American Historical Review* 114, no. 5 (2009): 1231–49; and *The Reaper's Garden: Death and Power in the World of Atlantic Slavery* (Cambridge, MA: Harvard University Press, 2008).

74. Ed White and Michael Drexler, "The Theory Gap," *American Literary History* 22, no. 2 (2010): 486.

75. David Kazanjian, "'When They Come Here They Feal So Free': Race and Early American Studies," *Early American Literature* 41, no. 2 (2006): 336.

Chapter 1 · *Zombies of Civic Virtue*

1. As Erica Armstrong Dunbar chronicles, enslavement in Pennsylvania began to unravel following the state's 1780 Gradual Abolition Act. In the ensuing decades, most African Americans living in the state were free or self-emancipated, and by 1830 only eleven enslaved persons resided in the state. Erica Armstrong Dunbar, *A Fragile Freedom: African American Women and Emancipation in the Antebellum City* (New Haven, CT: Yale University Press, 2008), 3–4.

2. Robert Levine, *Dislocating Race and Nation: Episodes in Nineteenth-Century American Literary Nationalism* (Chapel Hill: University of North Carolina Press, 2008), 80.

3. Mathew Carey, *A Short Account of the Malignant Fever, Lately Prevalent in Philadelphia: With a Statement of the Proceedings that Took Place on the Subject in Different Parts of the United States* (Philadelphia: printed for the author, 1793), 28–29.

4. Khalil Gibran Muhammad, *The Condemnation of Blackness: Race, Crime, and the Making of Modern Urban America* (Cambridge, MA: Harvard University Press, 2010), 3.

5. As Saidiya Hartman notes, "The law's selective recognition of slave humanity ... acknowledged the intentionality and agency of the slave, but only as it assumed the form of criminality." *Scenes of Subjection: Terror, Slavery, and Self-Making in Nineteenth-Century America* (New York: Oxford University Press, 1997), 80.

6. Scholars since Hartman have emphasized that there were of course exceptions, where the law recognized enslaved people's humanity beyond a liability to criminality, including remarkable instances of enslaved people who engaged the legal system as

subjects, which underscore nineteenth-century US legal pluralism. See, for example, Kimberly M. Welch's *Black Litigants in the Antebellum American South* (Chapel Hill: North Carolina University Press, 2018).

7. Kelly Marie Kennington, "Law, Geography, and Mobility: Suing for Freedom in Antebellum St. Louis," *Journal of Southern History* 80, no. 3 (2014): 575–604.

8. Stephen Smith, *Life, Last Words and Dying Speech of Stephen Smith, a Black Man* (Boston: n.p., 1797).

9. Martha S. Jones, *Birthright Citizens: A History of Race and Rights in Antebellum America* (Cambridge: Cambridge University Press, 2018), 11.

10. See Lindsey Andrews and Jonathan M. Metzl, "Reading the Image of Race: Neurocriminology, Medical Imaging Technologies and Literary Intervention," in *Edinburgh Companion to the Critical Medical Humanities* (Edinburgh: Edinburgh University Press, 2016), 242–59; and Priscilla Wald, "Blood and Stories: How Genomics Is Rewriting Race, Medicine and Human History," *Patterns of Prejudice* 40, nos. 4/5 (2006): 303–33.

11. Richard Iton, *In Search of the Black Fantastic: Politics and Popular Culture in the Post–Civil Rights Era* (New York: Oxford University Press, 2008), 13.

12. Dylan Rodriguez, "Criminal," in *Keywords for African American Studies*, ed. Erica R. Edwards, Roderick A. Ferguson, and Jeffrey Ogbonna Green Ogbar (New York: New York University Press, 2018), 59.

13. Barnor Hesse and Juliet Hooker, "Introduction: On Black Political Thought inside Global Black Protest," *South Atlantic Quarterly* 116, no 3 (2017): 443–56.

14. J. Hector St. John de Crèvecoeur, *Letters from an American Farmer* (New York: Oxford University Press, 1998/1782), 41.

15. Carey, *A Short Account*, viii, 30.

16. Carey, *A Short Account*, viii, 30–31, 31.

17. David Walker, *Appeal in Four Articles; Together with a Preamble, to the Coloured Citizens of the World, but in Particular, and Very Expressly, to Those of the United States of America*, ed. Peter P. Hinks (1829; Philadelphia: Pennsylvania State University Press), 2000.

18. Absalom Jones and Richard Allen, *A Narrative of the Proceedings of the Black People, During the Late Awful Calamity in Philadelphia, in the Year 1793: And a Refutation of Some Censures, Thrown upon Them in Some Late Publications* (Philadelphia: William W. Woodward, 1794), 6, 9–10.

19. Jones and Allen, *A Narrative of the Proceedings*, 3.

20. Jones and Allen, *A Narrative of the Proceedings*, 9–10.

21. Derrick Spires, *The Practice of Citizenship: Black Politics and Print Culture in the Early United States* (Philadelphia: University of Pennsylvania Press, 2019), 56.

22. Carey, *A Short Account*, 91.

23. Jones and Allen, *A Narrative of the Proceedings*, 3.

24. Carey, *A Short Account*, 91.

25. Carey, *A Short Account*, 77.

26. Jones and Allen, *A Narrative of the Proceedings*, 13.

27. Carey, *A Short Account*, 77.

28. Jones and Allen, *A Narrative of the Proceedings*, 12–13.

29. Jones and Allen, *A Narrative of the Proceedings*, 4.

30. Carey, *A Short Account*, 8.
31. Carey, *A Short Account*, 84.
32. Jones and Allen, *A Narrative of the Proceedings*, 5.
33. Jeannine Marie DeLombard, *In the Shadow of the Gallows: Race, Crime, and American Civic Identity* (Philadelphia: University of Pennsylvania Press, 2012), 171.
34. Spires, *The Practice of Citizenship*, 76.
35. William Cobbett, qtd. in Sarah R. Riedman and Clarence C. Green, *Benjamin Rush, Physician, Patriot, Founding Father* (Berkeley: University of California Press, 1964), 218.
36. Mel Y. Chen, *Animacies: Biopolitics, Racial Mattering, and Queer Affect* (Durham, NC: Duke University Press, 2012), 3.
37. Chen, *Animacies*, 4.
38. Robert R. Sullivan, "The Birth of the Prison: The Case of Benjamin Rush," *Eighteenth-Century Studies* 31, no. 3 (1998): 333–44.
39. Sullivan, "The Birth of the Prison," 335.
40. Jacquelyn C. Miller, "The Body Politic and the Body Somatic: Benjamin Rush's Fear of Social Disorder and His Treatment for Yellow Fever," in *A Centre of Wonders: The Body in Early America*, ed. Janet Moore Lindman and Michelle Lise Tarter (Ithaca, NY: Cornell University Press, 2001), 67.
41. Miller, "The Body Politic," 62.
42. Miller, "The Body Politic," 70.
43. Benjamin Rush, *An Enquiry into the Origin of the Late Epidemic Fever in Philadelphia: In a Letter to Dr. John Redman* (Philadelphia: from the press of Matthew Carey, 1793), 12.
44. Rush, *An Enquiry into the Origin*, 13.
45. Rush, *An Enquiry into the Origin*, 15.
46. Benjamin Rush, *Sixteen Introductory Lectures* (Philadelphia: Bradford and Inskeep, 1811), 386.
47. Rush, *Sixteen Introductory Lectures*, 391.
48. Elizabeth McAlister, "Slaves, Cannibals, and Infected Hyper-whites: The Race and Religion of Zombies," *Anthropological Quarterly* 85, no. 2 (2012): 459.
49. Stephan Palmié, *Wizards and Scientists: Explorations in Afro-Cuban Modernity and Tradition* (Durham, NC: Duke University Press, 2002), 66.
50. See Sarah Juliet Lauro's discussion of how the zombie "metaphorizes both slavery and slave rebellion" in *The Transatlantic Zombie* (Newark, NJ: Rutgers University Press, 2015), 29.
51. Lauro, *The Transatlantic Zombie*, 28.
52. Phillipe Ariès, *The Hour of Our Death* (New York: Knopf, 1981).
53. Monique Allewaert, *Ariel's Ecology: Plantations, Personhood, and Colonialism in the American Tropics* (Minneapolis: University of Minnesota Press 2013), 53.
54. Qtd. in Edward Allen Driggers, "The Chemistry of Blackness: Benjamin Rush, Thomas Jefferson, Everard Home, and the Project of Defining Blackness through Chemical Explanations," *Critical Philosophy of Race* 7, no. 2 (2019): 377.
55. Adam Smith, *Theory of Moral Sentiments*, ed. Knud Haakonssen (1759; New York: Cambridge University Press, 2002), 16.
56. Smith, *Theory of Moral Sentiments*, 16.

57. Swanwick is in fact one of the historical figures on whom Charles Brockden Brown's confidence man Tom Welbeck, a central figure in *Arthur Mervyn*, was based. See Peter Kafer, *Charles Brockden Brown's Revolution and the Birth of American Gothic* (Philadelphia: University of Pennsylvania Press, 2004), 90.

58. Carey, *A Short Account*, 82.

59. Samuel Otter, *Philadelphia Stories: America's Literature of Race and Freedom* (New York: Oxford University Press, 2010), 51.

60. William Cobbett, *Selections from Porcupine's Gazette*, vol. 7 (London: Printed for Cobbett and Morgan, at the Crow and Mitre, 1801), 234.

61. Cobbett, *Selections*, 249.

62. *A Report of an Action for a Libel: Brought by Dr Benjamin Rush, against William Cobbett* (Philadelphia: W. W. Woodward, 1800), 1, 3.

63. Rush, *Letters*, 2:794, qtd. in Otter, *Philadelphia Stories*, 51–52.

64. Benjamin Rush, *An Account of the Bilious Remitting Yellow Fever, as it Appeared in the City of Philadelphia, in the Year 1793* (Edinburgh: John Moir, 1796).

65. Spires, *The Practice of Citizenship*, 49.

66. Rush, *Sixteen Introductory Lectures*, 215.

67. Rush, *Letters*, 2:658, qtd. in Otter, *Philadelphia Stories*, 52.

68. Otter, *Philadelphia Stories*, 35.

69. Charles Brockden Brown, *Arthur Mervyn, Or Memoirs of the Year 1793* (New York: Holt, Rinehart and Winston, 1962), 122–23.

70. Brown, *Arthur Mervyn*, 122–23.

71. James Dawes, "Fictional Feeling: Philosophy, Cognitive Science, and the American Gothic," *American Literature* 76, no. 3 (2004): 440.

72. Sari Altschuler, *The Medical Imagination: Literature and Health in the Early United States* (Philadelphia: University of Pennsylvania Press, 2018).

73. Brian Waterman, "*Arthur Mervyn*'s Medical Repository and the Early Republic's Knowledge Industries," *American Literary History* 15, no. 2 (2003): 214.

74. Brown, *Arthur Mervyn*, 164.

75. Brown, *Arthur Mervyn*, 147. Brown clearly has in mind the Bush Hill hospital, set up temporarily at the Bush Hill Estate. He draws heavily on Carey's description here and elsewhere in the novel.

76. Brown, *Arthur Mervyn*, 165–66.

Chapter 2 · *The Convict's Corpus*

1. Abraham Johnstone, *The Address of Abraham Johnstone, a Black Man, Who Was Hanged at Woodbury, in the County of Gloucester, and State of New Jersey, On Saturday the the [sic] 8th Day of July Last: To the People of Colour. To Which Is Added His Dying Confession or Declaration. Also, a Copy of a Letter to His Wife, Written the Day Previous to His Execution* (Philadelphia: printed for the purchasers, 1791), last modified December 12, 2000, https://docsouth.unc.edu/neh/johnstone/johnstone.html, 34–35.

2. Johnstone, *Address*, 39.

3. See Stephen J. Hartnett, "The Hanging of Abraham Johnstone and the Turning of Terror into Hope, 1797," in *Executing Democracy*, vol. 1: *Capital Punishment and the Making of America, 1783–1807* (East Lansing: Michigan State University Press, 2010), 149–50.

4. Jeannine Marie DeLombard, *In the Shadow of the Gallows: Race, Crime, and American Civic Identity* (Philadelphia: University of Pennsylvania Press, 2012), 156.

5. Johnstone, *Address*, 49.

6. Johnstone, *Address*, 11.

7. Samuel Frost et al., *The Confession and Dying Words of Samuel Frost* (Worcester, MA, October 1793), col. 4. All future citations of Frost's "Confession" and "The Account of Samuel Frost" will refer to this edition.

8. Johnstone, *Address*, 4.

9. Much of this material has been digitized and is collected in the Archive of Americana database. Although Samuel Frost is by no means widely studied, two recent historians have attended to individual texts from the Frost archive. In *Murder Most Foul: The Killer and the American Gothic Imagination* (Cambridge, MA: Harvard University Press, 1998), Karen Halttunen draws on "The Account of Samuel Frost," published in at least three versions in 1793, as a piece of evidence for her compelling argument that ideas of the criminal as a moral monster were increasingly prevalent in the late eighteenth century (77, 262). Daniel A. Cohen incorporates a discussion of Bancroft's sermon in his argument that ministers began increasingly to explain deviance as a result of flawed education. See *Pillars of Salt, Monuments of Grace: New England Crime Literature and the Origins of American Popular Culture, 1674–1860* (New York: Oxford University Press, 1993).

10. Daniel A. Cohen offers a detailed account of the rise and development of American gallows literature in *Pillars of Salt, Monuments of Grace*. See also Daniel A. Cohen, "Blood Will Out," in *Mortal Remains, Death in Early America*, ed. Nancy Isenberg and Andrew Burstein (Philadelphia: University of Pennsylvania Press, 2003), 31–56; Ronald A. Bosco, "Early American Gallows Literature: An Annotated Checklist," *Resources for American Literary Study* 8 (1978): 81–105; and Thomas M. McDade, *The Annals of Murder: A Bibliography of Books and Pamphlets on American Murders from Colonial Times to 1900* (Norman: University of Oklahoma Press, 1961).

11. Halttunen, *Murder*, 1–6, 208–40.

12. Donna Hunter, "Race, Law, and Innocence: Executing Black Men in the Eighteenth Century," *Studies in Law, Politics, and Society* 20 (2000): 85.

13. For an explanation of how liberalism preceded the widespread use of the term, which did not appear until 1810, see Immanuel Wallerstein, *The Modern World-System IV: Centrist Liberalism Triumphant, 1789–1914* (Los Angeles: University of California Press, 2011), 2.

14. See Ed White for an alternative reading of Benjamin Franklin, who is usually understood as either an "exceptional individual" or an "embodiment of the system" (*The Backcountry and the City: Colonization and Conflict in Early America* [Minneapolis: University of Minnesota Press, 2005], 177). Arguing against this bifurcation, White explores Franklin's life and writings in relation to institutional structures, rather than prioritizing one over the other. He instead sees Franklin "as class agent, as booster, as local organizer" (178).

15. Wallerstein, *The Modern World-System IV*, 144.

16. See Colin Dayan's illuminating analysis of the resonances between the history of exclusion, especially in relation to race and slavery, and contemporary human rights

abuses in *The Law Is a White Dog: How Legal Rituals Make and Unmake Persons* (Princeton, NJ: Princeton University Press, 2011).

17. Charles Mills, "Racial Liberalism," *PMLA* 125, no. 5 (2008): 1394.

18. Mills, "Racial Liberalism," 1382.

19. Scholars focusing on early America have long debated the role of liberalism, with its emphasis on the individual, in shaping the new nation's political and cultural landscape. Vernon L. Parrington argues for the dominance of liberalism, which, in his view, subsumed republicanism, with its emphasis on civic duty, in the early United States. In the latter half of the twentieth century, the "republican synthesizers," J. G. A. Pocock, Bernard Bailyn, and Gordon Wood, popularized the view that republicanism was preeminent in the period and offered an alternative to liberalism. Elizabeth Maddock Dillon has convincingly shown that early American politics and culture in fact drew on liberalism to "appropriate and transfigure" the terms and values of classic republicanism, all the while retaining the individualist emphasis of classical liberalism. See Elizabeth Maddock Dillon, *The Gender of Freedom: Fictions of Liberalism in the Literary Public Sphere* (Stanford, CA: Stanford University Press, 2004), 142–61. See also Isaac Kramnick, *Republicanism and Bourgeois Radicalism: Political Ideology in Late Eighteenth-Century England and America* (Ithaca, NY: Cornell University Press, 1990).

20. Ajay Kumar Batra, "Reading with Conviction: Abraham Johnstone and the Poetics of the Dead End," *Early American Literature* 55, no. 2 (2020): 322.

21. Johnstone, *Address*, 9.

22. Serenella Iovino and Serpil Oppermann, "Material Ecocriticism: Materiality, Agency, and Models of Narrativity," *Ecozone* 3, no. 1 (2012): 76. See also Monique Allewaert, "Toward a Materialist Figuration, a Slight Manifesto," *English Language Notes* 52, no. 2 (2013): 61–77, which argues that a materialist literary studies methodology can successfully incorporate insights from not only from poststructuralism but also New Historicism: "A figurative materialism must study non-literary texts, here not primarily for the forms they offer (as Greenblatt's New Historicism did so brilliantly) but for the figurative operations on which they depend and that they transmit" (70).

23. As Diana Coole notes, "Agency has been central to modern conceptions of politics but it is a complicated and contested idea that seems to have fallen into both theoretical and historical crisis." "Rethinking Agency: A Phenomenological Approach to Embodiment and Agentic Capacities," *Political Studies* 53 (2005): 124.

24. Both Ed White and Matt Cohen have recently argued for the necessity of this kind of disciplinary "shift in perspective" in early American studies away from purely discursive formations. White examines backcountry cultures through the lens of "practical ensembles," arguing that "eighteenth-century actors understood themselves as living in a society of relatively fluid collective forms, and through these local building blocks they approached those matters we more loosely capture with generalities like 'politics,' 'economy,' or 'culture'" (*The Backcountry and the City*, 17). Elucidating complex communication networks, Matt Cohen argues against the ahistorical bifurcation between oral and print cultures that has structured much of the scholarship on early American culture, particularly in relation to Indigenous peoples. *The Networked Wilderness: Communicating in Early New England* (Minneapolis: University of Minnesota Press, 2010), 2.

25. Aaron Bancroft, *The Importance of a Religious Education Illustrated and Enforced* (Worcester, MA: Isaiah Thomas, 1793), 17.

26. See Ronald A. Bosco, "Lectures at the Pillory: The Early American Execution Sermon," *American Quarterly* 30, no. 3 (1978): 156–76.

27. Richard Slotkin, "Narratives of Negro Crime in New England," *American Quarterly* 25, no. 1 (1975): 10.

28. Cotton Mather, *Tremenda: The Dreadful Sound with which the Wicked Are To Be Thunderstruck* (Boston: B. Green, for B. Gray & J. Edwards, 1721), 26.

29. DeLombard, *In the Shadow of the Gallows*, 176.

30. My reading of Bancroft's sermon runs counter to a widespread consensus that execution sermons remained largely unchanged through the latter half of the eighteenth century. For example, both Bosco ("Lectures") and Halttunen stress that goal of the execution ritual was reconciliation, a healing of the fissure caused by the crime, wherein the criminal played the dual role of moral example and sacrificial Christ figure, putting evil in service of salvation (*Murder*, 41–49). Wayne C. Minnick argues that every execution sermon at least implied the existence of an all-powerful God, free will, the preeminence of life after death, and damnation for all sinners except those who repent through Jesus Christ ("The New England Execution Sermon, 1639–1800," *Speech Monographs* 35 [1968]: 77–89, 82). Bancroft's sermon fits these molds only at a stretch.

31. This embrace of liberal secularism is likewise apparent in the titles of other later execution sermons, such as *Warning against Drunkenness* (1816, David D. Field) and *A Discourse* (1825, Jonathan Going).

32. See Daniel A. Cohen's discussion of Bancroft's sermon in his explication of the growing emphasis early national ministers placed on faulty education as the source of deviance: "One might have expected that the case of a young man who had brutally murdered two of his elders would inspire a sermon arraigning the depravity and ingratitude of youth. Instead, Bancroft's discourse stressed the importance of juvenile education" (*Pillars*, 91).

33. Bancroft, *The Importance of a Religious Education*, 17.

34. Bancroft, *The Importance of a Religious Education*, 17–18.

35. Bancroft, *The Importance of a Religious Education*, 16–17.

36. For more on early American education more broadly, especially in relation to John Locke, see Gillian Brown, *The Consent of the Governed: The Lockean Legacy in Early American Culture* (Cambridge, MA: Harvard University Press, 2001). For the role of education in relation to liberalism, see Wallerstein: "Liberalism . . . preached that virtue could be taught, and it therefore offered the managed progression of rights, the managed promotion of passive citizens to the status of active citizens" (*The Modern World-System IV*, 147).

37. Bancroft, *The Importance of a Religious Education*, 21. It is useful to recall Michel Foucault's observation that, in the eyes of the state, the possibility of identification with the condemned is one of the shortcomings of public modes of punishment (*Discipline and Punish: The Birth of The Prison* [New York: Vintage, 1995]). In the United States, Benjamin Rush explicitly criticized public punishments because of this possibility of "misplaced" identification (*An Enquiry into the Effects of Public Punishments upon Criminals, and Upon Society* [Philadelphia: Joseph James, Chesnut Street, 1787]).

38. Bancroft, *The Importance of a Religious Education*, 20.

39. Bancroft, *The Importance of a Religious Education*, 20–21.

40. Bancroft, *The Importance of a Religious Education*, 23.

41. In Giorgio Agamben's terms, Frost is a figure of dehumanized "bare life" included in political life by means of exclusion (*Homo Sacer: Sovereign Power and Bare Life*, trans. Daniel Heller-Roazen [Stanford, CA: Stanford University Press, 1998]); Alexander Weheliye's corrective account assesses the centrality of race in constructing modern conceptions of what is included and excluded in the category of the human (*Habeas Viscus: Racializing Assemblages, Biopolitics, and Black Feminist Theories of the Human* [Durham, NC: Duke University Press, 2014]). See also Stacey Margolis, *The Public Life of Privacy in Nineteenth-Century American Literature* (Durham, NC: Duke University Press, 2005).

42. Dillon, *The Gender of Freedom*, 3, 17.

43. Johnstone, *Address*, 9.

44. Johnstone, *Address*, 11.

45. For an analysis of the integral, if submerged, roles of corporeality, textuality, and gender in liberal theory, see Dillon, *The Gender of Freedom*, 11–48.

46. Anonymous, "To the Public," in Johnstone, *Address*, 2.

47. For an illuminating discussion of Plummer's career as an "author-peddler" and the audiences he reached with broadsides like *Last Words and Dying Confession of Samuel Frost*, including the young poet John Greenleaf Whittier, see Michael C. Cohen, *The Social Lives of Poems in Nineteenth-Century America* (Philadelphia: University of Pennsylvania Press, 2015), 22, 1–39.

48. See Daniel A. Cohen and Louis P. Masur, *Rites of Execution: Capital Punishment and the Transformation of American Culture, 1776–1865* (New York: Cambridge University Press 1989).

49. Hartnett, "The Hanging of Abraham Johnstone," 125; and DeLombard, *In the Shadow of the Gallows*, 121.

50. As Daniel E. Williams writes, confessions in this period "exhibited a much greater concern for the imagination than they did for the conscience" (*Pillars of Salt: An Anthology of Early American Criminal Narratives* [Madison: University of Wisconsin Press, 1993], 13).

51. Literary critics and philosophers have become increasingly interested in the affect of disgust; see especially Sianne Ngai, *Ugly Feelings* (Cambridge, MA: Harvard University Press, 2005); Nicolae Morar, "Against the Yuck Factor: On the Ideal Role of Disgust in Society," *Utilitas* 2, no. 2 (2014): 153–77; Carolyn Korsmeyer, *Savoring Disgust: The Foul and the Fair in Aesthetics* (New York: Oxford University Press, 2011); and William Ian Miller, *The Anatomy of Disgust* (Cambridge, MA: Harvard University Press, 1998).

52. DeLombard, *In the Shadow of the Gallows*, 156.

53. Johnstone, *Address*, 6–7.

54. Batra, "Reading with Conviction," 339.

55. Johnstone, *Address*, 27.

56. Johnstone, *Address*, 14.

57. Johnstone, *Address*, 15.

58. See discussions regarding the question of authorship below.

59. Johnstone, *Address*, 10.
60. Johnstone, *Address*, 11.
61. Johnstone, *Address*, 11.
62. Johnstone, *Address*, 11.
63. Johnstone, *Address*, 13–14.
64. *The State Gazette of South Carolina* 55, no. 4242 (August 12, 1793): 2, col. 4; "Account."
65. I am grateful to Daniel A. Cohen for drawing my attention to Frost's connection to Shays's Rebellion. Arguing for the centrality of "backcountry" insurrections such as Shays's, White laments the tendency amongst historians to understand such events "as either localized versions of national phenomena or, worse, as so many *symptoms* of a broad unrest to be registered by the urban centers" (*The Backcountry and the City*, 2). See also Robert A. Gross, ed., *In Debt to Shays: The Bicentennial of an Agrarian Rebellion* (Charlottesville: University of North Carolina Press, 1993); and Leonard L. Richards, *Shays's Rebellion: The American Revolution's Final Battle* (Philadelphia: University of Pennsylvania Press, 2002).
66. "Account," col. 2.
67. *Thomas's Massachusetts, Connecticut, Rhode Island, New Hampshire & Vermont Almanack, with an Ephemeris, for the Year of our Lord 1793* (Worcester, MA: Isaiah Thomas, 1792).
68. The publisher of the printed version of Bancroft's sermon includes a footnote explaining that Frost had murdered his father (*The Importance of a Religious Education*, 22).
69. Adam Smith, *Theory of Moral Sentiments*, ed. Knud Haakonssen (1759; New York, Cambridge University Press, 2002), 11–12.
70. See Bruce Burgett's related argument about the necessary relationship between embodiment and the formation of the public sphere in the late eighteenth- and early nineteenth-century United States in *Sentimental Bodies: Sex, Gender, and Citizenship in the Early Republic* (Princeton, NJ: Princeton University Press, 1998).
71. Edward Cahill, *Liberty of the Imagination: Aesthetic Theory, Literary Form, and Politics in the Early United States* (Philadelphia: University of Pennsylvania Press, 2012), 12, 201. Paul de Man revived this integrative view: "The *aesthetic* is not a separate category but a principle of articulation between various known faculties, activities, and modes of cognition." "Aesthetic Formalization: Kleist's *Über das Marionettentheater*," in *The Rhetoric of Romanticism* (New York: Columbia University Press, 1984), 264–65.
72. See Richard Iton's *In Search of the Black Fantastic: Politics and Popular Culture in the Post–Civil Rights Era* (New York: Oxford University Press, 2008); as well as Giorgio Agamben's argument that the aesthetic becomes increasingly marginal as the "anthropological machine of humanism" grows. *The Open: Man and Animal*, trans. Kevin Attell (Stanford, CA: Stanford University Press, 1994), 29.
73. Cahill ultimately offers a different understanding of the force of aesthetic in the early United States. Arguing for the aesthetic as a mode of theorizing most useful for those interested in consolidating an elite, he demonstrates that aesthetic theory complemented the vision of the Federalists. Though "the political aims of Federalist criticism went unfulfilled [in the nineteenth century,] . . . its literary aims had a significant effect on nineteenth-century culture" (*Liberty of the Imagination*, 225). While I am

convinced by Cahill's argument, I am interested in an alternative tendency within the eighteenth-century discourse of the aesthetic, which he also notes, to give rise to "collective models of subjectivity" (12).

74. In the Boston broadside, the poem is retitled "A Poem on the Solemn Occasion."

75. Mark E. Kann has argued that a system of penitentiary punishment that denied liberty to a significant proportion of "citizens" on the margins became necessary in this period, as a solution to the problem of how to maintain order in a nation engendered by anti-patriarchal rhetoric. *Punishment, Prisons, and Patriarchy: Liberty and Power in the Early American Republic* (New York: New York University Press, 2005).

76. For lucid analysis of the centrality of the penitentiary in nineteenth-century American culture, see Caleb Smith, *The Prison and the American Imagination* (New Haven, CT: Yale University Press, 2011).

77. Dayan, *The Law Is a White Dog*, 60.

78. See *Salem Gazette* 3, no. 135 (May 11, 1784): 2, cols. 2–3; and *Vermont Gazette, or Freeman's Depository* 1, no. 49 (May 10, 1784): 3, col. 1.

79. *Columbian Centinel* 20, no. 9 (October 9, 1793): 3, col. 1.

80. These included the *Massachusetts Spy*, the *Daily Advertiser*, the *Essex Journal*, and the *New Hampshire Gazette*. By September, papers carried one of two main accounts, one longer and one shorter. Frost's demand of execution by hanging appeared in the shorter version. Newspaper coverage of Frost's first trial was sparse by comparison.

81. *Massachusetts Spy: Or, Worcester Gazette* 22, no. 1069 (September 26, 1793): 3, col 3.

82. Qtd. in Richard Moran, "The Insanity Defense," *Annals of the American Academy of Political and Social Science* 477 (1985): 28.

83. *Essex Journal & New Hampshire Packet* 491 (November 13, 1793): 3, col. 3.

84. For more on Plummer as author, see Michael C. Cohen, *The Social Lives*.

85. Johnstone, *Address*, 4.

86. Johnstone, *Address*, 5.

87. Johnstone, *Address*, 19.

88. Johnstone, *Address*, 21–22.

89. Johnstone, *Address*, 16.

90. Johnstone, *Address*, 16.

91. Johnstone, *Address*, 43.

92. Johnstone, *Address*, 46.

93. Johnstone, *Address*, 46.

94. Johnstone, *Address*, 8.

95. Bennett, *Vibrant Matter*; Sharon Krause, "Bodies in Action: Corporeal Agency and Democratic Politics," *Political Theory* 39, vol. 3 (2011): 317.

96. In the literary criticism of the past few decades, much-needed attention to historical and cultural context has largely replaced the aesthetic object as the heroic (liberal) agent, while the aesthetic object in turn becomes passive and inert. Rita Felski has suggested that to regain a robust view of the aesthetic, we need also to rethink agency: specifically, she calls for recognition of texts as nonhuman actors. Felski's understanding of text as "a fellow actor and co-creator of relations, attitudes, and attach-

ments" productively dismantles the static figuration of the artist as "a self-authorizing subject, an independent agent who summons up actions and orchestrates events" ("Context Stinks!," *New Literary History* 42, vol. 4 [2011]: 583, 590). But rather than renouncing the aesthetic as a result, Felski instead rightly points out that the distinctiveness of art "does not rule out connectedness but is the very reason that connections are forged and sustained" (584).

Chapter 3 · Outlaw Humanism

1. Peter P. Hinks's meticulously researched history continues to be the most extensive direct treatment of Walker's life and times, *To Awaken My Afflicted Brethren: David Walker and the Problem of Antebellum Slave Resistance* (University Park: Pennsylvania State University Press, 1997).

2. For a fuller treatment of the printing and dissemination of Walker's *Appeal*, see Hinks, *To Awaken*, 116–72; and Robert S. Levine, *Dislocating Race and Nation* (Chapel Hill: University of North Carolina Press, 2008), 67–118; and Lori Leavell, "'Not Intended Exclusively for the Slave States': Antebellum Recirculation of David Walker's *Appeal*," *Callaloo* 38, no. 3 (2015): 679–95.

3. Southern historian Clement Eaton's 1936 highly racist evaluation nevertheless offers valuable information regarding circulation and legal action taken against the pamphlet in "A Dangerous Pamphlet in the Old South," *Journal of Southern History* 2 (1936): 323–34.

4. Henry Highland Garnet's "A Brief Sketch of His Life," appended to his 1848 edition of the *Appeal* remains an important early source of biographical information on Walker. David Walker and Henry Highland Garnet, *Walker's Appeal, with a Brief Sketch of His Life by Henry Highland Garnet; And Also Garnet's Address to the Slaves of the United States of America* (New York: J. H. Tobbitt, 1848).

5. Eaton, "A Dangerous Pamphlet," 327–33.

6. For more on threats to Walker's life, see Darryl Scriven, *A Dealer of Old Clothes* (New York: Lexington Books, 2007); and Herbert Aptheker, *One Continual Cry: David Walker's Appeal to the Colored Citizens of the World, 1829–1830; Its Setting & Its Meaning* (New York: published for A.I.M.S. by Humanities Press, 1965).

7. Leavell, "Not Intended," 679.

8. For a provocative analysis of the dynamic agency of typography in early American print culture, see Marcy J. Dinius, "'Look!! Look!!! at This!!!!': The Radical Typography of David Walker's *Appeal*," *PMLA* 126, no. 1 (2011): 55–72. Dinius extends this analysis in her monograph, which represents an important development in Walker scholarship, taking seriously the creative contribution and legacies of his work, *The Textual Effects of David Walker's "Appeal": Print-Based Activism against Slavery, Racism and Discrimination, 1829–1951* (Philadelphia: University of Pennsylvania Press, 2022).

9. Qtd. in Eaton, "A Dangerous Pamphlet," 327–28.

10. Qtd. in Hinks, *To Awaken*, 119.

11. Cheryl A. Wall, *On Freedom and the Will to Adorn: The Arts of the African American Essay* (Durham: University of North Carolina Press, 2019), 41. See also Jane H. Pease and William H. Pease, "Walker's *Appeal* Comes to Charleston: A Note and Documents," *Journal of Negro History* 59 (1974): 287–92.

12. W. E. B. Du Bois, *Dusk of Dawn* (Piscataway, NJ: Transaction, 2007), 192.

13. Ian Finseth and Thabiti Asukile have both critiqued Sterling Stuckey's influential analysis of Walker as one of the originators Black nationalist thought in his seminal *Slave Culture: Nationalist Theory and the Foundations of Black America* (New York: Oxford University Press, 1987), especially pp. 98–137. Ian Finseth, "David Walker, Nature's Nation and Early African-American Separatism," *Mississippi Quarterly* 54, no. 3 (2000): 337–62; and Thabiti Asukile, "The All-Embracing Black Nationalist Theories of David Walker's Appeal," *Black Scholar* (1999): 16–24.

14. Tera Hunter, in *To 'Joy My Freedom* details the virulent racism that accompanied TB's nineteenth-century epidemiology; we could equally connect this back to yellow fever and forward to COVID-19 (Cambridge, MA: Harvard University Press, 1997), 187–218.

15. Ruth Wilson Gilmore, *Golden Gulag: Prisons, Surplus, Crisis, and Opposition in Globalizing California* (Berkeley: University of California Press, 2006), 28.

16. Christina Sharpe, *In the Wake: On Blackness and Being* (Durham, NC: Duke University Press, 2016), 17.

17. Sharpe, *In the Wake*, 14.

18. As Alicia Garza, picking up Audre Lorde's earlier thread, writes in response to the Charleston church shooting in 2015, "We were never meant to survive. We were stolen from our families and our land, brought to this country in the bottoms of boats, chained together like animals." Garza registers awareness that British colonies in the Americas, and later the United States, generated wealth directly, and deliberately, from Black alienation and exploitation. "We Were Never Meant to Survive: A Response to the Attack in Charleston," *Truthout*, June 19, 2015, https://truthout.org/articles/we-were-never-meant-to-survive-a-response-to-the-attack-in-charleston/.

19. Garza, "We Were Never Meant to Survive."

20. *Philadelphia Inquirer*, April 22, 1830, qtd. in Leavell, "Not Intended," 685.

21. Herbert Aptheker outlines the historical and cultural background of the *Appeal* in *"One Continual Cry": David Walker's "Appeal to the Colored Citizens of the World" (1829–1830)—Its Setting and Its Meaning* (New York: American Institute of Marxist Studies by the Humanities Press, 1965).

22. Vincent Harding explores the place of Walker in the struggle for Black liberation in his seminal *There Is a River: The Black Struggle for Freedom in America* (New York: Vintage, 1981), 75–100.

23. Elizabeth McHenry, *Forgotten Readers: Recovering the Lost History of African American Literary Societies* (Durham, NC: Duke University Press, 2002), 31.

24. Melvin L. Rogers, "David Walker and the Political Power of the Appeal," *Political Theory* 43, no. 2 (2014): 209.

25. When the *Appeal* was first published, multiple readers and reviewers cast doubt on whether Walker was in fact the author, claiming that he did not, could not, have the education required to produce such a learned and compelling work of literature. If modern-day readers do not doubt Walker's authorship, they rarely emphasize the erudition that marks the *Appeal*, preferring instead to emphasize its stridency. See Hinks, *To Awaken*, 117; and McHenry, *Forgotten Readers*, 31–33.

26. McHenry, *Forgotten Readers*, 31.

27. For analysis of the tangled histories of citizenship, rights and Black activism in the period, see Martha S. Jones, *Birthright Citizens: A History of Race and Rights in*

Antebellum America. Studies in Legal History (Cambridge: Cambridge University Press, 2018).

28. Terri L. Snyder, *The Power to Die: Slavery and Suicide in British North America* (Chicago: University of Chicago Press, 2016), 89–90.

29. For a fuller explication of outlaw status and its adjacency to civil and social death in Western legal traditions, see the discussion of Johann Fichte's *Science of Rights* (1796) in Bryan Wagner, *Disturbing the Peace: Black Culture and the Police Power after Slavery* (Cambridge, MA: Harvard University Press, 2009), 15–18; and Markus D. Dubber, "Citizenship and Penal Law," *New Criminal Law Review: An International and Interdisciplinary Journal* 13, no. 2 (2010): 209–11.

30. Qtd. in Hinks, *To Awaken*, 93; see also 102.

31. Du Bois, *Dusk of Dawn*, 192–93.

32. Finseth, "David Walker, Nature's Nation," 337.

33. Hinks, *To Awaken*, xxv.

34. McHenry, *Forgotten Readers*, 26, 27. Dinius, *Textual Effects*, 3.

35. Aptheker, *One Continual Cry*, 5.

36. Peter Thompson takes an opposed view, arguing for the ultimate secularism of Walker's work in "David Walker's Nationalism," *Journal of the Early Republic* 37, no. 1 (2017): 47–80. Thompson attends to theories of sovereignty, drawing examples from Missouri's assertion of its sovereignty as a state via John Scott, Missouri's delegate to Congress, for the purposes of excluding free Black people, and the United States' own declaration of its free and independent status. He holds that there is a tension insofar as Walker's assertion of the rights of African-descended peoples resembles white supremacist projects that proceed from the same premise but for the purposes of excluding Black people from citizenship, e.g., Senator James Barbour of Virginia, "Indians, free negroes, mulattoes and slaves! Tell me not that the Constitution, when it speaks of *We, the people*, means these" (qtd. on p. 69). Thompson's interesting analysis misses the necessity, for Walker, of a just God, rather than a political sovereign, in securing a universal humanity.

37. Indeed, Walker, who makes direct reference to Toussaint Louverture in the *Appeal*, was well aware of the history of Haiti; see Wall, *On Freedom and the Will to Adorn*, 39–40.

38. Thomas Jefferson, *Notes on the State of Virginia*, Documenting the American South, https://docsouth.unc.edu/southlit/jefferson/jefferson.html. All quotations are from the online edition.

39. Lewis R. Gordon, "Africana Philosophy as Modern Philosophy," in *An Introduction to Africana Philosophy* (Cambridge: Cambridge University Press, 2012), 31.

40. My emphasis. All Walker quotations are from the scholarly edition of the *Appeal* edited by Peter P. Hinks (Philadelphia: Pennsylvania State University Press), 2000.

41. Ian Frederick Finseth, *Shades of Green: Visions of Nature in the Literature of American Slavery* (Athens: University of Georgia Press, 2009), 177.

42. Eddie S. Glaude Jr., Wilson Jeremiah Moses, and Cheryl A. Wall all explore the *Appeal* in relation the American jeremiad tradition. Eddie S. Glaude, *Exodus! Religion, Race, and Nation in Early Nineteenth-Century Black America* (Chicago: University of Chicago Press, 2000), 19–44; Wilson Jeremiah Moses, *Black Messiahs and Uncle Toms:*

Social and Literary Manipulations of a Religious Myth (University Park: Pennsylvania State University Press, 1993), 38–46; Wall, *On Freedom and the Will to Adorn*, 46–48.

43. Gordon, "Africana Philosophy as Modern Philosophy," 21.
44. René Descartes, *Discourse on Method and Meditations on First Philosophy*, trans. Donald A. Cress (Indianapolis, IN: Hackett, 1998), 47.
45. Descartes, *Discourse*, 47.
46. Descartes, *Discourse*, 59.
47. Descartes, *Discourse*, 60.
48. Descartes, *Discourse*, 62.
49. Descartes, *Discourse*, 65.
50. Descartes, *Discourse*, 92.
51. The Latin phrase *cogito, ergo sum*, famously associated with Descartes, appears first in *Principles of Philosophy* (1644). Its first iteration comes in French in Descartes 1637 *Discourse on Method*, his opening foray into the problematic of skepticism, where he writes, "Je pense, donc je suis." He sets his response to skepticism out most fully in *Meditations on First Philosophy* (1641), as discussed above (*Discourse*, 18).
52. Timothy J. Reiss, "Descartes's Silences on Slavery and Race," in *Race and Racism in Modern Philosophy*, ed. Andrew Valls (Ithaca, NY: Cornell University Press, 2005), 19.
53. Joan Dayan, *Haiti, History, and the Gods* (Los Angeles: University of California Press, 1996), 204.
54. Descartes, *Discourse*, 60.
55. From *Discourse on Method*; qtd. in Reiss, "Descartes's Silences," 20.
56. Letter to Jean-Louis Guez de Balzac, qtd. in Reiss, "Descartes's Silences," 19.
57. Reiss, "Descartes's Silences," 17.
58. Aimé Césaire, *Discourse on Colonialism*, trans. Joan Pinkham (New York: Monthly Review Press, 2000), 56.
59. Césaire, *Discourse*, 42.
60. Césaire, *Discourse*, 42–43.
61. As Mansfield puts it in his decision, slavery is "so odious, that nothing can be suffered to support it, but positive law. Whatever inconveniences, therefore, may follow from the decision, I cannot say this case is allowed or approved by the law of England; and therefore the black must be discharged." Andrew Lyall, *Granville Sharp's Cases on Slavery* (Oxford: Bloomsbury, 2017), 233.
62. Descartes, *Discourse*, 47, emphasis added.
63. Descartes, *Discourse*, 47.
64. Descartes, *Discourse*, 62.
65. Gordon, "Africana Philosophy," 24.
66. Immanuel Wallerstein, *The Modern World-System IV: Centrist Liberalism Triumphant, 1789–1914* (Los Angeles: University of California Press, 2011), 144.
67. Cedric Robinson, *Black Marxism: The Making of the Black Radical Tradition* (London: Zed Press, 1983), 27.
68. Gordon, "Africana Philosophy," 32.
69. Andrew S. Curran, *The Anatomy of Blackness: Science & Slavery in the Age of Enlightenment* (Baltimore: Johns Hopkins University Press, 2011), 223–24.

70. Alexander G. Weheliye, *Habeas Viscus: Racializing Assemblages, Biopolitics and Black Feminist Theories of the Human* (Durham, NC: Duke University Press, 2014), 3

71. Lee Allen Dugatkin, *Mr. Jefferson and the Giant Moose: Natural History in Early America* (Chicago: University of Chicago Press, 2009), x.

72. Cf. Cristin Ellis, *Antebellum Posthuman* (Fordham, NY: Fordham University Press, 2018); and Erin E. Forbes, "Vegetative Politics from Crèvecoeur to Hawthorne," *J19: The Journal of Nineteenth-Century Americanists* 8, no. 1 (2020): 43–66.

73. Greta LaFleur emphasizes Jefferson's inconsistency throughout this text, noting in particular that while "Jefferson ardently refuses Buffon's characterization of Native Americans as feeble and dispassionate and urges the universal emancipation of slaves, he reverts to an anatomical explanation of racial difference in his discussion of African Americans; this passage points again to the coexistence of environmentalist and more rigid theories of human variety in works by the same authors, and even in the same texts." See Greta LaFleur, *The Natural History of Sexuality in Early America* (Baltimore: Johns Hopkins University Press, 2018), 58.

74. Marlene L. Daut, *Tropics of Haiti: Race and the Literary History of the Haitian Revolution in the Atlantic World, 1789–1865* (Liverpool: Liverpool University Press, 2015), 50.

75. C. L. R. James, *The Black Jacobins* (New York: Penguin, 1938, 2001), 20.

76. Britt Rusert notes that "Jefferson's *Notes* holds a complicated place in early African American culture. While antebellum Black newspapers routinely lambasted Jefferson for his damaging comments on African inferiority, contributors were just as likely to cull *Notes* for remarks on the despotism of slavery and the eventual inevitability of 'total emancipation' for the enslaved, thus making Jefferson an unlikely prophet for the coming of abolition." Britt Rusert, *Fugitive Science: Empiricism and Freedom in Early African American Literature* (New York: New York University Press, 2017), 35.

77. Curran, *Anatomy*, 213.

78. Curran, *Anatomy*, 211.

79. George M. Frederickson recounts that Carl Linnaeus's early attempt at human species' division "included some mythical and 'monstrous' creatures; but the durable heart of the schema was ... the differentiation among Europeans, American Indians, Asians, and Africans." *Racism: A Short History* (Princeton, NJ: Princeton University Press, 2002), 56.

80. Kevin Pelletier, *Apocalyptic Sentimentalism: Love and Fear in Antebellum U.S. Literature* (New York: Oxford University Press, 2015), 37.

81. Mark Dery, "Black to the Future: Interviews with Samuel R. Delany, Greg Tate, and Tricia Rose," in *Flame Wars: The Discourse of Cyberculture*, ed. Mark Dery (Durham, NC: Duke University Press, 1994), 179–80. Recent scholars including Alondra Nelson, Lisa Yaszek, Brit Russert have begun to rectify this neglect.

82. Individual agency is intimately linked to the definition of "the human" in the liberal tradition: in this view, to be human is to possess an individual will and the capacity to act according to that will; see Walter Johnson, "Agency: A Ghost Story," in *Slavery's Ghost: The Problem of Freedom in the Age of Emancipation* (Baltimore: Johns Hopkins University Press, 2011), 8–20.

83. Johnson, "Agency," 8.

84. Sterling Stuckey, *Slave Culture*, 378.

85. David Walker, "Speech to the Massachusetts General Coloured Association," *Freedom's Journal*, December 19, 1828.

86. McHenry, *Forgotten Readers*, 37, 40, 41.

87. As Rogers concludes, "Walker need not rely on a recognitive legal relationship to [call out the political standing of Black folks] because it is the practice of judging that illuminates one's political, indeed, citizenly standing" ("Political Power," 20).

Chapter 4 • *The Southampton Insurgency*

1. Saidiya Hartman, "Venus in Two Acts," *Small Axe* 26, no. 2 (2018): 3.

2. Lamonte Aidoo, "Genealogies of Horror: Three Stories of Slave-Women, Motherhood, and Murder in the Americas," *African and Black Diaspora: An International Journal* 13, no. 1 (2020): 40.

3. The trial record, seeming unable to choose among terms, refers to Turner as a "negro man slave." Henry Irving Tragle, *The Southampton Slave Revolt of 1831, A Compilation of Source Material* (Amherst: University of Massachusetts Press, 1971), 221.

4. Southampton County Court Records, qtd. in Tragle, *The Southampton Slave Revolt*, 221–22.

5. David F. Allmendinger Jr., *Nat Turner and the Rising in Southampton County* (Baltimore: Johns Hopkins University Press, 2014), 14.

6. Ultimately, "the rebellion involved more than forty rebels, nearly sixty white victims, dozens of witnesses, hundreds of militia, and many summary trials and executions." Alfred L. Brophy, "Nat Turner and the Rising in Southampton County. By Allmendinger, David F. (Baltimore, MD: Johns Hopkins University Press, 2014. Pp. xi, 401. $49.95.)," *Historian* 79 (2017): 106–7.

7. Gray's account brings the total to fifty-five (Nat Turner and Thomas R. Gray, *The Confessions of Nat Turner [. . . and] An Authentic Account of the Whole Insurrection* [Baltimore: Lucas & Deaver, 1831], in Tragle, *The Southampton Slave Revolt*, 22). Tragle, who adds material from Drewry and trial records, lists sixty murdered (*The Southampton Slave Revolt*, xv–xvii). Allmendinger, who excludes from his list of "white victims" the two apprentices at the Travis house (his sources, Gray and William C. Parker, indicate only two boys, Moore and Westbrook, with Westbrook being the apprentice), Catherine Whitehead's mother, the overseer at Nathaniel Francis's house, and a second child of Mrs. Caswell Worrell, lists fifty-five (*Nat Turner*, 288).

8. Turner and Gray, *The Confessions*, 311.

9. *Richmond (VA) Compiler*, August 27, 1831, in Tragle, *The Southampton Slave Revolt*, 48.

10. Samuel Warner, *Authentic and Impartial Narrative of the Tragical Scene* (New York: Warner & West, 1831), in Tragle, *The Southampton Slave Revolt*, 282.

11. Turner and Gray, *The Confessions*, 306.

12. Turner and Gray, *The Confessions*, 305.

13. Christopher Tomlins makes this point: "The legalities of the narrative, rather than of Gray's account of it, and the genre to which they belong, take their shape in his first sentence: 'You have asked me to give a history of the motives which induced me to undertake the late insurrection, *as you call it*.' From the outset, that is, Turner denies

that he and his interlocuter share a common understanding of what had occurred. From this moment we know that while Gray calls the event an insurrection Turner does not." *In the Matter of Nat Turner: A Speculative History* (Princeton, NJ: Princeton University Press, 2020), 48.

14. Herbert Aptheker, *Nat Turner's Slave Rebellion* (New York: A.I.M.S., 1966), 45.

15. Eugene D. Genovese locates slave revolts in the United States on a world-historical stage, alongside the Haitian Revolution. He argues that where earlier "guerilla" rebellions among enslaved people sought to establish local autonomy, after the Haitian and French Revolutions, slave revolts helped shape world politics by linking directly with international revolutionary movements. *From Rebellion to Revolution: Afro-American Slave Revolts in the Making of the Modern World* (Baton Rouge: Louisiana State University Press, 1981).

16. Tragle, *The Southampton Slave Revolt*, 135.

17. Allmendinger, *Nat Turner*, 101.

18. Allmendinger, *Nat Turner*, 336n99.

19. Alex Haley and Malcolm X, *Autobiography of Malcolm X* (New York: Penguin, 1965, 2001), 271.

20. Joseph Drexler-Dreis offers a complementary reading that robustly critiques masculinist readings of Turner and analyzes the role of African American Christianity in shaping Turner's "politics of belonging that cultivates an orientation beyond Man." "Nat Turner's Orientation beyond the Doctrine of Man," in *Beyond the Doctrine of Man: Decolonial Visions of the Human* (New York: Fordham University Press, 2019), 129.

21. Hartman, "Venus in Two Acts," 11.

22. Eric Gardner, "Accessing Early Black Print," *Legacy* 33, no. 1 (2016): 27.

23. Derrick R. Spires, "Genealogies of Black Modernities," *American Literary History* 32, no. 4 (2020): 613.

24. Tragle, *The Southampton Slave Revolt*, xi.

25. See Parramore, "Covenant in Jerusalem," for a fascinating and sensitive discussion of Gray and his potentially symbiotic, sympathetic relationship to Turner.

26. *Richmond (VA) Compiler*, in Tragle, *The Southampton Slave Revolt*, 89.

27. Allmendinger, *Nat Turner*, 302.

28. Meticulously analyzing the source material, Allmendinger ultimately does conclude that the insurgency originated with Turner.

29. Alfred L. Brophy, "The Nat Turner Trials," *North Carolina Law Review* 91, no. 5 (2013): 1818.

30. The specific retaliatory violence local to St. Luke's Parish seems to have been more limited than long thought. Carefully analyzing the tax lists from the following year, Allmendinger convincingly refutes the notion, held since the nineteenth century, that a "reign of terror" claiming the lives of as many innocent Black residents of St. Luke's Parish followed upon the heels of the August 1831 events. His evidence, tabulating taxation levied on enslaved persons, limits the possible number of "atrocities" or extralegal reprisals against those who did not take part in the insurgency to fourteen victims (*Nat Turner*, 203–7).

31. Harriet Jacobs, "XII. Fear of Insurrection", *Incidents in the Life of a Slave Girl* (New York: Norton, 2001), 54.

32. Qtd. in Peter H. Wood, "Nat Turner: The Unknown Slave as Visionary Leader,"

in *Black Leaders of the Nineteenth Century*, ed. Leon F. Litwack and August Meier (Urbana-Champaign: University of Illinois Press, 1991), 32.

33. About a month after the Insurgency, Thomas R. Gray had predicted that many Southampton citizens "will leave us" because "they never again can feel safe, never again can be happy" (letter in the *Constitutional Whig* [Richmond, VA], September 26, 1831, in Tragle, *The Southampton Slave Revolt*, 91). Yet Allmendinger, in his concluding chapter, shows that the vast majority of enslaving families in St. Luke's Parish who survived the insurgency in fact seemed to feel perfectly secure. They showed little to no inclination to limit the numbers of people they enslaved later in life but rather increased their holdings in both land and enslaved people (258–75).

34. Warner, *Authentic and Impartial Narrative*, 286.

35. *Richmond (VA) Compiler*, September 3, 1831, in Tragle, *The Southampton Slave Revolt*, 60.

36. *Constitutional Whig* (Richmond, VA), September 3, 1831, in Tragle, *The Southampton Slave Revolt*, 67.

37. *Norfolk Herald*, in Tragle, *The Southampton Slave Revolt*, 134.

38. *Norfolk Herald*, in Tragle, *The Southampton Slave Revolt*, 134.

39. *Norfolk Herald*, in Tragle, *The Southampton Slave Revolt*, 135.

40. William Lloyd Garrison, *Liberator*, September 3, 1831, in Tragle, *The Southampton Slave Revolt*, 63.

41. Garrison, *Liberator*, in Tragle, *The Southampton Slave Revolt*, 64.

42. Garrison, *Liberator*, in Tragle, *The Southampton Slave Revolt*, 64.

43. Wood, "Nat Turner."

44. Such problems are not helped by the fact that numerous mistakes get repeated across scholarly sources (see Allmendinger, *Nat Turner*, 301–5).

45. John Henrick Clarke, ed., *William Styron's Nat Turner: Ten Black Writers Respond* (Boston: Beacon Press, 1968); and Vincent Harding, qtd. in Drexler-Dreis, "Nat Turner's Orientation," 118.

46. Genovese, qtd. in Tomlins, *In the Matter of Nat Turner*, 23.

47. Tragle, *The Southampton Slave Revolt*, 4.

48. Turner and Gray, *The Confessions*, 303.

49. Tragle, *The Southampton Slave Revolt*, 4.

50. Tragle, *The Southampton Slave Revolt*, 5.

51. William Lloyd Garrison, "The Insurrection," *Liberator*, September 3, 1831, in Tragle, *The Southampton Slave Revolt*, 64.

52. Drexler-Dreis, "Nat Turner's Orientation," 113.

53. This aspect of the insurgency is usefully understood through the lens of performative studies; see e.g., Uri McMillan, *Embodied Avatars Genealogies of Black Feminist Art and Performance* (New York: New York University Press, 2016); Daphne Brooks, *Bodies in Dissent* (Durham, NC: Duke University Press, 2006); and Diana Taylor, *Performance* (Durham, NC: Duke University Press, 2016).

54. Tomlins, *In the Matter of Nat Turner*, xi.

55. This disparaging moniker notwithstanding, Aptheker actually discusses Gray very little, while relying on him as a source of information about "Nat Turner, the man" (*Nat Turner's Slave Rebellion*, viii and 42–43). Although critics like French have read Aptheker as disputing the authenticity of Gray's text, it is more plausible that Aptheker

instead meant to disparage the idea that "confession" is an apt term, as Turner's was an act of political rebellion in Aptheker's view, not a crime. Aptheker's gloss of *The Confessions* in his bibliography examines some of the controversy around the document's reliability but concludes, "As far as the present writer knows, it is genuine" (113). Scot French, *The Rebellious Slave: Nat Turner in American Memory* (Boston: Houghton Mifflin, 2004).

56. Thomas C. Parramore, "Covenant in Jerusalem," in *Nat Turner: A Slave Rebellion in History and Memory* (New York: Oxford University Press, 2004).

57. Caleb Smith, *The Oracle and the Curse: A Poetics of Justice from the Revolution to the Civil War* (Cambridge, MA: Harvard University Press, 2003), 157.

58. Tomlins, *In the Matter of Nat Turner*, xvi–xvii.

59. See Lara Langer Cohen and Jordan Stein, "Introduction: Early African American Print Culture," in *Early African America Print Culture*, ed. Lara Langer Cohen and Jordan Stein (Philadelphia: University of Pennsylvania Press, 2013).

60. William Sidney Drewry, *The Southampton Insurrection* (Washington, DC: Neal, 1900).

61. Alfred L. Brophy lists one B. Drewry among the seventeen justices who participated in the Nat Turner Trials and also owned enslaved people ("The Nat Turner Trials," 1849).

62. Aptheker, *Nat Turner's Slave Rebellion*, v.

63. Drewry, *The Southampton Insurrection*, 27.

64. Terri L. Snyder, *The Power to Die: Slavery and Suicide in British North America* (Chicago: University of Chicago Press, 2016), 26.

65. Drewry, *The Southampton Insurrection*, 28.

66. Aptheker, *Nat Turner's Slave Rebellion*, 35–36.

67. Allmendinger's research suggests that Turner's father may have been a man named Abraham, and his mother and grandmother women called Lydia and Nancy, enslaved by the Griffins (*Nat Turner*, 34).

68. Molefi Kete Asante, *100 Greatest African Americans* (Ann Arbor, MI: Prometheus Books, 2002), 299.

69. Drewry, *The Southampton Insurrection*, 27.

70. Warner, *Authentic and Impartial Narrative*, 296–99.

71. *Constitutional Whig* (Richmond, VA), September 26, 1831, in Tragle, *The Southampton Slave Revolt*, 93.

72. Turner and Gray, *The Confessions*, 308–9.

73. Ian Balfour, *The Rhetoric of Romantic Prophecy* (Stanford, CA: Stanford University Press, 2002), 1.

74. One goal here would be to read Turner not in the jeremiad tradition that Bercovitch outlines as being central to the American literary tradition but in the more strident, less self-congratulatory mode of biblical critique and prophecy.

75. Turner and Gray, *The Confessions*, 306.

76. Trial record as printed in Tragle, *The Southampton Slave Revolt*, 221.

77. Although Gray's claims regarding the legality of his pamphlet have been debunked, *The Confessions* is presented with all the official trappings one might want from a legal text and therefore, stylistically, it operates in a juridical discursive register. See David F. Almendinger Jr.'s *The Rising in Southampton*; as well as his "The Con-

struction of *The Confessions of Nat Turner*," in *Nat Turner: A Slave Rebellion in History and Memory* (New York: Oxford University Press, 2004), 2004.

78. See Almendinger, "The Construction of *The Confessions*."

79. Turner and Gray, *The Confessions*, 310.

80. We are reminded yet again of Poe's man of the crowd, the "type and genius of deep crime" as a book that does not permit itself to be read.

81. In this it resembles constructions like Eastern State Penitentiary, a building whose blank walls gave it an air of unreadability while its material citation of a gothic novel rendered it eminently readable.

82. Jeannine Marie DeLombard, *In the Shadow of the Gallows: Race, Crime and American Civic Identity* (Philadelphia: University of Pennsylvania Press, 2012).

83. Bringing together the frameworks of law and psychoanalysis, Christina Zwarg argues that "fear of slaves by definition was a fear of *things*, which is to say a fear of unwittingly exposing a lack of control over objects under possession, including one's dominion over oneself." "Who's Afraid of Virginia's Nat Turner? Mesmerism, Stowe, and the Terror of Things," *American Literature* 87, no. 1 (2015): 24, 50, 32.

84. Baptist, *The Half Has Never Been Told*, 24.

85. Turner and Gray, *The Confessions*, 307.

86. Snyder, *The Power to Die*, 90–91.

87. Turner and Gray, *The Confessions*, 307. The deliberateness of this sentence retains Turner's engagement with religion but indicates that the pamphlet did not seek to construct Turner as a religious fanatic who did not pose a rational or broad-based threat to the community of enslavers.

88. Drexler-Dreis, "Nat Turner's Orientation," 127.

89. Turner and Gray, *The Confessions*, 307.

90. Turner and Gray, *The Confessions*, 307.

91. Kyle Baker, *Nat Turner* (New York: Harry N. Abrams, 2008), 57.

92. Turner and Gray, *The Confessions*, 307.

93. Vincent B. Leitch, William E. Cain, Laurie Finke, and Barbara Johnson, eds., *The Norton Anthology of Theory and Criticism* (New York: Norton, 2001), 553.

94. Turner and Gray, *The Confessions*, 307.

95. Kenneth S. Greenberg suggests that Turner, simply in becoming a man named "Nat Turner" (a person with a story), struck an important blow against institution of slavery, which denied surnames to the enslaved. Kenneth S. Greenberg, "Name, Face, Body," in *Nat Turner: A Slave Rebellion in History and Memory* (New York: Oxford University Press, 2004), 3–23.

96. Turner and Gray, *The Confessions*, 317.

97. Mary Kempt Davis, *Nat Turner before the Bar of Justice: Fictional Treatments of the Southampton Slave Insurrection* (Baton Rouge: Louisiana State University Press, 1999).

98. A review that appeared in the *Liberator* just after the publication of *The Confessions* argues that the pamphlet will "serve to rouse up other leaders and cause other insurrection, by creating among the blacks admiration for the character of Nat, and a deep, undying sympathy for his fate. We advise the Grand Juries in the several slave States to indict Mr. Gray and the printers of the pamphlet forthwith; and the legislative bodies at the south to offer a large reward for their apprehension." William Lloyd Garrison, "The Confessions of Nat Turner," *Liberator*, December 17, 1831, 2.

99. Gustavus Stadler, *Troubling Minds: The Cultural Politics of Genius in the United States: 1840–1890* (Minneapolis: University of Minnesota Press, 2006), xxii.

100. Turner and Gray, *The Confessions*, 307.

101. Turner and Gray, *The Confessions*, 316.

102. Immanuel Wallerstein, *The Modern World-System IV: Centrist Liberalism Triumphant, 1789–1914* (Los Angeles: University of California Press, 2011).

103. John W. Blassingame, *The Frederick Douglass Papers, Series One*, vol. 5 (New Haven, CT: Yale University Press, 1992), 545–46.

104. For a thorough overview of this scholarship, see Elizabeth Maddock Dillon, *The Gender of Freedom: Fictions of Liberalism in the Literary Public Sphere* (Stanford, CA: Stanford University Press, 2004), 142–61.

105. For a brilliant analysis of the consequences of this dynamic relating to another African American of the nineteenth century, see Nell Irvin Painter, *Sojourner Truth: A Life, a Symbol* (New York: Norton, 1997).

106. Thomas De Quincey, "On Murder Considered as One of the Fine Arts," in *On Murder* (New York: Oxford, 2006), 29–30.

107. McMillan, *Embodied Avatars*, 8.

108. For a powerful rethinking of the nature, role and place of social death in African American cultural expression, see Vincent Brown, "Social Death and Political Life in the Study of Slavery," *American Historical Review* (2009): 1231–49; and V. Brown, *The Reaper's Garden: Death and Power in the World of Atlantic Slavery* (Cambridge, MA: Harvard University Press, 2008).

Chapter 5 · Fugitive Aesthetics

1. See Edgar Allan Poe, *Complete Poems*, ed. T. O. Mabbott (Champaign: University of Illinois Press, 2000), 342, hereafter cited parenthetically. As Kevin J. Hayes remarks, "Many commentators have used this memorable pair of prepositional phrases" to signal the distance between Poe's imaginative writings and their larger cultural context. Preface to *Edgar Allan Poe in Context*, ed. Kevin J. Hayes (New York: Cambridge University Press, 2013), xv.

2. Shira Wolosky, *The Art of Poetry, How to Read a Poem* (New York: Oxford University Press, 2001), 192–93; and Floyd Stoval, "The Conscious Art of Edgar Allan Poe," *College English* 24 (1963): 417–21.

3. Joan Dayan's invocation and summary dismissal of "Dream-Land" exemplifies this widespread tendency: "Much that is necessary to the sanctification of something called 'literariness'. . . is risked if we put Poe in his place, if we avoid the romantic image of a genius in 'Dream-Land,' 'Out of SPACE / Out of TIME.'" "Amorous Bondage: Poe, Ladies, Slaves," in *The American Face of Edgar Allan Poe*, ed. Stephen Rachman and Shawn Rosenheim (Baltimore: Johns Hopkins University Press, 1995), 196.

4. Paul Gilmore, *Aesthetic Materialism: Electricity and American Romanticism* (Stanford, CA: Stanford University Press, 2009), 1. For detailed analyses of the sometimes problematic indebtedness of the field of early American literature to the discipline of history, see the special joint issue of *Early American Literature* and *American Literary History* 22 (2010).

5. Edward Cahill, *Liberty of the Imagination: Aesthetic Theory, Literary Form, and Politics in the Early United States* (Philadelphia: University of Pennsylvania Press, 2012),

7. In 2004 *American Literature* published a special issue devoted, rather ominously, to "aesthetics and the end(s) of American cultural studies," edited by Christopher Castiglia and Russ Castronovo. More recent work in this area includes Russ Castronovo, *Beautiful Democracy: Aesthetics and Anarchy in a Global Era* (Chicago: University of Chicago Press, 2007); Gilmore, *Aesthetic Materialism*; Eric Slaughter, *The State as a Work of Art* (Chicago: Chicago University Press, 2009); Ivy G. Wilson, *Specters of Democracy: Blackness and the Aesthetics of Politics in the Antebellum U.S.* (New York: Oxford University Press, 2011); and the essay collection, Christopher Looby and Cindy Weinstein, eds., *American Literature's Aesthetic Dimensions* (New York: Columbia University Press, 2012). Much of this work has been influenced by the work of philosopher Jacques Rancière, especially *The Politics of Aesthetics: The Distribution of the Sensible* (New York: Continuum, 2004).

6. Exceptions include Weinstein's essay in *American Literature's Aesthetic Dimensions* on temporality in *Pym*; Rachel Polonsky, "Poe's Aesthetic Theory," in *Cambridge Companion to Edgar Allan Poe*, ed. Rachel Polonsky (New York: Cambridge University Press, 2002), 42–56; C. T. Walters, "Poe's 'Philosophy of Furniture' and the Aesthetics of Fictional Design," and Daniel J. Philippon, "Poe in the Ragged Mountains: Environmental History and Romantic Aesthetics," in *Edgar Allan Poe: Beyond Gothicism* (Newark, NJ: University of Delaware Press, 2011), 1–16 and 89–102.

7. Despite the relative anachronism of the term, which was not commonly used by English speakers during Poe's lifetime, Polonsky notes that "the word 'aesthetic' and its cognates have clung to the name of Edgar Allan Poe" ("Poe's Aesthetic Theory," 42).

8. *Ladies' Magazine and Literary Gazette* (January 1830). For a discussion of how Poe's pedantry was sometimes taken as evidence by his contemporaries that he lacked a spontaneous "genius"; see Scott Peebles, *The Afterlife of Edgar Allan Poe* (Rochester, NY: Camden House, 2007), 15. For a historicized account of genius in late nineteenth-century America, see Gustavus Stadler, *Troubling Minds: The Cultural Politics of Genius in the United States, 1840–1890* (Minneapolis: University of Minnesota Press, 2006). For an analysis of the concept of genius in the early national period, see Cahill, *Liberty of the Imagination*.

9. Toni Morrison, *Playing in the Dark: Whiteness and the Literary Imagination* (New York: Vintage, 1993), 32. Morrison was pushing back against a long held consensus, that, in the words of T. S. Eliot, "there can be few authors of such eminence who have drawn so little from their own roots, who have been so isolated from their surroundings" ("From Poe to Valéry," *Hudson Review* 2 [1949]: 329). William Carlos Williams early on took exception to this view, arguing in 1925 that Poe was "intimately shaped by his locality and time." *In the American Grain* (repr., New York: New Directions, 1956), 216.

10. For an overview of the wealth of historical and contextual studies of Poe, see James M. Hutchinson's introduction to Philippon, *Beyond Gothicism*, x.

11. T. S. Eliot, qtd. in Polonsky, "Poe's Aesthetic Theory," 45.

12. Colin Dayan, *Fables of Mind: An Inquiry into Poe's Fiction* (New York: Oxford University Press, 1987), 14, 83.

13. Although excluded from the ecocritical canon that emerged in the 1990s, Poe's work is clearly engaged with what Matthew Taylor has termed "the complex nature-culture imbrications currently at issue in much ecocriticism and science studies

discourse." See "The Nature of Fear: Edgar Allan Poe and Posthuman Ecology," *American Literature* 84 (2012): 363.

14. Colin Dayan, *Fables of Mind*, 91.

15. Polonsky, "Poe's Aesthetic Theory," 43.

16. Along similar lines, Paul de Man noted three decades ago that the "continuity between depth and surface" is "the most problematic issue with which the theory of poetry will have to deal." "Form and Intent in American New Criticism," in *Blindness and Insight: Essays in the Rhetoric of Contemporary Criticism* (Minneapolis: University of Minnesota Press, 1983), 23.

17. Simon Gikandi, "Race and the Idea of the Aesthetic," *Michigan Quarterly Review* 40 (2001): 325.

18. Saidiya V. Hartman, *In the Break: The Aesthetics of the Black Radical Tradition* (Minneapolis: University of Minnesota Press, 2003), 68; *Scenes of Subjection: Terror, Slavery and Self-Making in Nineteenth Century America* (New York: Oxford University Press, 1997), 36. See also Wilson, *Specters of Democracy*.

19. See John Gerald Kennedy and Liliane Weissberg, eds., *Romancing the Shadow: Poe and Race* (New York: Oxford University Press, 2001).

20. Colin Dayan, *Fables of Mind*, 14, 9. See also Colleen Glenney Boggs, who reads Poe in relation to Latour's "two senses" of representation (of things and of citizens) in *Animalia Americana: Animal Representations and Biopolitical Subjectivity* (New York: Columbia University Press, 2013), 110.

21. Maurice Lee offers an incisive analysis of the interrelation of chattel bondage and philosophical movements in the antebellum period in *Slavery, Philosophy and American Literature* (New York: Cambridge University Press, 2005). Building on Lee's insights, I aim to connect Poe to the philosophical discourse of the aesthetic in relation to the political history of race and enslavement.

22. My citations are drawn from the June 1844 version printed in *Graham's*.

23. Like "Dream-Land," "Dreams" suggests that the happiness of the speaker has not been lost but rather displaced, while "Visits of the Dead" tells of a lonely soul encountering the spirits of the departed.

24. This review appeared in the *Yankee and Boston Literary Gazette*, September 1829.

25. Joan Dayan, *Fables of Mind*, 8.

26. J. O. Bailey explores this invocation of this northern realm in relation to contemporary polar explorations in "The Geography of Poe's 'Dream-Land' and 'Ulalume,'" *Studies in Philology* 45 (1948): 512–23.

27. Edgar Allan Poe, *Poetry and Tales*, ed. Patrick F. Quinn (New York: Library of America, 1984), 281.

28. G. R. Thompson, ed., *Essays and Reviews* (New York: Library of America, 1984), 1331.

29. Poe, *Poetry and Tales*, 457.

30. cf. Joan Dayan, *Fables of Mind*, 93, 104.

31. Benjamin F. Fisher, "Poe and the Gothic Tradition," in Polonsky, "Poe's Aesthetic Theory," 72.

32. Hutchinson, introduction to Philippon, *Beyond Gothicism*, x–xi.

33. See Nancy Armstrong and Leonard Tennenhouse, "The Problem of Population and the Form of the American Novel," *American Literary History* 20 (2008): 667–85;

Leonard Tennenhouse, *The Importance of Being English: American Literature and the British Diaspora, 1750–1850* (Princeton, NJ: Princeton University Press, 2007); and Siân Silvyn Roberts, *Gothic Subjects: The Transformation of Individualism in American Fiction* (Philadelphia: University of Pennsylvania Press, 2014).

34. Leslie Fiedler, *Love and Death in the American Novel* (New York: Anchor, 1992), 142.

35. Charles Brockden Brown, "To The Public," in *Edgar Huntley* (New York: Penguin, 1988), 3.

36. Roberts, *Gothic Subjects*, 6.

37. Roberts, *Gothic Subjects*, 7.

38. Roberts, *Gothic Subjects*, 19.

39. Roberts, *Gothic Subjects*, 19.

40. Hutchinson, introduction to Philippon, *Beyond Gothicism*, xi.

41. Daniel O. Sayers, "Diasporan Exiles in the Great Dismal Swamp, 1630–1860," *Transforming Anthropology* 14, no. 1 (2006): 10–20. For a description of how Poe and his contemporaries turned to the swamp for its "dark gothic qualities," see Rebecca McIntyre, "Promoting the Gothic South," *Southern Cultures* 11, no. 2 (Summer 2005): 40. See also David Miller, *Dark Eden: The Swamp in Nineteenth-Century American Culture* (New York: Cambridge University Press, 1989).

42. See Sylviane A. Diouf, *Slavery's Exiles: The Story of the American Maroons* (New York: New York University Press, 2014).

43. Joan Dayan, *Fables of Mind*, 15, 134.

44. Miller, *Dark Eden*, 6.

45. Monique Allewaert, *Ariel's Ecology: Plantations, Personhood and Colonialism in the American Tropics* (Minneapolis: University of Minnesota Press, 2013) 18.

46. Elise Lemire, "'The Murders in the Rue Morgue': Amalgamation Discourses and the Race Riots of 1838 in Poe's Philadelphia," in Kennedy and Weissberg, *Romancing the Shadow*, 194.

47. As Diouf has remarked, "Such was the reputation for isolation of the Great Dismal Swamp that two years after Emancipation, one could hypothesize that some of them still did not know they were legally free" (*Slavery's Exiles*, 209). See also Lawrence Buell, "Wetland Aesthetics," *Environmental History* 10 (2005): 670–71; and William Howarth, "Imagined Territory: The Writing of Wetlands," *New Literary History* 30 (1999): 509–39.

48. The swamp originally covered more than 1.3 million acres. See Daniel O. Sayers, "Landscapes of Alienation: An Archeological Report of Excursions in the Great Dismal Swamp," *Transforming Anthropology* 15 (2007): 150.

49. Daphne Brooks, *Bodies in Dissent: Spectacular Performances of Race and Freedom, 1850–1910* (Durham, NC: Duke University Press, 2006), 104–5.

50. Walters, "Poe's 'Philosophy of Furniture,'" 7.

51. As Miller writes, "That the Dismal Swamp fascinated Poe is little to be doubted" (*Dark Eden*, 41). See also Robert Morrison, "Poe's 'The Lake: To—,'" *Explicator* 7 (December 1948): 36–37; and Burton R. Pollin, "Edgar Allan Poe and John G. Chapman: Their Treatment of the Dismal Swamp and the Wissahickon," *Studies in the American Renaissance* (1983): 245–74.

52. Poe, *Poetry and Tales*, 387. Walters has suggested that this painting "was such a popular image that it became a conversational idiom" ("Poe's 'Philosophy of Furniture,'" 7).

53. Thomas Moore, "A Ballad: The Lake of the Dismal Swamp," in *The Poetical Works of Thomas Moore, Collected by Himself*, vol. 2 (London: Longman, Orme, Brown, Green, and Longmans, 1840–41), 223–25.

54. Poe, *Essays and Reviews*, 85.

55. Poe, *Essays and Reviews*, 19.

56. Poe, *Essays and Reviews*, 25. For a provocative reading of "The Raven" that connects Poe's aesthetics to race, see Betsy Erkkilä's work on the raven as an African American voice in "The Poetics of Whiteness: Poe and the Racial Imaginary," in Kennedy and Weissberg, *Romancing the Shadow*, 41–74.

57. For an exploration of how literary representations of grief challenge normative temporal and historical frameworks, see Dana Luciano, *Arranging Grief: Sacred Time and the Body in Nineteenth-Century America* (New York: New York University Press, 2008).

58. P. Sayers, Brendon Burke, and Aaron M. Henry, "The Political Economy of Exile in the Great Dismal Swamp," *International Journal of Historical Archeology* 11, no. 1 (2007): 72.

59. Herbert Aptheker, "Maroons Within the Present Limits of the United States," reprinted in *Maroon Societies, Rebel Slave Communities in the Americas*, ed. Richard Price (Baltimore: Johns Hopkins University Press, 1996), 152.

60. Sayers, Burke, and Henry, "The Political Economy of Exile," 72.

61. Poe, *Essays and Reviews*, 763.

62. Henry Wadsworth Longfellow, *Complete Poetical Works*, www.gutenberg.org/files/1365/1365-h/1365-h.htm.

63. I am indebted to Joan Dayan's excellent discussion of Poe in relation to Longfellow ("Amorous Bondage," 194).

64. Quoted in David Allmendinger, *Nat Turner and the Rising in Southampton County* (Baltimore: Johns Hopkins University Press, 2014), 9.

65. Tommy Lee Bogger, "Maroons and Laborers in the Great Dismal Swamp," in *Readings in Black and White: Lower Tidewater Virginia*, ed. Jane H. Kobelski (Portsmouth, VA: Portsmouth Public Library, 1982), 2.

66. Quoted in Sayers, Burke, and Henry, "The Political Economy of Exile," 74.

67. Sayers, Burke, and Henry, "The Political Economy of Exile," 73.

68. Barnor Hesse, "Escaping Liberty: Western Hegemony, Black Fugitivity," *Political Theory* 42 (2014): 289. For a related discussion of the inherently "fugitive" nature of justice in relation to the reparations debate, see Saidiya Hartman and Stephen Best, "Fugitive Justice," *Reparations* 92 (2005): 1–15.

69. Hesse, "Escaping Liberty," 37.

70. Immanuel Kant, *Critique of Judgment*, ed. and trans. Paul Guyer (New York: Cambridge University Press, 2000), 186–87.

71. Glen A. Omans, "'Intellect, Taste, and the Moral Sense': Poe's Debt to Immanuel Kant," *Studies in the American Renaissance* (1980): 123–67.

72. Geoffrey Hartman, "Toward Literary History," *Daedalus* 99 (1970): 365.

73. Poe, *Essays and Reviews*, 314.

74. Kenneth Silverman, *Edgar A. Poe: Mournful and Never-Ending Remembrance* (New York: Harper Collins, 1992), 61–62.

75. Polonsky, "Poe's Aesthetic Theory," 44.

76. Lee, *Slavery, Philosophy and American Literature*, 49.

77. Poe, *Essays and Reviews*, 13.

78. Jonathan Elmer, *Reading at the Social Limit: Affect, Mass Culture and Edgar Allan Poe* (Stanford, CA: Stanford University Press, 1995), 34.

79. Poe, *Essays and Reviews*, 319.

80. For a discussion of Poe's attitude toward originality in relation to the widespread culture of reprinting in his era, see Meredith McGill, *American Literature and the Culture of Reprinting* (Philadelphia: University of Pennsylvania Press, 2003).

81. Johannes Fabian, *Time and the Other: How Anthropology Makes Its Object* (New York: Columbia University Press, 1983), 144. For a discussion of the "often ignored disaggregating potential of this period's literature and its peculiar account of time," see Lloyd Pratt, *Archives of American Time: Literature and Modernity in the Nineteenth Century* (Philadelphia: University of Pennsylvania Press, 2009), 2–3. For a related discussion of the historical potential of nonnormative modes of inhabiting time, see Elizabeth Freeman, *Time Binds: Queer Temporalities, Queer Histories* (Durham, NC: Duke University Press, 2010).

82. Daylanne English, *Each Hour Redeem: Time and Justice in African American Literature* (Minneapolis: University of Minnesota Press, 2013), 24. For a discussion of the distributed agencies that contributed to the eventual, nonsynchronous emancipation of enslaved Americans beyond "a dramatic moment of jubilee," see Christopher Hager, *Word by Word: Emancipation and the Act of Writing* (Cambridge, MA: Harvard University Press, 2013), 24.

83. John Ernest usefully maps the nonchronological coordinates of African American literary history in "Choreographing Chaos: African American Literature in Time and Space," *Chaotic Justice: Rethinking African American Literary History* (Durham: University of North Carolina Press, 2009).

84. The NRSV translates the relevant lines from Revelation 9–11 as follows: "I saw ... those who had been slain because of the word of God ... given a white robe, and ... told to wait a little longer, until the full number of their fellow servants, their brothers and sisters, were killed just as they had been."

85. Poe, *Essays and Reviews*, 582.

86. See especially Susan Buck-Morss, *Haiti, Hegel, and Universal History* (Pittsburgh, PA: University of Pittsburgh Press, 2009); Simon Gikandi, *Slavery and the Culture of Taste* (Princeton, NJ: Princeton University Press, 2011); and Jennifer Greeson, "The Prehistory of Possessive Individualism," *PMLA* 127 (2012): 918–24.

87. Bruno Latour, "How to Talk about the Body? The Normative Dimension of Science Studies," *Body & Society* 10 (2004): 207.

88. Monique Allewaert, "Swamp Sublime: Ecologies of Resistance in the Plantation Zone," *PMLA* 123 (2008): 354.

89. For an expansive and lucid account of the limitations and possibilities of new historicism, see Alan Liu, *Local Transcendence: Essays on Postmodern Historicism and the Database* (Chicago: University of Chicago Press, 2008).

90. For an analysis of how Poe's critique of Enlightenment tenets overwhelms his proslavery position, see Betsy Erkkilä, "Perverting the American Renaissance: Poe, Democracy, Critical Theory," in *Poe and the Remapping of Antebellum Print Culture*, ed. J. Gerald Kennedy and Jerome McGann (Baton Rouge: Louisiana State University Press, 2012); and Erin E. Forbes, "From Prison Cell to Slave Ship: Social Death in 'The Premature Burial,'" *Poe Studies* 46 (2013): 46–47.

91. Lee, *Slavery, Philosophy and Literature*, 45.

92. Wilson has made a similar argument about the need to return the aesthetic to its political and historical foundations, in order to "offer a reading of a subversive black aesthetic" concerned with "the affective possibilities of aesthetics as a model and a means through which collectivities can fulfill the unfinished work of democracy" (*Specters of Democracy*, 8).

93. Angus Fletcher, *A New Theory for American Poetry: Democracy, the Environment, and the Future of Imagination* (Cambridge, MA: Harvard University Press, 2006), 227.

94. Fletcher, *A New Theory*, 227.

95. Edgar Allan Poe, *The Narrative of Arthur Gordon Pym of Nantucket*, ed. Richard Kopley (New York: Penguin, 1999), 220.

96. Leland S. Person, "Poe's Philosophy of Amalgamation: Reading Racism in the Tales," in Kennedy and Weissberg, *Romancing the Shadow*, 205.

Conclusion • New Forms of Crime

1. Karla F. C. Holloway, *Legal Fictions: Constituting Race, Composing Literature* (Durham, NC: Duke University Press, 2014), 50.

2. Lisa Marie Cacho, *Social Death: Racialized Rightlessness and the Criminalization of the Unprotected* (New York: New York University Press, 2012).

3. Frederick L. Hoffman, *Race Traits and Tendencies of the American Negro* (New York: Macmillan, 1896), 225.

4. Abraham Johnstone, *The Address of Abraham Johnstone, a Black Man, Who Was Hanged at Woodbury, in the County of Gloucester, and State of New Jersey, On Saturday the the [sic] 8th Day of July Last: To the People of Colour. To Which Is Added His Dying Confession or Declaration. Also, a Copy of a Letter to His Wife, Written the Day Previous to His Execution* (Philadelphia: printed for the purchasers, 1791), last modified December 12, 2000, https://docsouth.unc.edu/neh/johnstone/johnstone.html, 7.

5. Brian Baaki, "White Crime and the Early African American Press: Elements of Reporting and Reporting in New York's *Freedom's Journal*," *American Periodicals* 29, no. 2 (2019): 123–25.

6. Hoffman, *Race Traits*, 217.

7. Arthur MacDonald, *Criminology* (London: Funk & Wagnalls, 1893), 103.

8. MacDonald, *Criminology*, 102, 104.

9. MacDonald, *Criminology*, 103.

10. Cesare Lombroso, *Criminal Man*, trans. Mary Gibson and Nicole Hahn Rafter (Durham, NC: Duke University Press, 2006), 284–5.

11. W. A. Coffey, *Inside Out* (New York: New York State Prison, 1823), 76.

12. Coffey, *Inside Out*, 20–21, my emphasis.

13. Vincent Brown, "Social Death and Political Life in the Study of Slavery," *American Historical Review* 114 (2009): 1248.

14. Frantz Fanon, *Black Skin, White Masks*, trans. Charles Lam Markmann (New York: Grove Press, 1967), 10.

15. Christina Sharpe, *In the Wake: On Blackness and Being* (Durham, NC: Duke University Press, 2016), 93.

16. Andrew S. Curran, *The Anatomy of Blackness: Science & Slavery in the Age of Enlightenment* (Baltimore: Johns Hopkins University Press, 2011), 223–24.

17. Fanon, *The Wretched of the Earth*, 250.

18. Gayatri Chakravorty Spivak, "Can the Subaltern Speak?," in *Colonial Discourse / Post-Colonial Theory: A Reader*, ed. Patrick Williams and Laura Chrisman (New York: Columbia University Press, 1994), 66–111.

19. Spivak, "Can the Subaltern Speak?," 71, 70; c.f. Walter Johnson, "Agency: A Ghost Story," in *Slavery's Ghost: The Problem of Freedom in the Age of Emancipation* (Baltimore: Johns Hopkins University Press, 2011); Rita Felski, *The Limits of Critique* (Chicago: University of Chicago Press, 2015); Stephen Best, "On Failing to Make the Past Present," *Modern Language Quarterly* 73, no. 3 (2012), 453–74; Stephen Best and Sharon Marcus, "Surface Reading," *Representations* 108 (2009), 1–21.

20. Denise Ferreira da Silva, "1 (life) ÷ 0 (blackness) = $\infty - \infty$ or ∞ / ∞: On Matter beyond the Equation of Value," *e-flux Journal* 79 (2017), www.e-flux.com/journal/79/94686/1-life-0-blackness-or-on-matter-beyond-the-equation-of-value/; and Joseph Drexler-Dreis, "Nat Turner's Orientation beyond the Doctrine of Man," in *Beyond the Doctrine of Man: Decolonial Visions of the Human* (New York: Fordham University Press, 2019).

INDEX

Illustrations are indicated by page numbers in *italics*. Fictional characters are alphabetized by first name.

abolitionism, 48, 95, 120
Address of Abraham Johnstone, The . . . (Johnstone), 57
"Address to the African Masonic Hall" (Stewart), 2
aesthetics, 4, 25; Blackness and, 17; crime and, 6, 25; criminal genius and, 20; De Quincey and, 154; fugitive, 23, 165–87; gallows literature and, 86; genius and, 127; in Kant, 83–84; Poe and, 166–68; Turner and, 132, 148, 157, 162–63; Walker and, 102
African Methodist Episcopal Church, 38
Agamben, Giorgio, 9, 208n41, 209n72
agency: Black history and, 98; collective, 39; convicts and, 7–8, 69; corpses and, 45–46; creative genius and, 4; criminal genius and, 40; fugitives and, 18, 22; humanity and, 215n82; law and, 28; liberalism and, 16–18, 20–21, 23, 25, 31–32, 40, 44, 60–63, 69–70, 93; neurodivergence and, 55; outlaws and, 11; posthuman extensions of, 19; radical, 156–57; of Turner, 147–49; voluntarism and, 59; yellow fever and, 39
Alexander, Michelle, 3
Allen, Elisha, 55, 79, 218n33
Allen, Richard, 23, 28, 31–37, *35*, 37–39, 52
Allewaert, Monique, 46, 173, 185, 205n22
Allmendinger, David F., 134, 138, 217n30, 219n67, 219n77
Altschuler, Sari, 51
"American school," 10

animacies, 40
"Annabel Lee" (Poe), 177
anti-Blackness, 11
Appeal to the Coloured Citizens of the World (Walker), 24, 95–130, *101*, 106, 212n25
Aptheker, Herbert, 102–3, 133, 150, 177–78, 218n55
Arabian jurisprudence, 2–3, 29
archvillain, 134–35
Ariès, Phillipe, 46
Armstrong, Nancy, 171
Arthur Mervyn (Brown), 50–52, 204n57
Asukile, Thabiti, 212n13
Authentic and Impartial Narrative of the Tragical Scene (Warner), 140–41, *141*, 141–43, 151, 174

Baaki, Brian, 189
Babo, 5, 154
Bailey, J. O., 223n26
Bailyn, Bernard, 205n19
Baker, Kyle, 148, 150, 159
"Ballad, A: The Lake of the Dismal Swamp" (Moore), 174–76
Bancroft, Aaron, 62–63, *65*, 65–69, 75–76, 192, 207n30
Bancroft, George, 67
Banneker, Benjamin, 14, 16
Baptist, Edward, 157
Barbous, James, 213n36
Bartelby, the Scrivener (Melville), 42–43
Barthes, Roland, 61

Batra, Ajay Kumar, 60, 76
Baumgarten, Alexander, 12
beauty, 12–13, 123
Beloved (Morrison), 150
Benito Cereno (Melville), 154
Bennett, Herman L., 2
Bennett, Jane, 18
"Berenice" (Poe), 173
Bernasconi, Robert, 12
Best, Stephen, 119
Bird, Robert Montgomery, 96
Birth of a Nation, The (2016 film), 17, 147–48
"Black avenger" trope, 16–17
Black criminality, 7; disease and, 31; individualism and, 28; liberalism and, 28; as perpetual idea, 30–31; racialization and, 3–4; in Stewart, 2; Turner and, 149; in Walker, 98–99; yellow fever and, 28
Black Man, The, His Antecedents, His Genius, and His Achievements (Brown), 13–14
Black nationalism, 97, 127
Blackness, 4; as absence, 49; aesthetics and, 17, 25; anti-Blackness, 11; criminality and, 28; in Curran, 194–95; darkness and, 125; degendered, 15–16; fugitivity and, 22; genius and, 17; materiality and, 195; in Rush, 46; in Sharpe, 97
Black people: incarceration of, 38–39; legal status of, 29–30; legislation against, 99, 111; Poe and, 166; Walker's *Appeal* and, 96
Black Skin, White Masks (Fanon), 8
Black Thunder (Bontemps), 145
bloodletting, 41, 48
Blumenbach, Johann Friedrich, 122–23
Boerhaave, Hermann, 40
Bontemps, Arna, 145–47
Bosco, Ronald A., 207n30
Brooks, Daphne, 174
Brooks, Joanna, 200n69
Brophy, Alfred L., 138
Brown, Charles Brockden, 4, 23, 50–52, 160, 171–72, 204n57
Brown, John, 1–2, 146
Brown, Vincent, 193–94
Brown, William Wells, 5, 13–14, 16, 148
Buffon, Comte de, 72n215, 116, 122
Burgett, Bruce, 209n70
Burke, Edmund, 12

Cacho, Lisa, 7–8, 189
Cahill, Edward, 84, 209n73
Calvinism, 63
capitalism, 43, 111, 114, 157
Carey, Mathew, 7, 28, 32, 33, 36–39, 48–49, 52
"Cask of Amontillado, The" (Poe), 173
Césaire, Aimé, 19, 112
Chapman, John Gadsby, 174, 176
Chen, Mel, 40
Christianity, 103–4, 162, 217n20
citizenship, 17, 20, 30, 32–34, 59
civilization, 11
Civil War, 3, 11
Clarke, John Henrick, 145
Clotel, 5
Cobbett, William, 48–49
Coffey, W. A., 192–93
Cohen, Daniel A., 86, 205nn9–10, 207n32, 209n65
Cohen, Matt, 205n24
Coleridge, Samuel Taylor, 182, 184
collectivism, 95, 121–22, 199n48
collectivities, 6
"Colloquy of Monos and Una, The" (Poe), 170–71
colonialism, 2, 10, 32, 97, 112, 115, 126, 172
colonization, 125
commodification, 42, 123
commodity, 157
Confessions of an Opium Eater (De Quincey), 170
Confessions of Nat Turner. . . . (Gray), 21, 134, 136–38, 137, 145–46
"Conqueror Worm, The" (Poe), 171
convict, 7–8, 18, 59–62, 70, 75, 83, 93
Coole, Diana, 205n23
Cornish, Samuel, 190
corpses, 28, 31–32, 40, 43, 45–47, 50, 88, 140, 193
COVID-19 pandemic, 212n14
Crania Americana (Morton), 10
creative genius, 4, 12, 14, 84, 154, 173, 189
Crèvecoeur, J. Hector St. John de, 11, 32
crime: aesthetics and, 6, 25; definitions of, 11; in Halttunen, 8; in Poe, 155–56; slavery and, 6, 11, 100; as subject in fiction, 6
criminal genius, 4–6; agency and, 40; as liminal state, 190; personhood and, 10–11;

social death and, 195–96; Southampton Insurgency and, 134–35; Tuner and, 162–63; as voluntarist, 18–19; in Walker, 95. *See also* genius
criminality. *See* Black criminality; racialized criminality
criminology, 9–10, 190–92
Critique of Judgment (Kant), 160, 181–82
Cubitt, William, 3
Curran, Andrew S., 116–17, 119, 194–95

Daut, Marlene, 117
Davis, Rebecca Harding, 5
Dayan, Colin, 166–67, 178, 205n16
Dayan, Joan, 111, 221n3
"Day in a Railway Car, A" (Poe), 174
dehumanization, 8–9, 18, 60–61, 67, 119–21, 208n41
DeLombard, Jeannine, 38, 55, 75, 119, 121, 156, 201n69
de Man, Paul, 209n70, 223n16
de Pauw, Abbé, 116
depravity, 60
De Quincey, Thomas, 12, 15, 23, 154–55, 164, 170
Dery, Mark, 127–28
Descartes, René, 100, 109–13, 115, 124, 127–28, 214n51
dignity, 67–68, 119, 121
Dillon, Elizabeth Maddock, 68
Dinius, Marcy, 102, 211n8
Diouf, Sylviane A., 224n47
disavowal, 75–76
disease, 40–43
disgust, 75, 208n51
divinity, genius as, 14
"Domain of Arnheim, The" (Poe), 171
Douglass, Frederick, 14, 21, 163–64, 188
"Dream, A" (Poe), 168
"Dream-Land" (Poe), 25, 165–71, 173–77, 180–87, 221n3
"Dreams" (Poe), 168
Dred (Stowe), 148, 179
Dred: A Tale of the Dismal Swamp (Stowe), 5
Dred Scott case, 30
Drewry, William S., 149–50
Drexler, Michael, 25
Drexler-Dreis, Joseph, 147, 158, 217n20

Du Bois, W. E. B., 28, 96, 102
Dunbar, Erica Armstrong, 201n1
DuVernay, Ava, 3

Eastern State Penitentiary, 38–39, 220n81
Eaton, Clement, 211n3
Eliot, T. S., 166, 222n9
Ellis, Cristin, 19
Ellis, Havelock, 9–10
Elmer, Jonathan, 183
embodiment, 83
Emerson, Ralph Waldo, 12, 199n48
English, Daylanne K., 183
Enlightenment, 5–9, 11, 13, 22–26, 40, 58, 77–78, 102–4, 110–15, 125–30, 160, 183, 195, 199n48, 277n9
epidermalization, 31
Essay on Man (Pope), 84
eugenics, 12, 15–16, 18, 22, 25, 122–23
Evers, Medgar, 96
evil, 5, 8, 108, 110, 113, 130, 147
exceptionalism, 1
execution sermons, 63–67, 66, 67–69, 75, 207n30

"Fairyland" (Poe), 168–69
"Fall of the House of Usher, The" (Poe), 173
Fanon, Frantz, 8, 19, 31, 193, 195
Felski, Rita, 210n96
Fiedler, Leslie, 171
Finseth, Ian, 102, 107, 212n13
Fisher, Benjamin F., 171
formalism, 17, 149, 165–67, 200n55
Forten, Charlotte L., 14
Foucault, Michel, 207n37
Fourteenth Amendment, 30
Frankenstein (Shelley), 160
Franklin, Benjamin, 59, 163, 205n14
Franklin, H. Bruce, 3
Franks, Bobby, 5
Frazier, E. Franklin, 129
Frederickson, George M., 215n79
Free African Society, 34, 37
Freedom's Journal, 100, 189–90
French Revolution, 41, 80, 217n15
Frost, Samuel, 20, 23–24, 52, 55–63, 67–75, 71–74, 78–94, 205n9, 208n41, 208n47, 209n65

fugitive, 18
fugitive aesthetics, 23, 165–87
fugitivity, 11

gallows print, 56–57, 62, 67–70, 71–74, 76–86, 88–91
Galton, Francis, 12
Gardner, Eric, 136
Garner, Margaret, 150
Garnet, Henry Highland, 95–96, 211n3
Garrison, William Lloyd, 143–44, 146, 152–53, 156
Garza, Alicia, 98, 212n18
gender: collective imaginary and, 147; collectivist understanding of, 199n48; degendered Blackness, 15–16; hierarchies, 21, 25; as permanent, 199n48; racialization and, 19
genius: Black, 14, 16, 104, 124; Blackness and, 17; in Brown, 13–14; creative, 4, 12, 14, 25, 84, 154, 173, 189; in De Quincey, 15; as divinity, 14; as elite, 12; as feminine, 15–16; as impossible aspiration, 13; in Jefferson, 124; in Kant, 22, 181–82; as masculine, 12; masculinity and, 12–15; racialization of, 15; racialized agency of, 11; softness of, 14; talent versus, 13–15; as transgressive, 20; as white, 12; in Young, 14–15. *See also* criminal genius
Genius of Universal Emancipation (Lundy), 143, 162
Genovese, Eugene D., 145–47, 217n15
Gikandi, Simon, 12, 15, 167, 199nn36–37
Gikandt, Simon, 12–13
Gilmore, Paul, 165
Gilmore, Ruth Wilson, 97, 189, 195
Gordon, Lewis R., 104, 109, 115
Gothic fiction, 8, 171–72, 185, 195, 220n81
Gray, Thomas R., 22, 133, 136–37, 146, 148, 218n33
Gray, William, 37
Great Dismal Swamp maroons, 20, 23, 25, 95, 151, 172–81, 173, 175–76, 178
"great man," 5
Great Seal of the United States, 15
Greenberg, Kenneth S., 220n95

Haiti, 27–28, 41–44, 48, 80, 104, 118–19, 131, 217n15
Halttunen, Karen, 8, 56, 207n30

Hanno, Joseph, 64, 68
Hartley, David, 40
Hartman, Geoffrey, 182
Hartman, Saidiya, 26, 131, 136, 167, 201nn5–6
Hartnett, Stephen J., 54–55, 75
"Haunted Palace, The" (Poe), 171
Hawthorne, Nathaniel, 4, 183–84
Hayes, Kevin J., 221n1
Hereditary Genius (Galton), 12
heroic treatment, 41
Herskovits, Melville, 128–29
Hesse, Barnor, 19, 31, 181
Hester Prynne, 4
Higginson, Thomas Wentworth, 144, 146
Hinks, Peter P., 102, 211n1
Hirsch, Nathaniel D. Mitron, 12
Hoffman, Frederick L., 189–90
Holloway, Karla F. C., 188
Hooker, Juliet, 19, 31
Hooton, David, 95
"How to Write a Blackwood Article" (Poe), 170
Hugh Wolfe, 5
humanism, 37–38, 62–63, 93–94; Descartes and, 115; liberalism and, 20, 87, 93; objecthood and, 157; Walker and, 115, 122, 129–30
humanity, 8–9, 40, 60–61, 104; agency and, 215n82; dignity and, 119–20; in Walker, 113–16
Hume, David, 12, 105
Hunter, Tera, 212n14
Hurricane Katrina, 7
Hutchinson, James M., 171–72

imperialism, 12, 183
incarceration, 3–4, 8, 20, 38–39, 86, 189, 193
Incidents in the Life of a Slave Girl (Jacobs), 139, 179
individualism, 12, 18, 21–22, 24, 28, 62, 75, 163, 188–89
intelligence, 5, 12, 62, 140, 155, 157–58, 160–62, 188–89
In the Break (Moten), 18, 67
Iton, Richard, 31

Jackson, Zakiyyah Iman, 19
Jacobs, Harriet, 139, 179
James, George Payne Rainsford, 148

Jefferson, Thomas, 15–16, 99–100, 104, 114–19, 121–27, 190
Jim Crow, 3, 8, 135, 189
Johnson, Walter, 21, 120
Johnstone, Abraham, 23–24, 54–64, 57, 68–70, 75–78, 84–86, 90–94
Jones, Absalom, 23, 28, 30–34, 35, 36–39, 52
Jones, Martha S., 30
jurisprudence, 2–3

Kann, Mark E., 210n75
Kant, Immanuel, 12, 22, 83–84, 160, 181–82, 184
Kazanjian, David, 26
Keith, Leonard, 200n55
Kendi, Ibram X., 16
Kennedy, J. Gerald, 185
kindness, 14
King, Martin Luther, Jr., 96
Kings, Book of, 67

labor, 17
LaFleur, Greta, 215n73
"Lake, The" (Poe), 168, 174, 177
Lake of the Dismal Swamp, The (Chapman), 174, 176
Larkin, Edward, 21–22
Lauro, Sarah J., 44
Leavell, Lori, 96
Lee, Maurice, 223n21
Leopold, Nathan, 5–6
Letters from an American Farmer (Crèvecoeur), 11
Levine, Robert, 27
liberalism, 205n19; agency and, 16, 18, 21, 23, 25, 31–32, 40, 44, 69–70, 93; belonging and, 84; citizenship and, 17, 20, 34; convicts and, 69; evil and, 8; exclusion and, 59–60, 85, 88; execution sermons and, 68; historiography and, 18; humanism and, 20, 37–38, 60, 62–63, 87, 93; identity and, 17; individualism and, 21–22, 24, 28, 75; racial, 61; republicanism and, 163; taste and, 13; voluntarism and, 53
Liberator, 143–44, 153, 220n98
liminality, 11, 190
Linnaeus, Carl, 9, 114–15, 215n79
literacy, 99

Liu, Alan, 200n67
Locke, John, 10, 17, 160
Loeb, Richard, 5–6
Lombroso, Cesare, 9–10, 190–91
Longfellow, Henry Wadsworth, 178–79
Louverture, Toussaint, 14, 48, 118, 131, 144
Lundy, Benjamin, 143, 162

MacDonald, Arthur, 25, 190
Malcolm X, 96, 135
Mallarmé, Stéphane, 165
"Man of the Crowd, The" (Poe), 155–56, 163
masculinity, 9, 26, 61, 188; "Black avenger" trope and, 16–17; genius and, 12–15, 22; Turner and, 135, 147, 217n20
Massachusetts General Coloured Association, 100, 129
materialism, 18–19, 40, 62, 83, 181
Mather, Cotton, 9, 64–65
Mather, Increase, 65
McAlister, Elizabeth, 43
McHenry, Elizabeth, 99–100, 102, 129
McMillan, Uri, 164
McTeigue, James, 166
Medical Inquiries and Observations upon the Diseases of the Mind (Rush), 42–43
Melville, Herman, 5, 42–43, 154
Memoirs of Carwin, the Biloquist (Brown), 160
Mendoza, Breny, 199n38
Miller, David, 173, 224n51
Miller, Jacquelyn C., 41
Mills, Charles, 12, 60
Milton, John, 154
Minnick, Wayne C., 207n30
Missouri freedom suits, 29, 198n30
Moore, Thomas, 174–76
Morrison, Toni, 150, 157, 166, 222n9
Morton, Samuel George, 10
Moten, Fred, 18, 167
Mountain, Joseph, 64
Muhammad, Khalil Gibran, 28
murder, 8, 49, 51, 53–56, 61–67, 76, 81, 83, 97, 103, 108, 132, 150
"Murder Considered as One of the Fine Arts" (De Quincey), 15, 23, 154
music, 124
Myth of the Negro Past, The (Herskovits), 129

Naimou, Angela, 3
Napoleon, 5
Narrative of Arthur Gordon Pym, The (Poe), 186, *186*
Narrative of the Life of Frederick Douglass, an American Slave (Douglass), 164, 188
nationalism, 39, 127
Nat Turner (Baker), 148, 150, 159
Neal, John, 168–69
Negro in the American Rebellion, The (Brown), 148
neuro-criminology, 31
neurodevelopmental disability, 58
neurodivergence, 24, 55, 58–59, 95
New Historicism, 25, 132, 165–68, 184–85, 200n67
New Jim Crow, The (Alexander and DuVernay), 3
new materialism, 18–19, 62, 93, 206n22
Newton, Isaac, 160
Notes on the State of Virginia (Jefferson), 115–17

objecthood, 157
objectification, 18, 21, 69, 122–23, 147, 157
Observations on Man, his Frame, his Duty, and his Expectations (Hartley), 40
Ocuish, Hannah, 64
Old Dominion, The (James), 148
Oleson, James C., 5–6
Olmstead, Frederick Law, 140
Omans, Glen A., 182
"On Imagination" (Wheatley), 196
Ormond (Brown), 50
Othello (Shakespeare), 154
outlaw, 95, 151, 153, 178; agency and, 11, 18, 21; Black politics and, 19, 31, 194; humanism and, 98–100, 114, 128; as legal status, 158

Paradise Lost (Milton), 154
Parker, Nate, 17, 147–48
Parramore, Thomas C., 148
Parrington, Vernon L., 205n19
Patterson, Orlando, 193–94
Pechméja, Jean de, 117–18
Pelletier, Kevin, 126
penal reform, 3, 38–39, 46, 192
penitentiary, 3, 10, 46, 53, 86, 191, 193, 210n75
Pennsylvania, 41, 45, 201n11
person, 10

personhood, 8, 10–11, 40, 84, 164, 201n69
Philip, M. NourbeSe, 26
"Philosophy of Composition, The" (Poe), 167, 177
"Philosophy of Furniture, The" (Poe), 174
Pierrot, Gregory, 16
"Pit and the Pendulum, The" (Poe), 173
Playing in the Dark (Morrison), 157, 222n9
Plummer, Jonathan, 70, 90, 208n47
Pocock, J. G. A., 205n19
Poe, Edgar Allan, 8, 23, 163; aesthetics and, 154–56, 165–73; bereaved lover as poet, 176–78; genius and, 25, 180–87
police power, 4
Polonsky, Rachel, 167, 182
Pope, Alexander, 84
posthumanism, 18–19
Powers, Thomas, 64
premature death: racism as vulnerability to, 97–98, 100, 158, 195
Price, Fortune, 64
property, 17, 91
Prosser, Gabriel, 145
punishment: in Foucault, 207n37; slavery as, 29
purity, 83–84, 166, 180
"Purloined Letter, The" (Poe), 155, 187

Race Traits (Hoffman), 189
racialization: criminal genius and, 5; criminality and, 8, 10, 23; of genius, 15; genius and, 11; of liberalism, 68; personhood and, 8–9; slavery and, 3–5, 129–30
racialized criminality, 2–4, 10, 19, 69, 84, 93, 166, 189–90
racialized criminalization, 3
Rancière, Jacques, 17
Raven, The (film), 166
"Raven, The" (Poe), 171, 177
Raynal, Abbé, 116–18
Read, Thomas, 54, 63
recovery histories, 13, 26, 147–48
Redpath, James, 179–80
refinement, 12–13
reputation, 49, 84, 91, 140–41
respectability, 2, 4, 11, 30–31, 47, 122
respectability politics, 62, 76–77
Revelation, Book of, 226n84
ritual violence, 10

Roberts, Siân Silvyn, 171–72
Robinson, Cedric, 114
Rodriguez, Dylan, 10, 31
Rogers, John, 65
Rogers, Melvin L., 99, 216n87
Romancing the Shadow: Poe and Race (Weissberg), 185
Roman jurisprudence, 2–3
Romans, Epistle to, 112–13
Rusert, Britt, 215n76
Rush, Benjamin, 23, 28, 30, 39–46, 48–50, 79, 191–92, 207n37
Russell, E., 70
Russwurm, John B., 190

Saint Domingue, 27, 48, 119, 140. *See also* Haiti
Samuel, Book of, 65, 67
Sancho, Ignatius, 16
sanitationism, 27, 45
Sayers, Daniel O., 172, 180
Schomburg, Arthur, 16
Scott, John, 213n36
Second Great Awakening, 65
self-determination, 21, 39, 60, 129, 135, 163, 172, 189, 194
"Self-Made Men" (Douglass), 163
self-making, 50, 68
sermons, execution, 63–67, 66, 67–69, 75, 207n30
settler colonialism, 2, 10, 32, 112, 115, 126, 172
Shakespeare, William, 154
Sharpe, Christina, 97–98, 193
Shays's Rebellion, 80–81, 84, 209n65
Shelley, Mary, 160
Shelley, Percy Bysshe, 11
Sheppard Lee (Bird), 96
Short Account of the Malignant Fever, A (Carey), 7, 32, 33
Silverman, Kenneth, 182
sins, in execution sermons, 65, 85
"Slave in the Dismal Swamp, The" (Longfellow), 178–79
slavery, 1–3; aesthetics and, 12–13; children and, 157–58; Christianity and, 103–4; crime and, 6, 11; criminal justice and, 100; Descartes and, 111–12; in Jefferson, 118; justification of, 9; legal status in, 29; Missouri freedom suits, 29, 198n30; in Pennsylvania,

201n1; as punishment, 29; racialization and, 3, 129–30; refinement and, 12–13; in Walker, 103–8, 120–21; wealth and, 197n4; zombification and, 43
Slavery and the Culture of Taste (Gikandi), 12–13
Smith, Adam, 46–47, 83
Smith, Caleb, 148–49
Smith, Edward, 95
Smith, Elihu Hubbard, 51
Smith, Stephen, 29, 31
Smith, Sydney, 1, 4, 197n4
Snyder, Terri L., 100, 150, 158
social death, 79, 193–96, 201n73, 213n29, 221n108
Southampton Insurgency, 21–22, 131–64
sovereignty: slavery and, 2–3
species: genius and, 12, 15; racialization and, 9, 55, 60, 69, 77, 112, 114, 117
Spillers, Hortense J., 16, 19, 193–94
Spires, Derrick, 32, 36, 49, 136
"Spirits of the Dead" (Poe), 168
Spivak, Gayatri, 195–96
Stadler, Gus, 162
Stewart, Maria W., 1–2, 4, 79
storyworlds, 5
Stowe, Harriet Beecher, 5, 148, 179
Stuckey, Sterling, 128–29, 212n13
Styron, William, 145, 147–48
subjectivity, 20, 23, 44, 63, 93, 195, 210n73
swamp, 169, 172–73. *See also* Great Dismal Swamp maroons
Swanwick, John, 28, 45–48, 50, 204n57
sympathy, 46–47
Systema Naturae (Linnaeus), 9, 114, 117, 215n79

talent, genius versus, 13–15, 124
Tamerlane and Other Poems (Poe), 168
Taney, Roger B., 30
Taylor, Matthew, 222n13
Tennenhouse, Leonard, 171
Teprell, Matthew, 95
Theory of Moral Sentiments, The (Smith), 47
"thing power," 18
Thirteenth Amendment, 3–5
Thomas, Isaiah, 70
Thompson, Peter, 213n36
Tomlins, Christopher, 148–49, 216n13
Tompkins, Kyla Wazana, 19

"To Toussaint L'Ouverture" (Wordsworth), 144
Tragle, Henry Irving, 133–34, 136, 145–46, 216n7
transcendence, 69, 83–84, 105, 130, 153–54, 165, 168, 170, 182–83, 199n48
Travis, Joseph, 132–33, 216n7
treadmill, 3
tuberculosis, 96–97, 212n14
Turner, Benjamin, 132
Turner, Nancy, 20, 24, 131, 133, 150, 157, 159, 219n67
Turner, Nat, 17, 20–21, 24, 52, 95, 131–64

Vesey, Denmark, 145
vice, 36, 40
Victor, Orville, 161
virtue, 31, 36, 39–40, 44, 59, 77, 84–85, 163, 188, 207n36
"Visits of the Dead" (Poe), 168
voluntarism, 38, 81, 93, 194; agency and, 18–21, 40, 44, 46, 53, 61–63, 86, 174; criminal genius and, 13, 59, 98, 154, 157, 162; legal subject and, 7; whiteness and, 15

Wagner, Bryan, 2–3
Walker, David, 8, 20, 23–24, 60, 94, 101, 106, 195–96; Allen and, 34; doubts on authorship, 212n25; on legal protections for free Blacks, 29–30; social death and, 79
Wall, Cheryl, 96
Wallerstein, Immanuel, 59
Warner, Samuel, 140–41, 141, 141–43, 151, 174, 180

Waterman, Brian, 51
wealth, slavery and, 1, 102, 111–12, 126, 197n4, 212n18
Wedgwood, Josiah, 119–20
Weheliye, Alexander, 19, 114, 116, 193–94, 208n41
Weissberg, Liliane, 185
Wells, Ida B., 28
Wheatley, Phillis, 14, 16, 196
White, Ed, 25, 205n14, 205n24
white depravity, 60, 190
whiteness, 11; beauty and, 123; creative genius and, 12; criminality and, 39; liberty as, 181; in Poe, 186; racialization of, 15; in Spires, 136; yellow fever and, 32
white supremacy, 18, 31, 98, 117–19, 121, 124, 135, 167, 189, 195, 213n36
will, disease and, 42–43
Williams, Charles, 38–39
Williams, Daniel E., 208n50
will to power, 15
Wilson, Ivy G., 17, 227n92
Wood, Gordon, 205n19
Wordsworth, William, 144
Wynter, Sylvia, 9, 17, 19, 114, 195

Yacob, Zara, 113
yellow fever epidemic, 23, 27–28, 31–53, *33, 35,* 54, 192–93, 212n14
Young, Edward, 14–15

zombie, 7, 18, 42–44, 47, 52, 97, 203n50
Zwarg, Christina, 220n83

www.ingramcontent.com/pod-product-compliance
Lightning Source LLC
Chambersburg PA
CBHW030539230426
43665CB00010B/959